BY MAX WILK

••

Every Day's a
MATINEE

*Memoirs scribbled on a
dressing room door*

W • W • NORTON & COMPANY • INC •

NEW YORK

FIRST EDITION

The text of this book was composed in Linotype Fairfield. Composition, printing, and binding were done by The Haddon Craftsmen, Inc.

Library of Congress Cataloging in Publication Data
Wilk, Max.
    Every day's a matinee.
    Includes index.
    1. Wilk, Max. I. Title.
PN2287.W459A33   791'.092'4 [B]   74–30082

ISBN 0–393–07491–9

1 2 3 4 5 6 7 8 9 0

Contents

INTRODUCTION   9

1 Matinees   15

2 The Summer of 1929   32

3 The Scarsdale Mouth   47

4 Black Mask   62

5 Pop Eldredge of New Haven   77

6 TITA on Tour   94

7 The Battle of Burbank   112

8 The Flying Typers   135

9 Shambles   159

10 Two Leading Ladies and One Dog   174
       And Did You Once See Tallulah Plain?   175
       Bogey's Baby's Harvey   183
       Yassoo, Melinaki!   192

11 A Covey of Comics   206

12 Leland   236

   INDEX   285

Illustrations

Joe Cook 17
Clark and McCullough 21
Laurel and Hardy 33
Charlie Chase 35
Rin Tin Tin 41
Will Rogers 45
The first *Maltese Falcon* 70
Warren William as Perry Mason 73
Mr. Berlin 97
The Class A pass 101
Parade to Burbank 113
Reagan, Murphy, and Merrill—the politicians 117
Ezra Stone and Joe Louis 119
Re-staging the war 125
The finale of World War II 127
What Price Glory?—Mark II 132
Film Men of the Air Force 139
Propaganda, Hollywood style 147
Miss Bankhead comments on the script 182
The second *Maltese Falcon* 191
Melina and Ari 203
The most Perfect of Fools, Ed Wynn 211
Mr. Buster Keaton 214
The great Professor Lamberti 216
Jimmy Durante 218
Olsen and Johnson, alas 220
Oliver Hardy 222
M. Jerry Lewis 226
Jonathan Winters 234
Leland Hayward and his two favorites 241
Hayward and General James Stewart 275

Introduction

ONE NIGHT, long ago in 1926, had you been in the orchestra at the Capitol Theatre on Broadway during the unspooling of a Metro epic called *The Flaming Forest*, which starred a long-since forgotten leading lady named Renee Adoree, you could possibly have found me there next to you. But to find me, you would have had to look hard in the dark. I was that terrified six-year-old who was under the seat.

I was crouched beneath it because what was taking place up there on the Capitol screen, with lovely Renee trapped in the log cabin directly in the path of the oncoming North Woods bonfire, was too vivid and terrible for any six-year-old to contemplate. So down there I cowered, escaping from the fantasy world, but I also couldn't resist sneaking an occasional look out of my sanctuary below, to find out what finally did happen up above to the trapped Miss Adoree.

Now that I come to think about it, perhaps that traumatic night at the Capitol could be symbolic of my entire succeeding affair ever since with that bitch-goddess we laughingly call show biz. . . . I have had my long spells crouched beneath the seat because of the harrowing moments she keeps providing, but I seem always to emerge from under there because I can't resist finding out how she (and I) are going to make out . . .

There's no question that my life could have been a good deal simpler—and duller—in the clothing business. After all, my grandfather scratched out a decent living selling heavy winter clothing to the Swedish and Finnish miners of the bleak Min-

nesota Iron Range, and that seemed to satisfy him. But I was
sired by his son, a quiet, amiable gent who turned his back on
storekeeping to go into the theatre. He met my mother while
he was out touring the country as an advance press agent for a
play. He wooed her and married her in Duluth, Minnesota, and
promptly took her off on a honeymoon ahead of another play, a
lurid melodrama which pioneered in dealing with the subject of
—*shhh!*—social disease. (Remember, this was in straitlaced
1914.) The title of that lulu was *Damaged Goods*, and in my
case, at least, the sins of the father were etc., etc. I was diseased,
all right. The symptoms manifested themselves by the time I was
in the first grade. Foot tapping to popular songs. Fascination
with the bright lights of Broadway. Ignoring schoolwork in favor
of *Photoplay* and *Silver Screen*.

I've been a walking epidemic ever since.

As I grew older and was exposed to the theatre, and to the
last dying gasps of vaudeville (FIVE ACTS THIS WEEKEND, PLUS
A FIRST-RUN FEATURE FILM, said the marquee at the RKO
Keith's in White Plains), one of the things that gnawed away
inside me, deep within my Rogers Peet knickers, was the growing
feeling that I'd been born—as that old comic strip used to put it
—thirty years too late. Why, oh why, had I missed out on all
those good old days? Those touring minstrel shows, the two-a-day
for B. F. Keith at the Palace—those Sunday night concerts which
Jolson gave at the Winter Garden—the lavish spectacles at the
Hippodrome, the shows at Hammerstein's Victoria, a jolly after-
theatre bird and bottle at Reisenweber's . . . all gone. And the
road—that wonderful institution, touring companies that crossed
and re-crossed the face of the country, playing a different town
each week . . . life upon the wicked stage, the showboats—the
whole marvelous long-gone scene sounded so much more interesting and alive than now . . .

One time, my father tried to set me straight on those good
old days. It may have been after I'd seen some movie musical
that dealt with show business at its most flowery hour, when
Diamond Jim Brady came to see Lillian Russell sing "Come
Down, My Evening Star," and derby-hatted agents burst into

dressing rooms to tell the nervous soubrette, "Listen, kid, tonight you've got to be great—guess who's out there, looking for the lead for his new Broadway spectacle—it's Charles B. Dillingham himself!"

I must have delivered myself of some delirious babble about how I wished I'd been around in the days when Jolson sang "Where Did Robinson Crusoe Go with Friday on Saturday Night?" and Bert Williams stopped the show with his "Nobody," and Anna Held took her milk baths, and nine musical comedies opened on any given night on Broadway (perhaps my time continuum was a trifle confused, but my impulse overpowered fact).

My father tried to put me straight. It was one of the few times he ever did a Judge Hardy with me. "You're wrong," he said, "dead wrong."

He'd begun his career in the business as a part-time usher in the legitimate theatre in Minneapolis, and he'd worked his way through college as a member of the *Tribune* drama department. Eventually he came to New York and secured a job as a traveling press agent ahead of the various attractions perpetrated on the public by William A. Brady. (The husband of Grace George, Brady was one of those legendary showmen whose primary business tenet consisted of a low morning bow in the direction of P. T. Barnum, and the uttered recitation of Barnum's litany that a sucker is born each and every minute.)

"It was a rough life and it was dirty," said my father. "Stop making it out pleasant; it never was. You traveled in day coaches with filthy seats and you stayed in fleabag hotels in towns that closed up every night at ten, you ate rotten food and you hit all kinds of bad weather, and most of the time you were lonely out there . . . No union to protect you from crook managers, and after a while, it was a grind . . . Why do you think all those actors and vaudevillians were so happy to sign contracts to stay in New York—or go to Hollywood and settle down? We all hated the road!"

His outburst was surprising. He was a quiet man, not given to bad-mouthing people, or shows, or even life styles. On

his office wall, in fact, he kept a small framed motto which
instructed, "IF WHAT YOU ARE ABOUT TO SAY IS NOT GOOD, KIND,
OR TRUE, DO NOT SAY IT." To live up to such a stricture while
conducting a complicated business office on behalf of the Warner Brothers for nearly thirty years must, at times, have been a
true herculean labor.

Besides, he seemed to love travel. Rather than settling down
with a best-seller, or a newspaper, his favorite reading was a
railroad timetable . . . any railroad's. All those years he'd crisscrossed the country, he'd acquired an enormous supply of vital
information about such pressing topics as the quickest route
between North Platte, Nebraska, and Rapid City, South Dakota,
or which railroad could take you across Missouri and out of it with
all possible speed (which is, even today, rather important to
know). And his greatest pleasure was not a sport; rather, it was
an evening game which we called "Forty-fourth Street Roulette,"
in which we would find a fortunate companion and spend the
time between 8:40 and 11:00 P.M. hitting the high spots of
whatever shows were currently running in all those theatres up
and down Forty-fourth and/or Forty-fifth . . .

So there was only one possible question after that outburst.
If it had all been so terrible back then, why had he left Minneapolis and a steady newspaper job to take on the distasteful
job of touring that rotten "road"?

He thought over the question.

"Well," he admitted, thoughtfully, "I suppose I was stagestruck."

Which served to explain my problem. According to the
Mendelian laws, I must have inherited his disease!

"You're right. I guess it was a disease," he said. "And it's a
tough one to shake," he warned.

He never did. When he died, at seventy, he had just completed a complicated set of negotiations between his good friend
Edna Ferber, George Stevens, the director, and Henry Ginsberg,
the producer, which resulted in the eventual filming of *Giant*,
and he'd spent the previous weeks on a tour of London theatres,
catching up on what was happening on Shaftesbury Avenue,

going to the Bolshoi, and taking tea with his pal Peter Ustinov . . .

So this is a random collection of reminiscences about *my* good old days. It's usually supposed to be a sign of old age when you start to reminisce. Your Tuesday-night poker-game acquaintances nod politely and go on dealing. Your seatmate on the 747 dozes as you ramble on about the past. Your children yawn, not so politely; your wife taps her foot as she waits for you to get to the snapper. *Let the old man run on, he'll be finished soon.*

Well, if that is Sun City looming up on my horizon, then so be it. For some strange reason known only to that psychiatrist I can't afford to bore with my recitative, the simple truth is that, just as it did when I was in my teens, the past has always seemed much more attractive to me than does the promise of the future. If I find old Al Jolson records more exciting than the latest LP by Kinky Friedman and his Texas Jewboys, if the memory of Gertrude Lawrence doing "Jenny" seems more winsome than the sound of some folk singer wailing away about his or her date on the barricades . . . if the echo of Moran and Mack doing their "Two Black Crows" routine makes me laugh harder than the so-called ripostes of Cheech and Chong, then I'm hopelessly stuck in time, and I refuse to move—in any direction except sideways. They *were* all better.

If this be slander, then go ahead and sue.

Because I don't think there's a judge in the land who'll rule in favor of Kinky, Joan, and Cheech. Any judge who's over fifty, anyway.

CHAPTER ONE

••••••••••••••••••••••••••••

Matinees

THE PHONE RINGS in our rented house in London; it is a call from a good friend. He's a gentleman named Donald Ogden Stewart, who also lives in N.W. 3, on a winding Hampstead street called Frognal. Mr. Stewart, who's in his late seventies, has had a long and successful career in America as a humorist, playwright, and screenwriter. He and his wife, Ella Winter, have maintained a small salon in their adopted British home. On weekend afternoons, one shares tea and cake with an assortment of other writers, artists, and traveling Americans. People enjoy Don, and he reciprocates by enjoying them.

Ella will pour the tea. What is left in the pot she will thriftily pour out into the dozens of potted plants and flowers in her living room. She has a theory that plants relish warm fluids, and her plants prove her correct by burgeoning. Don, thin and grey-haired, beaming happily behind his spectacles, will sit in a corner of the room, nodding to the conversation, and occasionally murmuring something witty.

This afternoon, he reports, he is having a very special visitor from the United States to tea. A lady named Kay Swift. "You must come up and meet her," he coaxes. "She's a wonderful pianist, and I think she's going to play for us. The reason I'm sure of it is that she's sent up a piano tuner from Chappell's, and he's been tuning the piano all morning. Maybe she'll play some of the songs from a show she and her husband wrote; it was called *Fine and Dandy*. Of course, you're much too young

to remember *that*," he adds, cheerfully. "It starred a man named
Joe Cook."

"And his stooge, Dave Chasen?"

"How would you know a thing like that?" inquires Don,
truly surprised.

Because I saw the show.

"You couldn't have," Don protests. "Why, you'd have to
have been a mere infant. That was in 1930."

Would he settle for my having been ten years old? And is
it not the same show in which some soubrette sang one of Miss
Swift's ballads called "Can This Be Love?"

"But how do you remember all that?" Don asks plaintively.
"Even I forgot that song . . . and I wrote the book for the show!"

The very first time I saw Joe Cook was in an earlier show,
called *Rain or Shine*, and I became his willing slave on the spot.
Joe was a cherubic, soft-spoken gent, and his comedic gifts
sparkled with irrational flashes of mild lunacy. He could sing a
bit, he could dance, he performed marvelous feats of juggling,
but he was at his most winning when his humor sneaked up from
behind and bit you where you weren't expecting it. This sort
of thing took place most often when he worked solo, in front
of the curtain. They'd be changing the scenery back there, and
Joe, beaming broadly, would emerge, carrying a rocking chair, set
it down, sit, begin to rock and chat.

The subject of his monologue would be the basic reason
why he could not and would not on this particular afternoon do
his world-famous imitation of four Hawaiians. (You must not
ask questions about the logic of this topic. In Joe's world, logic
didn't exist. If you didn't believe—for some captious reason known
only to yourself—that he could do a marvelous imitation of four
Hawaiians, then why for heaven's sake were you sitting there,
listening to him explain why he couldn't do it today?)

Joe's explanation would expand into a long, rambling tale
of how, as a boy in Evansville, Indiana, his mother had forced
him to take piano lessons. As Joe related it, his piano teacher lived

WOULD ANYONE believe that behind this amiable visage there lurked a true clown, a man capable of filling half an hour with laughter by merely explaining why he would not and could not imitate four Hawaiians? . . . Mr. Joe Cook. LEONARD MALTIN COLLECTION

all the way across town, and after hearing young Joe play a few notes on the first day of his lessons, the teacher had arbitrarily insisted that in future Joe could not use the piano teacher's piano. From now on, he must bring his own piano, which meant that every afternoon after school Joe would pick up the family piano, start out of the Cook home, head across Evansville to the piano teacher's house, and along the way he'd come to a traffic light, and while waiting for the light to change, he would put down his piano to take a breather, whereupon a complete stranger came up, sat down, and without so much as a by-your-leave, began to play Joe's piano right there on the street . . . and so on, and so on . . . until finally, after about five minutes' worth of this surreal fantasy, Joe would wind it up abruptly by saying, "and *that*, folks, is why I simply cannot do my imitation of four Hawaiians for you today." And pick up his rocking chair, beam at us, and depart the stage.

Joe also specialized in shorter takes, e.g., his joke about the husband who shot his wife with a bow and arrow because he didn't want to wake up the kids. But his lunacy came into its most elaborate flower when he showed us his famous prop machines. These huge Rube Goldbergian devices always involved a willing stooge, Dave Chasen (who later deserted performing to establish his famous rastaurant, probably on the valid theory that it is nice to get laughs, but difficult to eat them).

Cook would fill the stage with intricate pieces of machinery that consisted of real gears, pulleys, motors, winches, and cables. One such insanity—many years before Tinguely—was devised for the sole purpose of propelling Dave Chasen from one end of the stage, like some human bullet, in a graceful solo flight through the air into a large glass tank of water at the other end. Another, which Walter Kerr has lately recalled in one of his essays on modern-day theatre, was a device ". . . geared to hitting stooge Dave Chasen on the head, at the precise moment he was to strike a single note, on a triangle, to complete 'Three O'Clock in the Morning.' " But one of the purest of Joe's mechanized flights of fancy was a large thing—"thing" is the only applicable word to describe the collection of gears, pistons, and rods which sat on the stage—which Joe would explain to us was his new "Fruit and Flower Machine." He and Chasen would proceed to demonstrate. At the press of a button, a seat appeared from inside the thing, and protruded from one side, invitingly. Dave Chasen sat down on the seat, Joe pressed another button, gears whirled, clanked, pulleys squeaked, and suddenly a metal arm, to which was attached a large boxing glove, appeared and belted hapless Dave directly on the jaw. Down for the count went Chasen. "*Now*," Joe said, beaming with elegant logic, "he goes to the hospital, and his friends send him fruit and flowers."

In the words of Mr. George Jessel, the eminent eulogist, those, dear friends, were the halcyon days. Ah yes, those were the days when a musical comedy was musical and it contained comedy. Up and down Forty-second Street, the comedians reigned, and I was fortunate enough to be exposed to most of them. I believe I can remember the first matinee I was taken to; I can certainly remember the name of the show. It was called *The Ramblers*, and it starred two other glorious buffoons named Clark and McCullough.

How does one describe those two? They wore enormous raccoon coats, small flat fedora hats, and sported bamboo canes, which they flicked at everything and anyone that passed their way. Paul McCullough had a small mustache, and Bobby Clark smoked cigars incessantly, his eyes twinkling through glasses. Not from Bausch & Lomb were Mr. Clark's optics; they were drawn around his eyes with a make-up pencil. This team of antic spirits never walked onto a stage, or off. They loped, they ran, they played leapfrog, they whooped and whistled, they whacked at anything in sight, leered at passing showgirls, sang, and danced, and their bundle of anarchistic attitudes made this young matinee-goer in from Scarsdale nearly sick with laughter.

The written word never does justice to great comedy. And since I was six years old when I was first exposed to Clark and McCullough, I can only set down remembered fragments of Bobby Clark. In his deft fingers, a cigar became all sorts of things; he could make it fly in and out of his mouth as if it were some demented guided missile. He might aim his Corona at some hapless lady and it would flicker at her like a tumescent snake; he could also flip it, six-shooter style, or twirl it until it became a drum major's baton . . . and all the while, he leered happily and his eyebrows went up and down, up and down. I remember him practicing other exotic skills. Using his bamboo cane as a golf club, he could drive a piece of wet laundry far across the stage, and, with unerring skill, arrange for said laundry to end up festooned across a pair of moose antlers on the stage wall. That took some doing. But Clark made it seem easy.

Mr. McCullough, his associate in lunatic ventures, was

given to loud cries of pleasure, and he could do intricate dance steps in which random pieces of stage furniture quite remarkably became his partner. All the while this went on, the two of them did cross-talk. Say a very fat lady passed their way, across the stage. What followed was this:

McCULLOUGH: Say, did you see *that?*
CLARK (*exuding clouds of angry cigar smoke*): I certainly did see that!
McCULLOUGH: Well, if you saw it, would you tell me what that *was?*
CLARK: I certainly will. The Graf Zeppelin just laid an egg! [*Assorted whoops*]

Another of their nifties I cherished went like so:

CLARK: I say! Did you know that my Rhode Island Red hen just laid me a square egg?
McCULLOUGH: No, I did not know your Rhode Island Red hen just laid a square egg! What do you think caused that?
CLARK: Why, it was strictly an act of Providence! [*Assorted whoops*]

All right, so their material hasn't passed the test of time as well as, say, the work of their contemporary, Eugene O'Neill. But his work doesn't read well, either. The point is, you need them up on a stage to perform it, just as you need Smith and Dale to do "Dr. Kronkheit," or W. C. Fields to deliver "The Temperance Lecture." Great comics and their material are symbiotic. (And, as Mr. Clark might say, that is definitely a two-dollar word.)

Others of my circle at Greenacres School in Scarsdale were out playing Saturday touch football, or going on nature walks, or occupying themselves with other staunch pursuits, calculated to build body and character. Not I. Once I had been infected by that first Saturday matinee at a live Broadway show, I was a goner. Hooked. Doomed, from then until now, to worship at the shrine of the musical show.

MESSRS. Bobby Clark and Paul McCullough, caught in a relatively calm moment before an imminent comedic storm. LEONARD MALTIN COLLECTION

Why was I infected? Well, first of all, it was free. I was always in on a pass.

During all those early years of my life, my father commuted each Saturday to his office. In those pre-automated days, everyone worked six days, and he was no exception. So every Saturday, at breakfast, free as I was from the disciplines of the second and third grade, and thoroughly stagestruck, I nagged at him to take me along with him, into the big city, away from the wilds of rural Fox Meadow, down to where the bright lights of the Apollo, the Eltinge, the Liberty, the Republic, the George M. Cohan, and the New Amsterdam theatres twinkled. Within a short pebble toss of 1476 Broadway, where he had his offices, all sorts of entrancing comics, singers, and dancers plied their seductive arts on Saturday afternoons. And he had a wondrous open sesame to their shows. As an ex–theatrical press agent, now a busy play broker, his name was known in most legitimate theatre box offices. When you walked in with him, there was no mundane nonsense about purchasing a ticket. And since he was as enamored of the theatre as I was—he'd begun his apprenticeship as an usher in Minneapolis when he was twelve, in order to get in to see the shows there—how could he deny a son who showed every symptom the same infatuation? Could a railway conductor bar his kid from riding trains, or a major-league ballplayer forbid his offspring to show up in the dugout?

But a six-year-old couldn't be allowed to wander alone around Times Square, and my father had work to do. So in we would go, on a commuter train, and he would send uptown for my cousin, Harold Buchman, then a reliable fifteen-year-old. (Harold has since become a successful screenwriter and playwright, his own theatrical bent based, he admits freely, on those same Saturday matinee free treats.) At noon, Harold would arrive, be handed a note by my father—some illegible scrawl on the back of an old envelope or on a piece of scratch paper—and the two rovers would hurry off to one of the nearby legitimate theatres.

We usually arrived in the lobby early. Harold would proffer my father's note through the box-office window, to whoever was behind the grate. That gent would glance at the note, grunt, nod with pursed lips, report to his confreres that Wilk had sent those g—d—kids around again, and instruct us to go stand in one corner until he could complete his dealings with the cash customers.

There we would stand, the two of us, not exactly orphans of the storm, but growing more and more insecure in that drafty outer lobby, waiting, waiting, as the ticket holders vanished inside. Behind the closed doors, we could hear the first sounds of the pit orchestra, as it struck up those first thrilling chords of the overture. By now the lobby was nearly empty. Had they forgotten us? Were we ever going to get in? There was a show starting in there—how could we bear to miss it after all this anticipation? It was an indelible exercise in suspense . . .

Finally, most often as the first strains of the show's hit tune filtered out to our anxious ears, the lobby door would open, and a hand would beckon us inside. Into the darkened theatre we went, down a wide aisle, eargerly following the man in charge. "Tickets?" demanded some faceless usherette. "Sit 'em on the end of this row here," the manager would instruct, and disappear, leaving me and Harold to slide gratefully into two unsold seats, to savor the brass section of the pit orchestra as it blared out the climax of the overture. We were safe, *inside*—with another show to enjoy for the next magic two hours!

Applause, and the pit conductor would take his bow, and then, with that peripheral nonsense out of the way, up went the curtain, and *zip!*—we were miraculously blasted off into Sunny Spain, Gay South America, the Wild Wild West—some figment of the librettist's imagination. One, two, and out came the boys and girls of the ensemble—Messieurs et Mesdames, Señors y Señoritas, et al., to go into their opening dance and song. Followed, after two peppy choruses, by the juvenile leads—he in a dapper double-breasted suit, his soubrette paramour in silk stockings, flared skirt, and cloche hat. They'd exchange a bit of dialogue, and then give us their opening duet. And then, at last —making his funny entrance . . . the clown.

In a rickshaw. On a camel. Out of a sedan chair, borne by

pretty chorines. From a manhole. Dropped by a passing balloon, by parachute (usually on his rear). Or propelled across the stage by an offstage cannon shot, to land at the leading lady's feet. Applause, laughter, and we were off.

For the next two hours, we were affianced—no, married—to Joe Cook, or to Clark and McCullough, and a raft of other such genies. Perhaps distance lends rosy euphoria, but in the case of the comics of the Broadway '20s, I do not think I'm being over-maudlin. My memory of Fanny Brice doing a comedy ballet in her tutu is not playing me false. She *was* hilarious. As was a clown named Herb Williams, who looked like a banker but did indescribable things to a grand piano, one which became his sworn enemy and seemed to be fighting back, a humanoid Steinway. There was also an elegantly turned-out fellow named Lou Holtz, who carried a cane and could spin out endless anecdotes about his good friend Sam Lapidus, and Sam's pals at the Itsy-Pitsy Social Club. One of them dealt with three members arguing over which of them was the most stubborn. To go into Holtzian detail would take paragraphs; suffice it to relate that one of them went to a dentist for his toothache. When the dentist inquired which tooth ached, Sam's friend said, "You're the dentist—*you* find it!" Whereupon the dentist selected a tooth at random and yanked it. "Was that it?" he asked. "I was so stubborn, I wouldn't tell him!" bragged Sam's friend. "He pulled every tooth in my mouth *except* the one that ached—and I still wouldn't tell him, which makes me the champion!"

Shall we summon up the shade of a brilliant little comic named Willie Howard, who with his straight-man brother, Eugene, specialized in sketches such as "Pay Him the Two Dollars," and in such marvelous bits as the Sextet from *Lucia*, sung along with some buxom ladies, whom Willie would urge to take endless bows, solely for the purpose of gaining a better view of their low-cut décolletage?

There was also a jolly chap named Victor Moore, with a strangely shaped head and a fumbling, shy mien, who endeared himself to audiences later by presenting them with the definitive characterization of an American vice-president, yclept Alexander

P. Throttlebottom. I also recall a certain Al Trahan, who purported to be the accompanist for a dignified lady soprano by the name of (this nobody could forget!) Yukona Cameron. While Yukona stood stage center, delivering the Bell Song from *Lakmé* in her long evening gown, Trahan, to one side of her at the grand piano, made it perfectly clear to us that he loathed her with a passion. As he played, he would mutter dire curses, or make an occasional vaguely obscene gesture in her direction. Unlike Herb Williams, Trahan had his rough times not with the piano but with the stool. As he spun it to raise or lower it, eventually it came off its spindle, and caused him to commit mayhem on his nether regions. Which also seemed to be Miss Yukona Cameron's fault.

Wasn't it a few years later that Mr. Bert Lahr began to bray his *gnong-gnong-gnong* at us out in front of the footlights, and to sing us a song of the virtues of a tree, whilst all manner of objects made of wood rained down on him from both sides of the stage? The memory of Bert, trapped in a steam cabinet and slowly melting away, while crying out donkey-like brays for assistance, is a choice one.

And then there was Ed Wynn.

How, in simple, flat declarative sentences, can one describe the essence of Mr. Wynn—who was, as he billed himself, the Perfect Fool?

Ed wore wild costumes, funny hats, strange flat shoes, and lisped in a high voice. Ed specialized in inventions. One of them was an eleven-foot pole for people you wouldn't touch with a ten-foot pole, what else? Another, which hung in the theatre lobby, was labeled "My Latest Invention for Making a Hole in One." It was a framed revolver. Ed also reduced grand opera to a comic shambles by describing the plot of great works. ". . . Carmen runth down the thtreet, throwing lockth of hair to her admirerth . . . Carmen . . . or Baldy, ath she ith later known . . ." he'd say, and giggle.

At a Wynn matinee, nothing was ever momentarily sane. If four jugglers were busily tossing Indian clubs up and down, Ed might silently appear at one end of the stage, bearing a step-ladder. He would set it down, climb up to the top of the ladder, reach out, catch one flying Indian club, and then climb down. Without saying a word, he would then exit, leaving the jugglers performing sans their club. A surrealist painter could have contrived nothing more definitive.

During intermission, suddenly you'd encounter Ed in the flesh, mingling with his paying customers in the lobby, puffing a cigar and calling, "Hurry up—finish your orange juith—the show's thtarting any minute in there!"

If, in the second act, we were transported to a speakeasy—these being the days of Prohibition—in which Ed was the bartender, and a tough gangster type demanded whisky "right off the boat!" Ed would assure him that this whisky was thertainly right off the boat—and thereupon he would reach behind the bar, pick up a model of a Spanish galleon, open it, and remove a bottle of newly distilled whisky.

Other Wynn lovers may rightfully cherish the scene in which another tough customer came in to announce that he was so hungry he could eat a horse. Whereupon Ed disappeared and then returned, leading onstage a genuine, full-sized mare. The reaction was a tornado of laughter, straight from the belly. Ed knew the value of a prop; no matter what it cost him to feed that horse, he knew she was worth every ounce of her weight in shock value.

But my own particular preference in Wynnsanity comes from a scene in a much later show of Ed's called *Hooray for What?* It had a lovely score by Harold Arlen and E. Y. Harburg, and came to New York in 1937. Ed portrayed a gentle inventor who'd invented a gas that would end war, and during the course of the story, he ended up in Geneva, at the League of Nations, our earlier model UN. There, in a Swiss park, he took a cat nap on a park bench. Above Ed, from the flies, there descended a small puppet, Ed on strings. Dangling above the sleeping comic, the puppet loudly announced that he was Ed's conscience. "I follow you wherever you go," he squeaked. "If you go into a restaurant, I go into a restaurant. If you sit down, *I* sit down. If you eat, *I* eat . . ."

Ed opened one eye and blinked upwards. "In that cathe," he remarked, a bit petulantly, "why don't you ever pick up the check?"

Eventually, alas, all second acts came to an end, and the assembled company came out, draped itself across the stage, and sang the finale. To the music of the pit band, the audience gathered up overcoats and hats and reluctantly started up the aisles, humming whatever hit song had been supplied to the show by the Gershwins, or Kalmer and Ruby, DeSylva, Brown and Henderson . . . Rodgers and Hart—all of them were busily supplying bright musical scores for those 1920s musicals.

Exhausted from enjoyment, cousin Harold and I would wend our way out to the lobby, where my father would collect me, and then Harold went his way and we went ours, back across town to Grand Central, where we caught a train back to Scarsdale, and reality.

During the ensuing week, my schoolmates were chanting school songs and dirty jingles. Not me. I was humming "You Took Advantage of Me," and "Button Up Your Overcoat," and "Oh Gee, Oh Joy!" When the piano teacher assigned me a selection called "Raindrops" for practice, I was ignoring it in favor of something I'd memorized by a man named Cole Porter, a lovely song called "You Do Something to Me." The reason I had it committed to memory is that it was reprised in the last six or seven minutes of a 1930 show called *Fifty Million Frenchmen*. Which I must have seen a round dozen times. Not the entire show, that is—merely those last six or seven minutes.

The show opened in the fall of 1929 . . . not exactly a good year for shows that appealed to the tired businessman. In the early, fine months of that year, the Warner Brothers, flushed with profit from their new invention, Vitaphone, had begun to spread out their empire. Part of their newly reaped cash from *The Jazz Singer* had been invested in *Fifty Million Frenchmen*, which starred William Gaxton, a sharp-tongued comedienne named Helen Broderick, and a dancer named Betty Compton, whose offstage hours were spent mostly in the company of New York's Mayor Walker.

Norman Bel Geddes had designed a production which was massive, authentically Paris, and very expensive. The show lumbered into Manhattan a scant month after the stock market crash of October. There have been better instances of bad timing, but not many . . .

There's little point in rummaging through the details of Herbert Fields' libretto, except to remember that it seemed to deal with Mr. Gaxton's exploits as a playboy in Paris, where he had made a bet that he could function for a stated period of time sans cash. If he succeeded, then Genevieve Tobin, the lovely leading lady, became his bride. You could get away with a plot like that in those days, but don't try it out on Clive Barnes next week, not even in a camp revival.

Thus, by 4:45 P.M. on those Saturday afternoons, Mr. Gaxton had desperately bet his all on a horse named Daisy, at the Longchamps race track. Daisy lost, whereupon Mr. G. tore up all his tickets. He was through. Someone led Daisy on-stage . . . yes, again a real horse. A swaybacked nag, a wreck of an equine, good for a solid batch of laughs as Gaxton sardonically described her tired frame. Off went Daisy, down went the lights, and Mr. G., his chances of winning Miss Tobin as low as the current stock market averages, stood in a spotlight and reprised "You Do Something to Me." The song was lovely, and it was a pure moment of old-fashioned schmaltz.

Since it was part of my father's job at Warner Brothers to check on the company's investment in the show, he'd stop by the theatre, with me in hand, and we'd duck inside the darkened house, and stand in the back for those closing minutes of the show. By the time we'd made seven or eight consecutive Saturday next-to-closings, I could do Gaxton's scene and song by heart.

Assuming you are interested in learning the eventual outcome . . . well, the Longchamps judges, at two minutes before the final curtain, announced a foul. Guess who was declared actual winner of the race? . . . If you don't know the answer, your homework assignment is to study two decades' worth of Broadway librettos, in Burns Mantle's *Best Plays* (1920–40). Mr. Gaxton thereupon scrambled around the stage, picking up pieces of his torn-up tickets on Daisy, rushed to cash them in, won his bet, and went into a rapturous clinch with Genevieve Tobin. The company came out and went into a Cole Porter finale, but by that time we were halfway down the block, headed for the 5:26.

Daisy and those winning tickets and "You Do Something to Me" were not just a finale to that show; they were the curtain to an entire era. It was *finis* to that never-never land of carefree American tourists who'd spent the 1920s flinging their green-backs around gay, naughty Paree, tucking bills down the décol-letage of dancing girls at the Folies Bergère, gorging at Maxim's, joyfully dousing themselves with Lanvin perfume and Mumm's champagne, and treating the whole city as their private play-ground. *Fifty Million Frenchmen* closed soon afterwards, and our crosstown jaunt towards Grand Central Station meant passing through Times Square, where there were men lined up, not to buy theatre tickets, but at things called soup kitchens—homeless, unemployed men, huddled in shabby overcoats. And on cross-town street corners, other men stood, hopefully peddling apples from cardboard boxes, at a nickel per apple.

The theme song switched from "I've Got Five Dollars" to Messrs. Harburg and Gorney's "Brother, Can You Spare a Dime?" The Saturday matinees, with all those funny men onstage, all those wonderful clowns, began to vanish. One by one, those opulent, proud Forty-second Street musical houses, the Republic, the Eltinge, the New Amsterdam, the Erlanger, and the George M. Cohan—every one of them went dark. If they ever did reopen, it was for cheap burlesque, or as twenty-five-cent movie "grind" houses, showing double bills to audiences looking for a warm place to sleep for a couple of hours. Tired businessmen? Most of them were as broke as Mr. Ziegfeld, or any of the other producers who'd got rich by entertaining the people. Sure, there were cut-rate theatre tickets at Leblang's, or in the basement of Gray's Times Square drugstore, but who had a buck to spare for a legit show? And even provided you could mount a musical, post–1930, what the hell was there to be funny about?

Most of the Broadway comics found employment on the radio, and the price for listening to them was just about right. On your Atwater Kent, or Stromberg-Carlson, you got thirty minutes' worth for free (assuming you had the price of the electric bill). Ed Wynn, Eddie Cantor, Al Jolson, Fred Allen, Jack Benny . . . Burns and Allen—all of them made the transition over to NBC and CBS, and they thrived, not in sight, but through the speaker. Bobby Clark, he of the demented cigars and the painted eyeglasses, lost his partner, McCullough, but he went on solo, to star in *Strike Up the Band*, and many more hits. Jimmy Durante went out to Hollywood, and so did Ted Healy and his Three Stooges, and eventually the film studios engorged all the rest of them.

Joe Cook? Like a rare wine, he didn't travel. That fine insanity of his was never meant for the vast radio audience. In front of the cold eye of the movie camera, Joe's zaniness evaporated; on the screen he seemed simply brash. His success began to fade. He retired to his zany estate in New Jersey, where his home life was replete with humor. If you were invited to Joe's home, you were met at the door by a formal butler, who soberly took your hat and coat from you, ushered you inside, and then went over to the open window and threw your hat and coat out onto the lawn. Joe had himself a private golf course there; the ninth hole of his layout was specially designed by him to include a funnel-shaped green. Any guest whose shot landed on the green was thus guaranteed a hole in one. Joe had even installed a pipe, leading from the cup of the ninth hole, which carried your ball directly into his house, to a downstairs bar where one repaired to celebrate one's triumph.

He lived with mechanical gadgetry, but the technology of radio and talking pictures defeated him. Perhaps it was because Joe was a comic who could only thrive on direct contact with a live, breathing, laughing group of customers, who were sitting out there in his theatre, eight times a week. Two of them, his willing acolytes, were an eight-year-old in Rogers Peet knickers, in from Scarsdale, with his older cousin as a chaperon. And if they happened to be in the theatre on a pass, that didn't matter to Joe, I'm sure. He needed us laughing at him, and with him, to survive. That was his nourishment, and for a lovely while there, it was ours . . .

Don Stewart sits in his Hampstead living room, reminiscing with Kay Swift about the production of *Fine and Dandy*, which they both did forty years ago.

"You know something?" he says, as Miss Swift sits at the newly tuned piano, playing "Can This Be Love?" "That was the most pleasant writing job I ever took on. I sat down and I wrote the script, and I brought it in to Joe Cook, and he thanked me, and told me to go take a little vacation for myself, while he put the show into rehearsal. I never heard another word from Joe about anything—rewrites, changes, no problems at all. Opening night, he sent around tickets, I got out my white tie and tails, and we all went down to the theatre. Joe came out and did a wonderful show, full of those gags he'd thought up, or he'd ad-libbed, and those marvelous funny pieces of machinery—all that Cook nonsense. I didn't recognize a word of my book, and I didn't care—I was having much too good a time laughing at Joe!"

"Afterwards," says Don, "I went around backstage to congratulate him, and when I got to Joe's dressing room, he jumped up, threw his arms around me, shook my hand, and he said, 'Don—I want to congratulate you on a wonderful job! It's a lovely show!' And I said, 'Yes, it is—what show *was* that, Joe?' and he said, 'What do you care, Don? We're going to run a whole season!' " Don grins happily. "And do you know—it did?"

Yes, Don, I do know. I was there, at a Saturday matinee.

CHAPTER TWO

•••••••••••••••••••••••••••

The Summer of 1929

"SOMETIMES," said the late Bela Lugosi, in a long-forgotten B
horror film years back, "the mind plays funny tricks."

Yes, Bela, it is true. But not only in respect to monsters, half-
seen in the shadows of Stage 5. More often, as we grow older, it
is our own memory that plays capricious games with us. How
else can one explain a remembered experience from one's early
youth, in 1929 in Southern California, lying dormant for forty or
so years—and then suddenly reviving itself in the courtyard of
a new resort hotel on the slumbering island of Djerba, a few
miles off the Tunisian coast?

It is a warm July evening, and a breeze is blowing in off
the Mediterranean. The hotel has broad stone courtyards facing
the water; the entire complex has been designed by an architect
who believes in Frank Lloyd Wright as his prophet. Unfortunately, either the architect, or the hotel's owners, have forgotten
that Wright did most of his work in the pre-air-conditioning era
—and as a result, this brand-new edifice, sprawled across the
white Tunisian sands, contains three hundred and sixty-odd
barrackslike bedrooms that can become fearfully hot during
the summer months.

This morning, the young Frenchman, *M. le Directeur* of
Cultural Activities and Entertainment for the hotel, put up a
notice in the lobby that at 9 P.M. *ce soir* he will show a film in
the hotel lounge. But by that hour, the coolest place on hand is
out of doors, beside the large swimming pool. *M. le Directeur*,
who affects the native costume, a sheer white Tunisian burnoose

Two MEN who could get more comedy mileage out of a Model-T than old Henry Ford ever dreamed was possible. SPENCER BERGER COLLECTION

appliquéd with delicate embroidery, has set up his 16 mm. projector out of doors, and with his small audience adjusting itself comfortably into poolside lounges, the film begins. The light flickers against the dead-white walls of the hotel dining room, and there is the sound of music in the night, bright jazzy strains . . .

And what is the film that is about to be unreeled for these tourists, we half dozen sunburnt Italians and Germans and a very few French? (For the hotel is not doing well this first summer, and there are rumors of imminent disaster.) What is our Cultural Activity this Friday evening? It is nothing more *intellectuelle* than a collection of two-reel short subjects which star a large fat man named Babe Hardy, with a derby and a tiny mustache and a dark suit that is always too tight, and his partner, a wispy gent with a shock of straight-up hair, a bow tie, and the gift of instant weeping, Stan Laurel. Across the Tunisian wall flicker silent shadows of an angry Hardy pursuing a bekilted Laurel down the main streets of Culver City, California, circa 1929, past rows of parked touring cars and coupés and flivvers, and from around the pool here in Djerba, a few miles off the Tunisian coast, forty-four years after the fact, there comes scattered laughter.

Mr. Hardy pursues Mr. Laurel into the Southern California sunset, and now there are titles, and we are launched into another two-reeler of the period, one that involves an elegant ballet of destruction and mayhem to a line of parked automobiles, and I am laughing with everyone else, but from somewhere in the deeps of my subconscious I hear a voice; it wafts tantalizingly through my head, and it is saying, "Hey, my old man got the boys to do a real pip last week—they wrecked a whole lot of cars, and it's going to be a knockout!"

. . . he would have been about fifteen years old then, a stocky boy who lived a few hundred feet away from us in a large, comfortable California mission-style bungalow. His name was Roach, and his father produced two-reel comedies which starred a bunch of kids who were known to the world as Our Gang, and he also had a star who was a dapper little gent with a mustache named Charlie Chase. Along with Laurel and Hardy, Roach *père* had a

THE LAST great undiscovered silent-comedy star, Charlie Chase someday will be enshrined by the *cinéastes* and take his place along with the
others.

studio full of activity; in the years before 1929, much earlier on, he had discovered and starred the great Harold Lloyd in dozens of rapid-fire silent comedies.

All of this I was to learn in years to come, but in the summer of 1929, I was no *cinéaste*, I was a transplanted nine-year-old from a New York suburb, whose parents had come West for several months and subleased a small cottage in a strange and wonderful place in Santa Monica which was called the Uplifters Ranch. And that large boy named Roach down the street was a show-off and a braggart. Two-reel comedies? They were something you fidgeted through until the main feature flashed onto the screen.

It wasn't only the Uplifters Ranch that was a fantasy land that summer; the whole of Southern California was a violent culture shock for anyone who'd come from the calm streets of Scarsdale. Sunny, palm-lined boulevards stretched out into infinity through empty fields, where huge billboards announced, ON THIS SITE WILL BE ERECTED THE MIRACLE MILE. (The actual fact was to come much later than the prediction.) Our first stop, after the transcontinental hegira, was the Roosevelt Hotel; it stood opposite a wild and wonderful building called Grauman's Chinese, and from the hotel window, eight floors down, one could see the famous forecourt, with its hand- and footprints of the stars. One could lean out and hear music wafted up from below; through Mr. Grauman's loudspeakers came the strains of "Broadway Melody," the theme song from MGM's first all-talking-singing-dancing musical, which was enjoying a very successful run. Movie stars, real live movie stars, wandered hourly through the Roosevelt lobby, and Hollywood was real, it was alive, it wasn't the shadows you saw on the screen at the RKO White Plains on Saturday matinees—no sir, it was here, and this was where it all happened.

Pretty heady stuff for a nine-year-old, whose father had lately signed a contract to become an executive for the Warner Brothers, a motion-picture company whose fortunes had dramatically exploded from near bankruptcy overnight into lush prosperity, due to the technological change involved in films that talked. Vitaphone, as it was called, had been the dream of Sam Warner, and he had literally worked himself into an early grave in order to prove the commercial value of its invention. That night in New York when Al Jolson sang from the screen for the first time, he and Vitaphone catapulted the Warners into the front line of successful producers.

Throughout the 1920s, my father had been a successful literary agent and play broker, operating from his own small office at 1476 Broadway. Many times he had sold material to the then struggling Warner *frères*. (Somewhere in a trunk in my attic, there is a sheaf of postdated checks that Harry Warner gave him in payment for some story that he didn't have sufficient cash to pay for all at once, in the years when the Warners' most reliable money earner was a German shepherd named Rin Tin Tin.)

When the Warners became instant tycoons, they were prescient enough to realize their need for someone who could find them material for all the pictures they would make in the years to come, and they embraced Jake Wilk and signed him to a contract. "You've been selling stuff to us for a long time," said H. M. Warner. "Now you can start *buying* for us!"

The Uplifters Ranch was a vast, sprawling enclave of unspoiled flatlands and canyons. It had been turned into a private club some years before by farsighted Angelenos who wanted a rural setting in which they might live, swim, and ride, a short distance from the studios down in Hollywood, and the further downtown Los Angeles office buildings.

Under the eucalyptus trees was a large clubhouse, where members entertained their less fortunate guests who'd been passed through the gates by the guards. Nearby was a large swimming pool and cabanas, and in a canyon nearby were stables, stocked with members' horses. Small, winding roads led away through the trees up to terraced hillsides, on which were comfortable log-cabin cottages; the use of cars was discouraged, so small kids might play wherever they pleased. If one wanted to mount a horse and ride out onto the trails, they would lead him for miles through forests of scrub pine and cactus, or up into

the hills. Most trails finally ended at the far end of the ranch, out
at the pride of the Uplifters, its famous polo field.

Every weekend, the Uplifters fielded its own polo team,
led by an accomplished horseman named "Snowy" Baker. Crowds
of people from all over Hollywood drove out Sunset Boulevard
to sit in the bleachers and watch the Uplifters team play blue-
blood groups from Santa Barbara, or San Mateo, up the coast.

During the week, with fathers at work, things were fairly
quiet around the ranch. We played games on the streets, or
explored the trails on horseback, and swam. There was quite a
lot of peering through cracks in the wooden walls of the girls'
dressing rooms, as I remember. But come Saturday, that broad
green polo field was where it was all at. We came early to watch
the vans unload the strings of polo ponies that came in with the
visiting opponents; we gaped at the huge Packard roadsters and
Pierce-Arrows and Marmons as they pulled into the parking lot
behind the bleachers. The wicker hampers containing picnic
lunches, the silver hip flasks from which they drank toasts to
each other, the cheerful girls on their arms; truly, these were
demigods in the prime of life, to be examined and envied. No
matter how often their indolent grooms shooed us away, we
came back for yet another look. And then when the game began,
we sat in the bleachers and cheered on the brave Uplifters team.
For forty-eight hours a week, it was polo, polo, polo, with horses
racing up and down that field in the bright sunlight, the *thock*
of mallet on ball, and the drum of hoofbeats on turf. Who could
know that there was anything else going on in the world outside
those Uplifters' gates?

Sunday nights, in the clubhouse, there usually was a movie
shown. Since many of the members were producers, it was obviously an easy matter to procure first-run films. I seem to remember
some sort of a fracas that developed on the street between our
rented cottage and the one in which young Roach resided. He
had come out to tell us about the positive merits of one of his
father's latest efforts, but it was a losing battle. That summer,
talking pictures were all the rage, and Roach *fils'* loyalty to his
father was of little avail. "Who needs your father's rotten

pictures?" one of my older confreres sneered at him. "Those two dumb guys don't even *talk!*"

The ensuing fist fight, in which we all participated, was of no value in settling the argument caused by Sam Warner's invention. Sunday evenings, nobody came into the clubhouse while the silent comedy was unreeled; but as soon as it had ended, and it was time for the sound feature ("100% ALL TALKING!"), the screening room was packed. Perhaps his son couldn't, but Roach *père* could read (or hear) the *mene-mene-tekel* on that clubhouse screen.

The first time I saw an actual film studio was that summer. My father brought me with him to work, down Sunset Boulevard in a studio limousine cum driver, all those miles through empty fields that were to become Beverly Hills, and down the still nascent Strip, and finally up to the old Warner Sunset lot.

In that summer of 1929, before the Warners moved out to Burbank (they had just engorged the First National Pictures Corporation, as well as many other businesses allied with entertainment), their studio was a rather imposing structure, with a block front on Sunset Boulevard that consisted of a long imitation Greek façade, replete with high pillars and broad steps leading up to them. It was a sort of bastard Stoa-of-Agora style, and perhaps its design was out of deference to the Greek-American Skouras brothers, who had early on been Warner associates.

We went onto the lot through the front doors, past a studio policeman who tipped his hat, and then my father brought me down to a nondescript office building. There was inside it a suite of rooms with a large conference-type salon. These were his temporary headquarters while he was here from the East, where he had been made Eastern Story Editor. He had conferences scheduled throughout this morning, so he assigned a studio office boy to lead me out onto a sound stage, where I might actually watch a sound film being made. "Don't forget, now," instructed the lady who was serving as his secretary, "if you need to come back, or you get lost, just tell anybody your father is working here in the steam room."

Steam room? Conference room? Story department? What

did it matter what his office was called when you were nine years old and on your way into the very depths of a studio, to be a privileged witness of actual filmmaking? We hurried out and passed through long, nondescript studio streets, up this alleyway and down that one, and finally came to a door with a red light flashing over it. A sign read, "KEEP DOOR SHUT: RED LIGHT INDICATES FILMING!"

It was in the very first, primitive days of Vitaphone. The technology was rudimentary. The camera was encased in a sound-proof glass box, which rolled (not very often, since directors were unfamiliar with tracking shots, and the slightest vibration could set up booming echoes in the microphone) on rubber wheels. The fearless cameraman had to be locked inside that airless cubicle of glass while he operated his camera during a "take." The glass was to keep the sound of his camera motor from leaking out into the mikes on the set; if the hapless camera-man had to make a long scene—and in those days, the emphasis was strictly on dialogue, most of what was being shot on film being directly derived from the theatre—the poor chap would emerge at the end of the filming drenched in sweat and near suf-focation. It was a deadly serious business; when that assistant director yelled "Quiet! We're rolling—*this is a take!*" you held your very breath, lest you might inadvertently wheeze, or belch, and then be struck down from on high for having ruined some of Mr. Warner's film.

The name of the film which was being shot that morning in 1929 was *Tiger Rose*; that much I have never forgotten, but since I have far from total recall, I have researched it for my own edification. The director was a dapper Englishman named George Fitzmaurice, and the cast consisted of Monte Blue, a long-time Warner stalwart, a young Latin lady named Lupe Velez, the man who had played Christ for Cecil B. De Mille, H. B. Warner, Grant Withers, and . . . the ever popular Rin Tin Tin. The plot dealt with the pursuit of a wanted man through the frozen northern wastes by a fearless Royal Canadian Mountie. I have nothing else to report to the staff of *Cahiers du cinema* about the backstage goings on during the filming of *Tiger Rose* that

RIN TIN TIN,who for many years was the sole asset and major source of revenue for three struggling Warner brothers. JOHN ALLEN COLLECTION

summer's morning except that I lingered on the set for several hours, examining props—actual revolvers, etc.—and watching Lupe Velez playing a scene in a log cabin with fearless Monte Blue. Miss Velez was a beautiful, busty young lady, who seemed to be enjoying herself, and kept on very good terms with the cast and crew.

But in case you do not already know it, the physical aspects of filmmaking, that endless take and retake process of tiny one- and two-minute scenes, all the minutiae that go into the production of two or three minutes of usable film on any given shooting day, can eventually become extremely dull. Especially to this nine-year-old, who began to lose interest, and wandered off the *Tiger Rose* set. It was pushing lunchtime, and my stomach was issuing more seductive bulletins than was Miss Velez, so I started back in the general direction of my father's temporary GHQ. I was alone. The escort who'd brought me down on the set had long since returned to his gainful employment.

The Warner lot consisted of a dozen or so large sound stages, and it was easy for an eastern kid to lose his sense of direction—far too easy. Soon I was wandering this way and that, completely turned around; eventually, I heard a voice hailing me. It turned out to be a studio cop, an imposing man in a blue uniform, complete with pistol in holster—except that he was for real, and so was his gun and its bullets. He wanted to know where did I think I was going.

To my father's office. And who was my father? I gave the name, defiantly. He'd never heard of it, and was most unimpressed. Did I have a pass to get on the lot? No, I did not. Then what was I doing here on the lot? I was visiting! By whose authority? I tried to explain: my father—from the East—how I'd been out on the sound stage—and the more I babbled on in the face of this implacable authority, the less he believed a word of it. I was obviously an interloper, a foreign spy, a nine-year-old saboteur caught in the act. Why else would he clamp his large hand firmly around my arm and pull me off down the street?

Officer X triumphantly propelled a nine-year-old who was very near tears into a small security office a block away, and confronted his superior officer with his wriggling captive. Sergeant Y was even less inclined to believe my story than had been the first hawkshaw. "You say your father works here?" he demanded. "Okay, where does he work, then?"

"He works in the Steam Room!" I cried, with a certain amount of desperation.

"You mean he's with Abdul?" asked the studio cop, perplexed.

I was too young to know that Jack Warner, always the physical-fitness buff, had, even then, a burly Turk named Abdul as his personal masseur, exerciser, and sparring partner—and Abdul was to keep J. L. in the pink for many years to come.

The studio cop called a number on his phone and spoke to somebody on the other end. Then he hung up and stared at me with deepening suspicion. "Nobody in there ever heard of anybody named Wilk," he said. "Come clean, sonny."

I was obviously headed for Sing Sing.

No, wait. This was California. That meant a place named Folsom, didn't it?

With mounting panic, I protested that my father had nothing to do with anyone named Abdul, that he was here from New York on important business, that he had been assigned an office called the Steam Room, and he was waiting there for me right this minute.

The studio *polizei*, born cynics, bought none of it.

One of them took me by the arm and propelled me out the office door. The other one followed. Where were we going?

Off the lot.

"And then what?" I demanded, panicking at the prospect of being left alone to wander the friendless streets of Hollywood outside.

Neither of them replied, but continued to walk me down the studio street. Flanked by the two burly cops, I fought back tears. I didn't succeed. What had I done to deserve this kind of treatment? Suppose I had wandered off the set and gone off on my own? Was that any reason to be summarily ejected from the studio? It was, to use the Warner argot of the '30s, the very bummest of bum raps!

And if I was in dire trouble, where was the U.S. Cavalry, riding to rescue me from these two implacable villains?

It arrived just in time, and it was a voice behind me, an angry female voice, which was calling to the two policemen, "Where are you taking that boy? His father's been looking all over the lot for him!"

One of those capable secretaries from the Steam Room; obviously, she'd been searching high and low for an errant nine-year-old—and she'd located me, thank heaven. I was saved from being banished forever into that bright world that lay out on Sunset Boulevard . . . the world of the outs.

The cops were summarily put in their place. No amount of explanation that they were simply doing their job would serve to explain their gaffe. "I *told* them he worked in the Steam Room!" I insisted, as she led me away to safety.

The steam room where Abdul reigned I never got to see.
But I did shortly re-enter the one where my father sat, surrounded
by stacks of manuscripts and folders. He got up from his im-
provised desk and came over to me, obviously perturbed.
"*What* happened to you?" he demanded.
"Oh, nothing much," I said, once more in control of myself.
"I was arrested."

Came Labor Day, and we departed the Uplifters Ranch.
We rode through the empty fields of Beverly Hills, all neatly
laid out for the future boom times that lay ahead, down to
Union Station, got aboard a transcontinental express, and headed
back to the mundane East. The departure involved leaving behind a gentle polo pony named Duke whom I'd been allowed to
ride all that summer; being deprived of him was far more of a
wrench than it was to bid a careless goodbye to all the kids on the
tiny street on which we'd lived. Especially Roach *fils*, and his
bragging about those two silly silent comedians . . .

Less than six weeks after we returned to Scarsdale, something happened downtown in New York City, in a place called
the Stock Market . . . something grownups called The Crash.
After that happened, things began to change. Although one
couldn't foresee it at the time, there wouldn't be much more
weekend polo out at the Uplifters field, fewer visits by all those
rich young chaps from San Mateo, with their long Packard
roadsters, trailing behind them strings of polo ponies . . . As a
matter of fact, the Uplifters Ranch wasn't long for this world
itself. What people called the Depression soon took care of that
lovely, soft-focus place, and its euphoric life style . . .

Drive out Sunset Boulevard today, roll out towards the
Pacific on four- and six-lane stretches, and you will probably shoot
right past the canyon wherein lay that polo field. Down there
is a real-estate development, long since subdivided; that noble,
well-kept green turf where the Packards and the Pierce-Arrows
and the Cadillacs parked, those sunny afternoons years back,
is now dotted with neat rows of ranch-type and pseudo–Connecticut farmhouse colonials.

Over to the right, however, there is still one well-preserved

MR. WILL ROGERS, who would obviously prefer to be headed toward the polo field than in the direction of the links.

remnant of those affluent times. It's Will Rogers' Ranch, a vast piece of unspoiled acreage which that gentleman presented to the state of California as a bequest. Undisturbed, pristine, Will's comfortable green acres are still exactly as they were back on those 1929 weekends, when he'd slouch across Sunset on horseback, unshaven, be-jeaned, with his chewing gum going and his leathery face wrinkled in a permanent grin, to get in his day's worth of polo with the Uplifters team. Will played pretty good polo, and he certainly enjoyed the game; the spectators could hear him whooping and hollering with sheer pleasure as he raced up and down the field . . .

Perhaps it was Will's Indian ancestry that provided him with such an ingrained respect for the land. Whatever it was, there's not much else besides his ranch in Southern California that's left the way it was in that long-gone summer of 1929 . . .

The film is over. Bright white flickers across the wall in Tunisia, and *M. le Directeur*, in his long white burnoose, wishes to know if we have enjoyed the marvelous antics of those two brilliant *artistes*, Messieurs Laurel and Hardee?

He carefully rewinds the 16 mm. print, lays the reel back in its shipping carton, and closes the lid. The shipping label on the carton says it is due to travel tomorrow from Djerba to the Arab town of Kairouan, many miles inland across the desert.

One hopes that the Arab audience tomorrow night will also enjoy the antics of Messieurs Laurel and Hardee. Fortunately—or perhaps unfortunately—they will have no memories of the Uplifters Ranch, and the summer of 1929 . . . to distract their attention from the comedy.

CHAPTER THREE

The Scarsdale Mouth

LATELY, on the New York *Times* Letters to the Editor page, there has exploded a mini-controversy; it erupted from an angry piece written earlier by a nom-de-plumed divorced gent who seems to have fled suburban Scarsdale, and then drawn up a *j'accuse* damning the entire place. In his Op-Ed bill of particulars, he maintains that Scarsdale ruined his marriage and is warping his offspring with false values and insulation against any sort of reality. (Which could be immediately regained by moving back to Manhattan.)

In response, articulate Scarsdale property owners, stung, have overreacted by firing off salvos of defensive verbal missiles. Their defense of the barricades is admirable, but their time might have been better spent vacuuming the swimming pool. What they don't realize is that Scarsdale has always been everybody's dog to kick—everybody, that is, who couldn't afford to live there. Vaudevillians always had towns that were easy laughs. In Detroit, mention Hamtramck. In Chicago, you could get a roar by simply saying Cicero; in New Jersey, the magic word was Ho-Ho-Kus.

Scarsdale is a laugh name, too, available to all strata—those less affluent who had to settle for Yonkers or Valhalla, and at the other end of the scale, the hypersophisticates and free souls who considered Scarsdale's suburban ambience simply *stifling* . . . Over the years, everybody's had a crack at Scarsdale. A quarter of a century back, Frank Loesser pinned the town to the wall when he had Sky Masterson in *Guys and Dolls* sing-

ing to his lady love; he put down her dream of a potential husband, in "I'll Know," by scornfully telling her that she had picked
herself a Scarsdale Galahad, a breakfast-eating Brooks Brothers
type—remember? Later on, in *Butterflies Are Free*, didn't the
mother, an archvirago, come to Greenwich Village to reclaim
her wandering son, and from where? Scarsdale, natch.

A couple of weeks ago, in a long article on orthodontia,
another New York *Times* writer, discussing the cosmetic straight-
ening of teeth, harpooned the town again. According to her,
within the trade there is a name for the perfect set of uppers and
lowers. With their retainers all in and paid for, our dear little
pubescent consumer types are building the Scarsdale Mouth.

In the face of all this, it must take guts (plus a very good
credit rating) to move to Scarsdale, but friends of ours have
lately made the familiar leap out of a Manhattan apartment into
a large Scarsdale home. Undaunted by the snide jokes about
enclave life, they will educate their four children in Scarsdale's
excellent public-school system. For the fact is that the relatively
high cost of living in the heart of Westchester's highest-rent
district can still be justified in terms of the *quid pro quo* to be
gained by having your offspring trudge off to Greenacres School,
or to Fox Meadow Elementary, and whipping off in the MG or
the Mustang over to Scarsdale High. For years now, mother and
father have enfiefed themselves to the local banks on the tenet
that graduates of the Scarsdale school system inevitably go forth
into Later Life better fitted to cope, to excel . . . to Lead.

I could maintain that such a dream is strictly real-estate-
agent talk. After all, I grew up in Scarsdale, and nobody has ever
held me up as an example of true leadership; but then it could be
argued that I'm far from typical. I was, very early on in life, a
Scarsdale failure. A reject, a cull, a flunkout in first-year high
school. The Scarsdale school system did me no visible good whatsoever. Living on Fenimore Road until I reached manhood gave
me only a (pre-orthodontia) Scarsdale mouth.

Back in 1925, my parents delivered me up to the waiting
maternal arms of the Greenacres kindergarten, but three years

later, a ragged detachment of knicker-clad and beskirted small fry, with me in its ranks, marched down the quiet streets to a brand-new red-brick school two blocks in from Fenimore Road that was called, in honor of the development which it overlooked, Fox Meadow.

The year 1928, when we moved into the first class in 4-B, was a peaceful and pleasant one. The most excitement we'd encountered was Lucky Lindy's flight across the Atlantic, and then the current national election. Mr. Hoover, a Republican, was running against Al Smith, a Democrat. My parents were for Al Smith; that made him *my* candidate. In a town filled with Republicans, in a county even more so, my political position was far from popular. I remember a fist fight on a suburban street which erupted when I refused to concede that Al Smith was a no-good Catholic bum, and so was I for supporting him. I came home with broken glasses, bloody, unbowed, and anxious to find out what, exactly, *was* a Catholic?

We lived in a house at the corner of Fenimore and Fox Meadow roads, by the traffic light. Two doors away, for a couple of years, Al Jolson was our neighbor. He'd married Ruby Keeler and she'd persuaded him to desert Lindy's and Aqueduct for the quieter country life. Al stood the first few months of sitting in the garden and watching plants grow well enough, but after *The Jazz Singer* came out, plants palled. He packed up and took himself and family off to California. For the next two decades, however, his ex-manse was always known as the Jolson House, and was a popular stop for the Sunday drivers out for a ritual family sight-see.

Fox Meadow Road was, when we first arrived, a dirt track that led into a vast expanse of thick, undeveloped forest. The land had originally belonged to two ladies named Butler, and one could tramp for hours through fields and woods. Miles away, at the opposite end of Fox Meadow, the outer limits of Scarsdale were beginning to push towards us—we were up at the Hartsdale end, new settlers in the wilderness—but for the first few years, we were on the edge of a forest primeval. By the time the elementary school had been finished, the open land around it was rapidly being gobbled up. The accoutrements of civilization were all in, sewers, water mains, paved roads that crossed and crisscrossed the gentle fields and soft hills. One pedaled one's Iver-Johnson to school each morning past fresh excavations for houses. Heavy Mack trucks rolled by, architects and builders, landscapers, and the Peckham Road Company poured into the territory with all the enthusiasm of the crowd at the opening of the Cherokee Strip—each new crew striving to outdo the one across the street, it seemed, to throw up more opulent suburban dwellings . . .

Over the '20s, Fox Meadow began to resemble a vast surrealist smorgasbord of unplanned architectural styles. Scattered at random on precise lots, huge stone Tudor mansions with gables and leaded-glass windows reared up, cheek by jowl with modified Georgians, or relatively simple two-story New England colonials. Down the street there might emerge a scaled-down Carolina plantation home with pillared portico; next door to it would sprout a demure, red-brick Williamsburg mansion. Pumping up a hill, one could come upon a diminutive version of a Norman château, replete with mansard roofs and turrets, and around the corner from that improbable expensive folly, someone had commissioned a vast southern Italian villa, complete with Mediterranean-style red-tiled roof. It was an endless triumph of money over taste. Since, in those euphoric Hoover years, there was the wherewithal to indulge whatever whims one's architect suggested, what difference could it make that Anne Hathaway's cottage had a thatched roof totally unsuited to Westchester winters? With the help of one's willing builder, we could do the cottage roof in pale blue slate, shipped over from Italy, right?

The builders built, the families moved in, Packards and Pierce-Arrows and Buicks purred down the roads, and life in Scarsdale was pleasant enough. On the Fox Meadow playground, at recess, there was the usual outcropping of bullies, one or two of whom had, at an early age, taken upon themselves the ancient crusade of anti-Semitism. In those days, the Scarsdale population was mainly gentile, and whatever Jewish families appeared were treated with politeness, if not acceptance. Next door to us there lived a sober dentist with his wife and young daughter. Their house was a mere sixteen or so feet away, with a hedge between. For the entire period they were our next-door neighbors, a good twenty years, none of us ever set foot in their home, nor did they in ours. The hedge was a tacit Berlin Wall. Although it was less than a mile away, my father was never permitted to join the Scarsdale Golf Club—although my friends now assure me that today such barriers have collapsed, due, perhaps, more to economic than to social pressures.

My first encounter with race prejudice came in one of the Fox Meadow classrooms when a contemporary turned to me one day and casually snapped, "Hey, you—you dirty Jew . . ." In what must have been my first use of humor as a defensive weapon, I remember saying, "What do you want, you filthy Protestant?" (It was another word whose meaning I was unsure of, but it seemed to end the discussion.) We went on to more important matters, such as what movie was playing that weekend up at the brand-new RKO Keith's in White Plains, or last evening's radio chapter of "The Adventures of Chandu, the Magician" . . . or the length of Katherine Condon's underdrawers, visible when she rode her bicycle down Cohawney Road and the wind took her skirt . . .

Fox Meadow School was one of the first, if not the first, elementary schools that specialized in what has come to be called progressive education. To this day, I can provide no precise definition of that curriculum and what it meant; I can report on several tangibles that our principal, Mrs. Zyve, introduced to our daily school life. We kept pets, and learned from observing their daily habits a good deal about the home life of rabbits and chipmunks. In art class, we were encouraged to "express ourselves" through painting and clay sculpture, and we were given class "projects" to complete, i.e., the building of tree houses, and the establishment of a letter-writing program with children in faraway countries, by means of which paper bridge we were to clasp hands with other societies.

One element was conspicuous by its absence from our gentle course of studies (although I wasn't to discover this until my

first year at the more rigidly structured Scarsdale High School),
and that was discipline. We simply were not taught how to study.
Which explains why, a few years later, in the face of a report
card studded with D's, it would be mutually agreed upon by
my parents and Mr. Nelson at the high school that I might be
better off at an old-style New England boarding school where
less emphasis was placed on rabbits and the life style of Swedish
families and more on simply "beating the books." This should
not be used as a blanket indictment of the theories of Dr. John
Dewey as developed by Mrs. Zyve. They may have helped most
of my early classmates at Fox Meadow. They didn't work
for me . . .

In the winter of 1929–30, however, there began to appear
a series of hairline cracks in that hitherto unblemished life style.
Something had happened, down in New York where all our
fathers commuted to each morning from the New York Central
station, a something called The Crash. Radio comedians seemed
to be getting an instant laugh by referring to U.S. Steel stock, or
to Goldman, Sachs. (Sydney Weinberg, who ran that firm, lived
a few blocks away, but neither of his sons, who attended our
school, could enlighten us as to what had happened.) As winter
came, the weather turned very cold, and so did the atmosphere
inside the living room. In the papers, there were references to
Bankruptcy and Business Failures, Deficits and Losses. Men who
were World War I veterans were agitating for something called
a Bonus, and they were threatening to March on Washington.
President Hoover was saying that Prosperity Was Just Around
the Corner. Nobody seemed to believe him. These events were
for grownups; we continued our daily pursuits, but there were
signs and portents. Heretofore, allowances had been handed out
without a murmur; now, fifty cents for a matinee treat in White
Plains, or for a new model Fokker D-7, or a pulp magazine down
at the Hartsdale stationery store, wasn't as easily available . . . if at
all.

As time passed, at recess, there was strange gossip about
certain of our friends' parents. They weren't working any more,
some of them. One of our cronies, Walter Breck, became the first

tangible participant in a tragedy. The Breck family lived in a large house up off Mamaroneck Road, and Mr. Breck was a rotund, jovial gent given to making small jokes with us as he drove off for his weekend golf game. Suddenly, something happened which grownups discussed in hushed voices, in conversations that stopped when we came into the room. On the school playground, one of my smart-aleck pals confided that Mr. Breck had actually tried to throw himself out of a window in his New York office, but he'd been stopped. Why? Why would he want to kill himself? Because he'd been Wiped Out.

It was puzzling, an event far beyond our daily ken, which mainly involved touch football and one-o'-cat, and the furtive passing of Mutt and Jeff and Winnie Winkle dirty comic books. But soon enough we encountered further tangible signs of disaster at the Brecks'. Mrs. Breck no longer drove around town in the family Cadillac limousine. It vanished as if conjured away by Harry Blackstone—whose tricks were available as premiums on the back of a cereal box, for two box tops plus ten cents cash. When we went up to the Breck house to play, Mr. Breck could be glimpsed out in the large wooded back yard, wandering idly among the rhododendrons and azaleas. We watched him from a respectful distance. There were no more jokes; he did not even seem to know we were there. Somehow or other, we knew better than to ask Walter about any of the disasters that were taking place, or what plans his father had for the future.

Then, one Saturday afternoon, there took place an even more perplexing magic trick, on a bold scale. We pedaled up the hill to the Breck house, rang the doorbell, and yelled for Walter to come out. There was no answer. We peered into the windows. Some few pieces of furniture still remained inside, but the house was locked up tight, and empty. The Brecks were gone, overnight. Nobody seemed to know where they had gone to, and I have never seen or heard of Walter Breck since.

Theirs was far from the only empty house along those quiet Scarsdale streets in the next few years. Later on, my father was to explain about Mortgages, and what happened when you couldn't pay the Bank the Principal and the Interest. Something called Foreclosure took place . . . not the way it did in the movies, but for real. As things got worse, the banks, just as shaky as their distressed debtors in those dark days, began to tell the harassed householders that they should stay on in their large suburban homes even if the father might not be able to meet his payments. For it made no sense to leave that unsalable, unrentable suddenly white elephant house standing empty; far better to allow the family to go on living in it, taking care of it, and to pay some agreed-upon token sum as rent. "And there were times," my father remembered later, "when plenty of those men couldn't even pay *that* much—and the bank carried them anyway."

Those men? Engineers, advertising executives, lawyers, insurance brokers, bond salesmen . . . they'd all been successful enough to move into Scarsdale homes. Suddenly, nobody's father seemed to be working. One of my mother's closest friends, an engineer's wife, a charming lady who kept an immaculate house and never allowed anybody into it with muddy feet, underwent a remarkable transformation. Her husband had abruptly been fired; after twenty years with a large corporation, he was faced with the fact that nobody needed his expertise. Necessity turned his wife into a drawn-faced lady in corduroys who canvassed door to door to offer other families her services as a landscape gardener. Her husband brooded in their immaculate home, with the lights turned off to save electricity; she tramped home with muddy boots . . . and enough cash to maintain the family for the next few days.

President Roosevelt and his bold new plans for survival hadn't yet arrived on the national scene. Men in shabby overcoats, or old uniforms, began to wander down our streets, ringing Greenacres and Fox Meadow and Heathcote doorbells to ask for work, and if that were unavailable, simply a handout. Other men rang the doorbell to ask if the lady of the house was home, sonny, and might she be interested in buying this new vacuum cleaner, or this set of brushes, maybe? Or anything from the contents of that battered sample case . . . Tired men with cracked shoes, sometimes middle-aged ladies, standing on the front steps and staring hopefully at me as I went to fetch my mother. Who would come prepared to say no-thank-you, but end up inevitably listening to the salesman's tale of woe, and purchasing some token item that she didn't need.

One old gent we knew well. An austere German with mustache and pince-nez, erect, a burgher out of a George Grosz drawing, he'd been coming for years, long before this new Depression, to tempt my mother by selling her his line of Braden's fancy canned fruits and vegetables. Mr. Haas—I think that was his name—filled with pride in his wares, had always driven up to our home and toted two sample cases filled with canned goods into our kitchen. When he spoke, he sounded like Sig Rumann in the Marx Brothers pictures, his accent all guttural r's and sharp edges. "Der absolute finesht, dees est Brraden's besht," he would say, proudly. As the times got tougher, his customers vanished. Soon his Buick coupé was gone, and when he arrived, it was on foot, on each visit a bit more stooped, his shoulders dragged down, his forehead wet from the exertion of lugging those sample cases full of Finest Fancy Grade A this or that up the hill from the Hartsdale station.

Mother had seen him coming up the front walk, and when she went to open the door, she would be sighing. My father had already warned her about expenses. The movie business wasn't thriving; the Warner Brothers were hurting financially. Even though he remarkably still had a job and brought home a weekly salary, he lived with uncertainty. Nightly, as he checked the bills and paid them, he would quietly plead with her to try and cut down.

But how could she cut down on old Mr. Haas? She would bring him into her kitchen and he would accept a cup of her coffee and ja, ja, he would have one of her fresh-baked muffins (it probably was all the food he'd had on these endless, frustrating days when nobody needed Braden's, it seemed), and then he would hopefully spread out his samples, heavy cans of Fancy Yellow Cling Peaches, Kadota Figs in Syrup, Watermelon Rind Preserve, Grapefruit Conserve, Peaches in Brandy . . . Delicacies as useless in these times as Mr. Hoover. Blinking behind his pince-nez, he would open his order book, one that obviously had had few leaves ripped out so far this day . . . or perhaps this week? And wait hopefully for her order.

Downstairs in our basement there were still quite a few cans of Braden's, neatly stacked on shelves from his last visit. Who needed more goods shipped all the way from California when the local merchants were clamoring with any of their remaining customers to deliver an order, any order, from one or two blocks away? . . . But my mother could never bring herself to send him away without an order, to plod wearily down the Scarsdale streets beneath the weight of those two heavy sample cases—turned away by her? She hadn't the heart. She ordered less, but she ordered. She found some cash in her purse and paid him—that way my father would be unable to find the telltale stub in the checkbook. Mr. Haas would thank her profusely and congratulate her for still recognizing quality. "Value for der money, dot is vat counts," he would insist, and bid her a grateful goodbye. Down the walk he went, his overcoat flapping around his legs, bent over, a vestigial reminder of other times, disappearing down the street. All his life he'd placed his faith in Braden's Finest Fancy. Now he was too old to abandon it, even if the virtue of Quality would inevitably betray him . . .

And when the shipment arrived, my mother would quickly put the carton away in the basement so that my father would not see it. It was becoming more difficult for her to practice her small deceits in the name of charity, but she continued. If our neighbors were running up large unpaid bills at the local stores, she would insist on paying cash, and she also insisted on trading with Larry Soma, who ran an independent grocery on Central Avenue and wasn't able to cut prices the way the A & P and Grand Union did. When my father complained, she refused to budge. Larry needed help; he got it from her. Years later, Larry told me that her weekly orders had often been the margin between his being able to stay open and bankruptcy. "The chains could carry their customers—they had to. But not me," he said, "and she knew that, God bless her."

Grim-faced, my father arrived home from work one night

to announce that something had happened at 321 West 44th Street called a Cut. Harry Warner had called in all his executives and told them that business was rotten, and to conserve the company cash, they could expect a ten-percent cut in pay. That each of them had a contract which called for a stipulated weekly check meant nothing. It was a matter of survival, and even more so a few weeks later, when Warner held a second crisis meeting to announce a second ten-percent cut, and by the time 1932 loomed up ahead, there came a third. None of the Warner executives could object; nobody needed to remind a man who still had a job those days that 70 percent of one's rightful salary was better than a place in one of the long bread lines that could be seen everywhere in the Forty-fourth Street neighborhood.

The entire amusement industry was backed against the wall. Even with Bank Nites and Free Dishes, Glassware, Bingo, and Admission Prices 25¢ before 1 P.M., people didn't have the necessary 25¢. Out in California, Paramount was floundering in receivership. Uncle Carl Laemmle's Universal Studio was headed for the same 77-B; RKO-Radio was in dire straits; Harry and Jack Cohn were struggling to keep their tiny Columbia alive. Even the vast feudal Culver City domain of Loew's, Inc., where MGM had heretofore thrived, was feeling financial pain. (Years later, Donald Ogden Stewart was to tell me of the day when L. B. Mayer called in all his expensive stars and hired hands to impress on them the need to take a severe cut. "It was a superb performance," said Don, "something like a prayer meeting. L. B. got down on his knees and began to weep, and asked me to join him in a prayer—to save our beloved MGM. Naturally, I agreed to the cut and so did everybody else. It was a long time after that that I discovered—while *we* all took cuts —old L. B. never did.")

I full well realize the implicit irony in setting down here that 1932 was a dark and gloomy winter at 4 Fenimore Road. "The Waltons" we weren't. We had light, heat, a roof over our heads, food on the table, and a father who could meet his mortgage payments. Compared to the ghastly conditions suffered by unemployed coal miners and farmers who were being evicted from their lands, migratory workers searching for stoop labor, auto workers and steelworkers and small businessmen who were watching their world go quickly to hell, we were sitting on top of the world. I do not know how many of our family's relatives survived because of my father's weekly pay check, but I do know there were quite a few. I also know of his endless efforts to find jobs for many of his old confreres who had fallen on hard times, failed legitimate producers who were ecstatic to find work as company managers and ticket takers when he could place them. And my mother constantly substituted work for largess for local people who were in trouble. There was a French lady who had once been governess for my younger sister; if Mme. Sarthou had been fired, she would have instantly been out on the street. Long after my sister was well able to care for herself, Mme. Sarthou stayed on, cheerfully working for as much, or as little, as the family finances could bear. And when Mme. Sarthou's nephew Joseph, a skilled Basque mechanic who'd been working at the Marmon plant, building luxury automobiles, was pink-slipped, somehow he ended up living at our house, in a basement room, instead of in a bread line. "We don't need a mechanic around here!" my father protested, the day before he arrived. "He needs a place to live until he can find another job," said my mother. "How can we turn him away?"

Joseph came to stay, and remained for more than a year, helping out with odd jobs in return for room and board . . . for by that time, there simply was no spare cash with which to pay him. My father had come home one night with a really shocking piece of news. Cash was so tight in the Forty-fourth Street offices that Harry, Abe, and Jack Warner were desperately trying to keep the company afloat; all hands aboard that leaky vessel were ordered to take a *fifty*-percent cut. Until when? Until something miraculous like a smash hit film could surface and bail out the Warner Brothers.

That was a grim holiday season. Joseph kept busy around the house by tuning up every piece of machinery he could find. He was a mechanic and he couldn't stand inactivity. Out in the garage was a three-year-old Buick sedan. He washed and polished it until it gleamed. Then he decided to overhaul the car. Grimly, he took its engine apart and did a valve job, with his own tools. He worked on the pistons, and anything else that moved. He took out the huge clutch and washed the plates, and put it all back together again, and when he had it tuned, that big Buick engine purred like a satisfied Persian cat. It's safe to say that no General Motors product before or since ever operated at such an optimum level as that old Buick which he tinkered with, endlessly, day after day, in that cold, dark winter of 1932.

One brisk winter evening, my father came up the steps from his commuter train, rummaged in his briefcase, the old one in which he carried home galley proofs and playscripts every night, and handed me a phonograph record. It was a promotion record, on the Brunswick label—Brunswick was a subsidiary of Warners, purchased in an earlier, more affluent time when the company was flush with profits from Vitaphone. We put it on the old RCA phonograph, and heard the spiel that heralded the coming of a new Warner film. An excited announcer gave a speech that promised great excitement, stars, dancing girls, and laughs, and then the Vitaphone orchestra, conducted by Leo F. Forbstein, struck up a medley of some of the song hits from the picture, written by Harry Warren and Al Dubin. We were treated to fragments of "Shuffle Off to Buffalo," "Petting in the Park," and then, for a big finale, a new tenor named Dick Powell sang a chorus of the title song, a fast-paced number that sang of the joys of Forty-second Street.

The record ended. "Gee," I said, "I hope that's a hit."

"You're not the only one," said my father, with a sigh.

We had a new president, a Democrat named Roosevelt, and his clear voice was heard on the radio, and we saw him in the newsreels, telling us that the only thing we had to feah was feah itself. The first few weeks of Mr. Roosevelt's administration were rocky indeed. In order to save the country's banks from going under, Mr. Roosevelt declared something called the Bank Holiday. Whatever that meant, none of us at Fox Meadow School knew enough about economics to figure out, but its tangible result was that for the next week you got your recess milk and graham crackers without having to fork up the customary two cents in cash. It was my first experience with the miracle of credit . . .

Smack in the middle of that Bank Holiday, when people in New York were taking cabs and paying for them with IOUs because nobody had any cash, the Warners sent *Forty-second Street* out to the theatres. The Warner publicity department, run by a dynamic gent named Charlie Einfeld, devised a massive promotional stunt, which involved sending a train packed with movie stars all the way from California across the country to New York, for the film's opening. On the train were Bebe Daniels, Lyle Talbot, Leo Carillo, Veree Teasdale, Eleanor Holm, the swimmer, Bette Davis (far more agreeable to such hoopla back then than she might be later on), and a chorus line of Busby Berkeley's finest tappers.

By the time the *Forty-second Street* Special arrived in New York, the banks had reopened. The picture was a smash hit. If ever there was an example of the right film for the right time and place, it was that happy musical. (Which had been made in the Burbank studio without anybody telling Darryl Zanuck, the production head, because, as Zanuck had heretofore been fond of saying, "Musicals are dead at the box office.")

Soon there was to be an NIRA, and a Blue Eagle, and something called the Civilian Conservation Corps. Prohibition would end, and beer would flow, at three bottles for a quarter . . . There would be a Works Progress Administration, and an AAA, and a CWA, and all sorts of other bold devices proposed by Mr. Roosevelt, who was bent on getting the economy back into gear. If we'd touched rock bottom and were back on our way upwards, then it's always seemed to me that we began the long climb upwards to the tapping of eighty-odd pairs of dancers' feet, and the sound of Warner Baxter saying to Ruby Keeler, "You're going out there a nobody—but you're coming back a star!"

In a matter of weeks after *Forty-second Street* had opened, there was sufficient cash in the Warner tills to restore executive salaries, and my father came home from his office with far fewer worry lines around his eyes. There were still four or five bad years ahead, but at least now there was a sense of optimism. There were still plenty of jokes about Goldman, Sachs, true, but soon the Busby Berkeley girls would be happily telling us that "We're in the Money."

And how could anybody possibly make a liar out of them?

Years later, after World War II, we moved away from Scarsdale. My parents sold 4 Fenimore Road, where we'd grown up. Where Joseph had lived in the basement room and spent hours in a cold garage dissecting our Buick. The kitchen where old Mr. Haas had sipped coffee and hopefully spread out his samples. The front walk where all those nameless wanderers had trudged up to ring our bell and plead for a handout. The library where my father would sit up each night, poring over books and play-scripts and newspapers, endlessly hunting for material that might later turn up as the basis of a Warner Brothers Vitaphone hit . . . some of them still unspooled each night on Channel 5, tangible reminders of his judgment.

Sure, Scarsdale today is a quiet, affluent suburb, content with its good life, the tennis and the golf, the ten-speed bikes and the Mercedes, the catered parties and the well-chosen art hanging on the wall. The well-tended gardens and immaculate lawns, nicely setting off all those safe houses . . . which once sheltered terrified families with no bank balances and little prospect of anything. Perhaps the town *is* too secure in its afflu-ence . . . that's what the angry writer on the *Times* Op-Ed page was complaining about, isn't it, that the town was insulating his kids against the reality of harsher existence elsewhere?

Well, then again, I'm not so sure about the gentleman's desire for immersing his offspring in harsh reality. We all had a very good exposure to it, back there in 1931 and 1932, et seq. And I'm here to tell you, it was the sort of learning experience I'd just as soon not expose my kids to, thank you. Once was plenty. Let them find their insecurities somewhere else.

••••••••••••••••••••••••••

CHAPTER FOUR

Black Mask

IN A FAR CORNER of the attic are numerous boxes of old magazines. Stored by my two sons, they have been stowed away for safekeeping, and for several years now they have been gathering a fine patina of dust.

In one carton are stacks of ten-year-old magazines that deal with the subject of hot-rodding. A decade ago—how did time undergo such a re-engineering?—both adolescent boys were avid devotees of the noble art of putting together tiny plastic car models, and then modifying them with tiny silver camshafts, oversized wheels and hubs, misshapen bodies, bedecking the result with exotic mini-paint jobs, all in the style of the mystical cult of street-rods.

Stuffed in the other cartons are dozens of monthly science-fiction magazines, and in the last one is a carefully filed run of an underground newspaper which flourished several years ago—the *East Village Other*. By their reading shall ye see their rites of passage . . .

We are going through one of our periods of housecleaning, in a vain attempt to dispense with some of the accumulated clutter, and my wife wants to know if we can't possibly get rid of all those dusty cartons up there. If not all—at least *some?* . . .

No, we cannot. The two young men rarely agree on much, but on this point they are a united front. They insist that the contents of those cartons are precious. It's not merely the sentimental value of all those yellowing pages which concerns them. Don't we understand that the material in those stacks is rare, and is becoming even rarer by the hour? Why, those magazines are absolutely collector's items . . .

I am tempted to snicker.

A rare-book auction at Parke-Bernet, in which eager dealers vie with each other for slightly worn copies of 1959 model-builder's handbooks? Ludicrous.

But then I decide against comment. For I know something about collecting. Especially magazines.

Take, for instance, the *Black Mask* caper . . .

It all began back in the very early 1930s.

A very rough time, true. But the vintage years of the pulps.

Radio was first beginning to exert its powerful influence on the American audience. Some of the well-meaning ladies of the Scarsdale, New York, Fox Meadow School PTA became alarmed at the ugly prospect of what this new time-consuming medium might do to pervert the reading habits of their tender grade-schoolers. A grass-roots letter campaign began. Anxious matrons flooded the networks in New York with protest; the burden of their thesis wasn't (as it would be years later) why their Johnny couldn't read—it was Johnny Listens So Much to That Radio that Johnny *Won't* Read!

Downstairs, our mothers were writing letters. They should have done a little checking. Upstairs, we *were* reading.

Unfortunately, we weren't gorging our eyes on exactly the sort of tomes that they had in mind. Up in our rooms behind closed doors, or down in the basement, in the garage, we were turning pages, hypnotized by pulp magazines. All of us—everyone in the male population of the fifth grade at Fox Meadow—were hopelessly enslaved to such absolute *dreck* as *Amazing Stories, Detective Fiction Weekly, War Tales, Short Story Magazine, Doc Savage, Adventure, The Shadow, Railroad Stories, G-8 and His Battle Aces.* Whatever literary *schlock* was being peddled, we devoured it, and looked hungrily for more.

Future generations would riffle through comic-book pages. Not us. We read.

Dr. DeHart, an earnest English teacher, insisted that we get

through certain books. Fenimore Cooper, Mark Twain, Hawthorne; he even had us tackling some of the work of an Englishman, a bloke named Dickens. (Remember, this was all back a
good quarter century B.S.—Before Salinger.) Reading such heavy
junk was a chore to be dispensed with as soon as possible; if one
didn't get through those assignments, one wasn't going to pass, so
one gritted his teeth and slogged through *The Last of the
Mohicans* and *The House of the Seven Gables* and *A Christmas
Carol,* impatiently waiting for that last page so that one could get
down to the *real* reading at hand . . . this month's copy of whatever goody had been acquired from the Hartsdale cigar-store
pulp rack, down there by the railroad station. *Battle Stories . . .
that* was reading . . .

Not that any of us had enough cash to sustain our literary
blood lust. Perhaps the most affluent of my acquaintances could
swing one twenty-five-cent pulp every couple of weeks. The
rest of us settled for a less ostentatious fifteen-center. Either investment bought you three or four hours' worth of high adventure; stiff-backed and covered with glossy paper, a pulp usually
contained a novelette (BOOK LENGTH! it often said, proudly, on
the cover), five or six short stories with a minimum of art work on
their title pages, a section of laudatory Letters to Ye Ed, and at the
back a seductive Coming Next Month in Our Next Slam Bang
Issue, with a list of titles attached . . . On the back cover of the
mag (they always referred to themselves by that cheery nick-
name) was often an ad for the International Correspondence
Schools that promised earnings as high as $50 a week in return for
nighttime study. Or there might be an ad which promised BIG
MONEY FOR GROWING MUSHROOMS IN YOUR CELLAR. Often, there
was a puzzle contest: a trick drawing of a landscape, above which
it screamed WIN $$$$! FIND THE SIX HIDDEN FACES IN THIS PIC-
TURE—HURRY!—CONTEST CLOSES SHORTLY! Any hapless goof who
clipped the coupon below soon learned his lesson; within
days, a formidable carton of forty-eight bottles of cheap toilet
water—or flower seeds—or cheap candy—would arrive at the
family mailbox, with instructions from some far-off Fagin that

one was to peddle the lot to one's friends and neighbors for 25 cents per, remit the proceeds promptly to Contest Puzzle GHQ, after which one would move on to Phase Two of the Giant Competition . . .

There were also interesting smaller ads, for surplus World War I equipment, or from outfits in Hollywood, California, who guaranteed, from their anonymous P.O. Box Number 19, that you had talent, and there was big money to be made in selling your original songs to the movie producers, and then there were the ads for trusses.

But on the cover of any pulp . . . ahh—those action-packed tableaux. Virile trappers wrestling giant grizzly bears. Huge steam engines racing across burning bridges towards safety. Grim-faced doughboys bayoneting ugly Germans. Lean cowboys, their twin .44s blazing at unshaven rustlers. Wildly decorated Fokker D-7s, high in the blue, locked in eternal combat with heroic Allied pilots in Spads and Sopwith Camels, ominous gleaming cigar-shaped Martian vehicles descending on a burning Manhattan skyline . . . Years before Roy Lichtenstein was to impress it on the world, *we* knew that stuff was Art.

Drunk with action adventure—blazing bullets, fists of steel, iron men with grim jaws inexorably closing in for the kill, etc., etc.—we gulped down the latest copy and went desperately hunting for more, more, and since none of us had sufficient capital to sustain the habit, we developed our own bourse. We swapped. On the Fox Meadow School playground, at recess, or in a friend's basement, two fifteen-cent Western mags and some fast talking could bring you one twenty-five-cent *Battle Stories*. Most World War I stuff, as I remember, usually commanded a higher trading value than the somewhat staid *Short Story*, or *Argosy*, and all those cheaper Street & Smith magazines which featured Doc Savage, the adventurer, or that hooded nemesis of crime, The Shadow, were very hot items. Only weirdos went for the exotic early science-fiction books of Dr. Hugo Gernsback—in fact, one book was named for them—*Weird Tales*. It was a bit too high-brow for our exchange . . .

But there was one pulp magazine that I never swapped. A unique monthly called *Black Mask*. That one, I decided early on, was for reading . . . and *keeping*.

After all, I was a *Black Mask subscriber*.

How had I come by that exalted status? Certainly not by clipping a coupon and mailing in the required two dollars per year; no indeed. Who had two dollars cash in those years? No, my subscription was strictly graft, courtesy of the editor himself.

Captain Joseph T. Shaw was a Scarsdalian, and a good friend of my father, who would often take the same 8:18 into New York with him. An affable gent, grey-haired and mustached, a trim veteran of World War I, he seemed, the first time he appeared in our living room, much more like some insurance executive, or a banker, than the editor of a thriving pulp magazine, on whose pages were private detectives doing battle with the underworld.

Somehow or other, Shaw learned from me that I was a secret pulp addict, and that made us mutual fans, and we stayed so from then on. Shortly afterwards, he suggested that I try *his* magazine on a steady basis.

I must have mumbled some excuse about my lack of funds. He accepted that shortage with a careless shrug. After all, the whole country was in the same awkward mess. "Don't worry about that," he said cheerfully, and winked. "I'll put you on the free list."

It began to arrive, once a month, in a brown manila wrapper. There it sat, on the hall table, all mine, waiting for me to get home from those boring 5B English classes at Fox Meadow, to drop my schoolbooks, slide the latest issue out of its wrapper, trot upstairs to my room, slam the door shut . . . and fall to engorging its contents.

True enough, the monthly covers of *Black Mask* had just as high a violence quotient as did the other current pulps. There were all those familiar cowering women being protected by staunch detectives, the ugly criminal types, always unshaven, shooting it out with bluecoats, powerful cars careening away from robbed banks, all the standard stuff. It was inside, starting on page 5, after the ads, that "Cap" Shaw's magazine was different from the rest. Although I couldn't have foreseen it at the time, he was becoming one of the most powerful influences on modern-day American crime fiction. Up to that period of the early '30s, most pulp writing was pure hackwork of the most mechanical sort, churned out by ink-stained wretches at a fixed price, a penny a word. The upper-class, hard-cover detective stories were all terribly genteel, and mostly a monopolistic game, in the hands of a few English authors. Shaw, and the authors he induced to write for him, changed all that, and he did it in the pages of a pulp.

What was beginning to appear between those covers was a whole new genre of crime fiction, created by men who were *writing*. Today, critics refer to it in historical terms as "the hard-boiled school." Back in 1931, however, the taste-makers and the critics hadn't a clue that it was there. How could they? None of them would admit to reading such popular entertainments as a mag that was designed to separate the hoi polloi from a monthly quarter. Poor deprived intellectuals—they were deprived of a heady experience, one that this eleven-year-old was enjoying mightily. But had any of the critics picked up a copy of *Black Mask,* he would have soon discovered that there was a sharp difference between it and the mechanical stuff in all the other pulps. The Street & Smith hacks dealt in broad-stroked, un-motivated hack-plot slam-bang escapades, populated with cartoon-strip characters. Not Shaw's authors. Under his tutelage, they learned to write lean prose, to create character tensions. The dialogue was stripped down, laconic, revealing. Shaw's people were dealing with people . . .

Make no mistake about it, Shaw's writers *were* his people. Somewhere, somehow, he was finding them, recognizing their talents, and then encouraging them to write the sort of stuff he wanted for his mag. He supported them, buying their short stories, providing them with a steady market; it was a good arrangement for all hands. Shaw's stable would become reliable sources for *Black Mask's* table of contents. Soon, the short-story writers were moving on to novelettes, and then forty- and fifty-page novels, with fully developed plots and well-fleshed charac-

ters. As they developed for Shaw, they were developing for themselves . . . and for his faithful readers.

So if an editor is known by the company of writers he keeps,
let us pay ample tribute to Captain Shaw's roster.

For several issues, I'd been reading short, tersely written
stories about a character who worked for a detective agency, and
who went by the name of the Continental Op. He was a Califor-
nia-based bloodhound, and the adventures in which he figured
were peopled with fascinating characters. Then, one remarkable
month, there appeared the first installment of a five-part serial,
by the same author. "The name on the office door read 'Spade &
Archer'" was the opening line, and that was enough of a hook
to get me through that first installment as if I'd just graduated
from a speed-reading course. Alas, I was left panting for the
next four installments like some poor hooked fish who's been
dropped on the riverbank.

That night, when my father returned from New York, I
confronted him with this injustice. I complained bitterly about
the torture of this fiendish serial form. Who could have invented
such a swindle? To start a story, build up suspense, and then shut
it off abruptly—leaving this impatient reader to wait an interminable four weeks for the next installment! *Rotten!*

And what might be the name of this exciting new story?

I ran upstairs and brandished my latest copy of *Black Mask*.
He studied the title. He noted the author's name, and then he
nodded sympathetically. "Tell me what it's about," he said. I
gave him a quick précis of the plot—as far as it went.

"Let me see if I can get you the next four installments from
Cap Shaw," he said, and tucked my copy of the magazine into
his worn briefcase.

I might have realized that his interest wasn't purely altruistic—after all, he was a story editor with the sharpest eyes and ears
and radar in the business—but I merely took his gesture for
parental solicitude. At the time . . .

It was a couple of weeks before he returned with the
promised bounty. My copy, and the ensuing four installments, in
galley proof, of *The Maltese Falcon*, by Dashiell Hammett.

"Sorry you had to wait for these," he apologized. "But I had to have one of my readers do a synopsis of the book to send out to California before I could bring it home to you."

Synopsis? . . . of a *Black Mask* story? *Why?*

"Oh, I thought maybe there might be a movie in this," he said, casually making the understatement of that, or any other, year. "The studio seems to agree with me, and so we've made a deal to buy the movie rights."

Because *I* had brought him my copy of the magazine?

He nodded. "So now you can go finish reading it," he said, handing over the whole works. "Here—you've earned them. Provided you've finished your homework, that is."

If I felt any sense of triumph over our joint coup, it was dispelled the following fall, when Warner Brothers produced *The Maltese Falcon* as a film, starring Bebe Daniels and Ricardo Cortez. It wasn't a very good picture, on that we both agreed. How could they have bitched up such a damn good plot? I protested.

My father shrugged. "It happens," he sighed.

It was some ten years later, after countless B-picture remakes of the Hammett classic by Brynie Foy (he was fondly known at Warners as "The Keeper of the B's"), that John Huston came along to rescue Hammett's story, and to make it into the great film that it always will remain . . . and, I suppose, to justify our original faith in that *Black Mask* novel.

The stack of *Black Masks* grew too high for a bookshelf, so they were carefully consigned to an attac storeroom. Would that I had also kept those Hammett galley proofs . . . but no matter, I had the actual magazines, and, thanks to Cap Shaw's largess, they continued to come. Every month his mag plunged me headlong into that fascinating landscape somewhere far away from suburban Scarsdale, to city streets and offices and speakeasies . . . the world of the Continental Op, and someone named Cameo Kirby. A hypnotic scene, in which guns were gats and roscoes which spat and/or ka-chowed, opening up holes in gangsters— who were also referred to as "gunsels." Cops were thick-skinned bluecoats, detectives had persistently throbbing hangovers from

A SCENE from the first version of *The Maltese Falcon* (1931), with which you can win parlor games by identifying the first Sam Spade and his secretary, Effie. JOHN ALLEN COLLECTION

rotgut booze, their fee was a green sawbuck a day, women were frails, and very often not to be trusted . . . and the ritual-like unraveling of who was doing what to whom, and why, was known as a caper.

Justice wasn't always on the side of law and order. Plenty of the lowest characters on those pages were the solidest of citizens. Corruption was dealt with as an everyday fact of life. Shaw wasn't afraid to flout conventional moralities; his authors often depicted authority and its police arm as being for sale to the highest bidder. Conversely, his present-day Robin Hoods were not very likable men, who lived by their wits, far outside the law. *Black Mask* provided me with a survey course in cynicism. Sprawled on a secure couch in a safe Scarsdale library, I learned that politicians were not altruists, that a wife might cheat on her husband, nay, even plot to get rid of her lord and master . . . that honesty wasn't always the exclusive property of the property-owner. Heady stuff—very far from the simplistic morality of staid old Fenimore Cooper, or Nathaniel Hawthorne.

And a hell of a lot more exciting. The stories had pace, and they moved with the speed of a streamlined train. That was Shaw's recipe . . . *Move it forward, but tell me what makes the people tick as we go, and wind it up with a K.O. at the end.*

He ran a first-class incubator and academy, and his authors have long since proved out his faith in their talent. Along with the unique Dashiell Hammett, some of his regulars were Raoul Whitfield—who was to write a first-rate *roman policier,* a lost classic called *Green Ice*—George Harmon Coxe, who is still writing hard-cover mysteries forty years later, and Frederick Nebel, who soon after matriculated into published thrillers and the *Saturday Evening Post* elite. All of them, and many others, were polishing their craft for Shaw, and their output was considerable. But then, at a mere penny a word, it had to be, didn't it?

He kept on turning them up for his monthly table of contests. Soon after *l'affaire Maltese Falcon,* my father and I stumbled across another piece of buried treasure. Shaw began to publish a series of stories about a young lawyer out West who regularly turned detective in order to defend his clients from an unjust law system. The author was himself a lawyer, and his name was Erle Stanley Gardner. I whizzed through his first Perry Mason adventure; I had to share my excitement with someone. That night, I proudly thrust the copy of *Black Mask* across the dinner table at my father. He peered at the title, "The Case of the Howling Dog."

"Good?" he inquired.

"Neat!" I assured him.

He tucked the copy into his briefcase, and off it went to the city.

When he brought up the subject of Perry Mason again, some days later, he was beaming cheerfully. "Pretty sharp stuff," he agreed "We've bought the rights to that story for a picture. By the way, I've spoken to this Erle Stanley Gardner—he lives out in California—and I told him that you were the one who was responsible for our getting the first look at his story. He was tickled to hear it . . ."

Who needed to join the Boy Scouts? I was already a scout.

A year or so later, Gardner went into hard covers, the first book of the literally scores of detective novels he was to turn out over the next three decades. There arrived at our house a copy of the book, inscribed by the author to me. It has, alas, long since been pilfered from the shelf, but as I recall what he wrote (who could forget it?), he went into some detail over my literary judgment, the result of which had been to launch Perry Mason on the screen.

The actor who portrayed Mason was Warren William, and the picture, again, didn't live up to our expectations. A quarter of a century later, when Gardner and I corresponded about a television project (nobody would have dropped him as a pen pal, would he?), he summed up the situation. "It was nice of you and your old man to get Perry into films," he wrote, "but thank Heaven, I was smart enough to see that those studio guys would run old Perry into the ground with their assembly-line operation . . . So I got him back, and I kept him off the screen, until television . . . where I figured he'll have a much longer career."

MANY YEARS before Raymond Burr, Warren William was the first Perry Mason. Here he is in *The Case of the Lucky Legs*, with Patricia Ellis and Lyle Talbot (1935). With great foresight, Erle Stanley Gardner retrieved the rights to his character and made himself and Mr. Burr millionaires. JOHN ALLEN COLLECTION

You figured right, Mr. Gardner . . .

There were some empty shelves in our attic, and after three or four years of Captain Shaw's extraordinary munificence, I'd established up there a very satisfactory five-foot shelf of *Black Mask* crime fiction, suitable for rainy-afternoon browsing—but never for swapping or trading.

Even though my literary tastes where broadening—I was becoming an itchy devotee of such forbidden fruit as *Spicy Detective* and *Spicy Western*, where the plots weren't much, but the bedroom action was a bit more explicit—I never deserted *Black Mask*, and then I began to pay some attention to the work of one of Shaw's latest discoveries, a writer named Raymond Chandler.

His stories dealt with Southern California, and his heroes were private detectives, tough and yet intuitive, capable of absorbing vast amounts of physical punishment and bonded bourbon. His prose was spare, his plots complex. When he finally hit his stride and tackled a full-length novel, it took very little time for a prestigious publisher to put *The Big Sleep* into hard covers. That one was an instant out-of-the-ball-park hit, but it had been sold before publication to Warner Brothers. For some time, I'd been waving copies of Chandler's early stories at my father. He needed no further prompting; he was prepared for that novel with a contract and a corporate check for the screen rights.

I'd undoubtedly spent too much time reading pulps instead of required textbooks, for not long afterwards, by mutual consent of the authorities at Scarsdale High School and my family, I departed from the local school system and was sent off for remedial tuition at a strict and structured New England boarding school.

It must have been several years later that I went prowling up in the attic, in search of my shelf of childhood treasure, that file of *Black Mask*. But there was no sign of the copies I'd stored up there, not a single one.

What had become of my precious hoard of the Continental Op, of Cameo Kirby and Perry Mason, Sam Spade, and all the rest of my hero figures? Had somebody moved them to another corner of the attic?

No such luck.

All those junky old magazines? Gone. Taken away last year by someone from the Salvation Army, as part of one of those convulsive clean-up campaigns which gratify the need for neatness that some mothers are prone to . . . Just like that. She'd had them all taken away! . . . But hadn't she understood their literary worth? Their intrinsic value?

Certainly not. A trashy pulp magazine—all those copies had been cluttering up the attic. But I must understand that there was nothing personal about her feelings—hadn't she given away years' worth of *National Geographic*, and *Yellow Book,* and even a long green-backed file of old copies of the *American Mercury*? (Yes, that same treasure house of early H. L. Mencken, and George Jean Nathan, Ernest Hemingway, and dozens of other 1920s authors.)

I didn't give a damn about the *Mercury*—although I should have. For it was almost too painful to consider that somewhere, in a filthy Salvation Army warehouse, carelessly tossed into a corner, forlorn, forgotten, turning yellow, and coming apart at the seams, were all those seventy-odd copies of Captain Shaw's largess that I'd husbanded so carefully.

It was quite a while before I was able to swallow my bile and try to conquer the frustration induced by my mother's thoughtless act.

Captain Shaw eventually retired. Other, less skillful hands took over the operation of his magazine. Perry Mason, Philip Marlowe, Sam Spade . . . they had all become stars, worth a hell of a lot more than a penny a word. The new editors were obviously unable to afford Shaw's writers, and *Black Mask* degenerated into just another cheap pulp. Shaw had been midwife to a new school of fiction . . . and who is to deny that for an editor such an epitaph isn't as good as he'd have wanted?

Some years ago, on my way home through Grand Central, I picked up a copy of a magazine of detective fiction, edited by

Ellery Queen. Old reading habits die hard . . .

In it was a small advertisement, signed by the editors—
Manfred Lee and Frederic Dannay (Ellery Queen, to the world).
It seemed they were advising their readers that they wished to
acquire copies of an obscure magazine long since out of print,
a pulp published in the late '20s and early '30s. Would anyone
help them to locate issues—one, two, ten, *any*—of *Black Mask*
magazine? It was valuable source material for a project they
planned to start—a survey of the source material of American
crime fiction. They were prepared to negotiate price—but cost
was not an object.

I had nothing to sell them.

But even if I still had that valuable file of *Black Mask*s
they were seeking, I'm not sure I'd be prepared to part with it.

So . . . we will not be tossing out those cartons of magazines
that our sons have left sitting up there in the attic. Those aren't
simply hot-rod magazines, and science-fiction books, and underground papers we're storing for them. They're footnotes to *their*
youth.

CHAPTER FIVE

•••••••••••••••••••••••••

Pop Eldredge of New Haven

TAKE A LEFT off the Connecticut Turnpike, swing onto the Oak
Street connector, turn right at its end, and head the car in the
direction of the Taft Hotel, that once proud hostelry which stood
as a New Haven landmark throughout the '20s and '30s. There
you will see, dwarfed on one side by the moldering Taft, on the
other by a stark new parking building, a modest marquee which
reads SHUBERT. That, traveler, is a legitimate theatre, one of the
last of a vanishing category—a tryout house, on whose stage, for
more than half a century now, Broadway producers have rolled
the dice with their new shows.

Time was when tryout theatres could be everywhere on the
eastern seaboard. Up and down the Jersey shore went impresarios,
taking their newly mounted musicals and comedies and three-act
mysteries to such exotic opening-night locales as Asbury Park and
Atlantic City. Pittsburgh; Wilmington, Delaware; Hartford;
Cleveland; Detroit—in days past they also served as incubators
for shows. (According to the collected letters of Groucho Marx,
his good friend Harry Ruby once opened a show called *Helen of
Troy, N.Y.* in the rural surroundings of Fairmont, West Virginia.
Once, that is.)

Over on the Turnpike is the new Long Wharf arena-style
theatre, where a repertory company plays each season, and up on
Chapel Street, Dean Brustein of the Drama School has instituted
a Yale Repertory, but the Shubert, that plain little legit house a

few yards from the New Haven green—where many a brooding playwright has sat and contemplated self-destruction—is
practically the only true tryout theatre left to New York
producers. And in these days of rising production costs and
shrinking audiences, who can tell how much longer that Shubert
marquee will remain lit?

One should not think of such depressing prospects. Should
a new show be opening tonight at the Shubert, the audience will
come filing in through those swinging glass doors, the curtain
will go up at 8:40 or so, and the first act will begin. For the
next two hours, as it has for years, the New Haven audience will
sit in judgment. It is a peculiar mix in those Shubert seats; some
of the crowd consists of professionals, up from New York for an
early look. They will be agents who have clients in the cast or on
the production staff, film people up to scout the show's possibilities, a few dogged investors who have backed the show, plus loyal
friends and well-wishers, pseudo and real, of everyone. Sprinkle
in some Yale students and faculty, then suburbanites from lower
Fairfield County or down from Hartford; the rest of the house is
a die-hard core of locals. Those New Havenites are the ones who
regularly gamble their ticket money on this game of theatrical
roulette, all of them betting seven dollars or more per seat that
tonight they will be in on the premiere of a new *My Fair Lady*
or *A Streetcar Named Desire*. Oh yes, they opened here, right in
this very house.

More often than not, they will lose that seven dollar bet.
But like all dedicated gamblers, Shubert audiences keep on coming back to that 8:40 wheel every opening night. Bless them.
Sans their support, the management would starve . . . and sooner
or later the Shubert will be replaced by a condominium full of
people watching TV.

Which would be a severe loss. Shubert openings provide one
with drama on both sides of the proscenium. Going into the
theatre around 8:20, one can easily spot the nervous playwright,
already fortified by double vodka martinis around the corner at
Kaysey's, smiling wanly at his fond relatives. There's the director, gaunt, eyes red from lack of sleep, followed by his faithful

assistant, with her ever-ready clipboard and pocket flash, her
handbag full of his supply of Gelusil and Valium. Glance at the
back of the orchestra during the performance itself—it's a piece of
real estate usually reserved for standees, but that's only after the
show's opened and got good notices. Tonight that area is a
truncated track populated by nervous pacers, a crew of production people, technicians, and the producer himself, perhaps, all
muttering curses at missed cues up there on the brightly lit stage,
holding heads over malfunctioning scenery during muffed scene
changes. Shubert intermissions are replete with tense lobby scenes
between huddled groups of partisan pros, all of them with high
stakes riding on tonight's venture, whose tensions can often
explode into argument. Out there, lines are being drawn for post–
third-act-curtain battles. Sometimes the poor playwright isn't
even waiting for the end; he's headed out into the night for
Kaysey's bar to refuel *now*. And when the final curtain comes
down, the audience will applaud (the paying customers perhaps
not as enthusiastically as, say, the producer's family claque) and
file out into the night. There will be shrugs and protests if it's
a flop, or smiles of satisfaction, less often, if the show has a
fighting chance.

Follow everyone to Kaysey's, and there, in various booths, the
second of tonight's shows is on, played usually over heaping
plates of food and medicinal drink. Classic confrontations will
ensue as formalized as anything in the Roman arena. Playwright
will lock horns with director over botched-up casting and scenes,
director will accuse playwright of resisting changes, actors will
throw tantrums over big scenes which didn't play, agents will
defiantly argue on behalf of their clients, everyone will accuse
everyone else of sabotage, paranoia, and ineptitude, there will be
in-fighting, furies, alarums and excursions all through the night
. . . and tomorrow the painful but hopeful process known as
"fixing" will commence.

Whether or not the repairs will be sufficient to bring about
a successful opening night in New York, several weeks hence,
is really problematic. Perhaps the producer will bring in a new
director to take over; he may scout around desperately to secure

the services of some other playwright, a good "fixer-upper" to help out his own weary author. The pressures of time, and of hostile audiences, and of a dwindling bankroll are immense. From tomorrow on, it's The Clutch—times ten. "Anybody can call himself a producer," my father once told me. "All he has to do is to raise the money for a production, cast it, and bring it up to the New Haven Shubert. But *my* definition of a producer is the guy who opens a show in New Haven, and sees it's in trouble—and three weeks later brings it into New York a hit. *That's* a producer . . ."

This night, the play we are going up to see, in its premiere performance, is the latest venture of Morton Gottlieb. For three years now, he has had a big hit running, both on Broadway and in films . . . *Sleuth*. He is one of the few working producers left on the bleak Broadway scene, and we have close ties. We were undergraduates at Yale, more years ago than either of us cares to remember. Both of us are therefore Yale/Shubert alumni. We served our apprenticeship in those orchestra seats beyond the glass lobby doors. The two of us have grown grey together in thirty-five-odd years attendance at Shubert tryouts . . .

My first taste of Shubert roulette was in the fall of 1937, when I was a bright-eyed and bushy-tailed Yale freshman. Late one Thursday afternoon, my father arrived from New York with a seductive invitation. Dinner, and then the Shubert. A new play was opening that night—did I wish to join him?

He didn't have to twist my arm, especially as regards the meal. Yale Freshman Commons was notorious for the substandard food served to hapless poor little lambs. After dinner, we went down to the Shubert and into the lobby, where he secured his tickets—they had been left in his name, as always—and we went in to the show. Time has washed away everything about the show, its name and/or cast. But I certainly have never forogtten the events of the intermission.

We made our way out to the Shubert's vast, drafty lobby. Standing by the door which leads to the box-office was a medium-sized man of indeterminate age, wearing a dark, immaculately cut suit. His face was cocoa brown, from either the sun or a sun lamp—so burnt umber, in fact, that he might easily have been mistaken for an American Indian. The resemblance to Sitting Bull was accentuated by a sharp nose, sunken cheeks, and a pair of deep-set eyes, which now were carefully scanning the lobby. When he spotted my father, he waved. The gesture indicated that we were to come over.

When he spoke, it was in a high, small voice. "How are you, Jake? How did you like the show?

My father shrugged. "Too early to tell, Mr. Lee," he said. "Maybe after the next act we'll know better . . ."

"Don't go back to New York without telling me," remarked Mr. Lee. "I want to know what you think."

My father proceeded to introduce me to this gentleman. He explained that I had just begun my freshman year at Yale. Mr. Lee examined me with those keen eyes. Did I like the theatre? he demanded. With as much enthusiasm as was proper, I nodded. Yale mores frowned on too much overt enthusiasm; Eli under-graduates dispensed hauteur to the outside world. But I ventured the fact that I'd come to Yale with the specific aim of studying playwriting at the famous Drama School.

"Good, good," said Mr. Lee. "We need new playwrights, eh, Jake? Tell you what. I'll speak to the manager here and have him give you a couple of seats for the shows. How would you like that?"

Two seats for Shubert shows, during its busy season?

My hauteur was demolished. I managed to stammer out that I'd love such an arrangement.

"Good, good," said Mr. Lee, and went off to speak to some-one else.

After we'd moved out of his earshot, I demanded of my father the circumstances of such extraordinary bounty. "Who was that guy?" I asked. "What does he actually have to do with this theatre?"

"Well, for one thing, he owns it," my father said, smiling. "He's Mr. Lee Shubert."

Him I'd heard of. Who hadn't? Around the theatre, the name Shubert was equivalent to the name of Colonel Jake Ruppert at Yankee Stadium. "Do you think he meant it—or was he just pulling some sort of a gag?" I asked, still bewildered.

"Oh, I don't think so," said my father. "One thing about Mr. Lee—he's tough to get an answer from, but when you get one, he keeps his word."

The next morning, cynicism set in. Obviously Mr. Lee had been indulging in some sort of flash gesture. Who could count on a lobby promise, so casually granted, with such carelessness? Besides, Lee Shubert was a big man, with a huge theatrical empire to operate. Did big men remember such trivia as a promise of free seats?

A letter dropped into my Yale Station mailbox, typed on Select Theatres stationery, written by a Mr. Jack Morris. All it said was "Please give the enclosed letter to Mr. David Eldredge, manager of the New Haven Shubert." The second letter in the envelope was couched as economically as the first. It read, "Please see to it that Mr. Max Wilk, who is bringing you this note, is provided with two complimentary seats to all our forthcoming attractions at the Shubert Theatre." And it was signed "Lee Shubert."

Two free seats . . . to *all* forthcoming attractions!

That afternoon, I strolled down Chapel Street towards the Shubert, my feet several inches off the pavement.

In subsequent years, I've carried in my pocket large sums of cash, three-day passes from the U.S. Army—once, even, a letter of identification from General of the Army George C. Marshall himself (in facsimile, true, but nonetheless just as valid)—but no other piece of paper has ever made my inside pocket glow with the heat of that terse note from that office on West Forty-fourth Street.

The Shubert lobby was empty. It was four in the afternoon. That evening, a new play was to open. I walked up to the box-office window and presented my letter to the man inside. "I'd like my two seats, please," I said.

He opened the letter and read it. Then he read the second. He read them both a second time. His eyes opened wider. He studied the documents carefully. Then, hoarsely, he said, "Just a minute." He vanished into the deeper confines of the box office. I heard a discussion inside. Voices were raised. Then another man appeared at the ticket window and peered through the bars at me.

He would have been in his early sixties, and was somewhat stooped. His hair was white, and he wore a pince-nez, which was attached to his waistcoat with a black ribbon. He was middle-aged and a solid citizen in everything save his clothes, which were made in the best New Haven Ivy League tailored tradition, of soft, expensive Scottish tweed. He was small, but he exuded the air of a successful man, secure in his status, monarch of his own domain, and at this moment was somewhat condescending to the Yale freshman who stood patiently waiting for his largess outside the box-office window.

"Where'd you get this letter?" he demanded, without even introducing himself.

That rocked me back on my heels. "In—in the mail," I said. "It . . . came *today*."

"Well, *I* don't know anything about this," he told me curtly.

"Didn't Mr. Lee Shubert say anything about it?" I asked, defensively.

He didn't even deign to answer that. He turned away.

I hadn't expected such a shocking lack of cooperation from the local management. Even if I weren't a customer, didn't I have some rights? "But he himself told me he was going to speak to Mr. Eldredge about this!" I protested. "Where's Mr. Eldredge?"

"I'm Eldredge!" he snapped. "I'll have to call New York. How do I know this letter's not a fake?"

Lack of cordiality I could stomach. But to be accused of such duplicity was a low blow, and I began to lose my temper. "Look—are you calling me a crook, or something?" I brayed.

"I said I was going to call New York!" he said. When he slammed the door of his inner office, that was the end of that.

I stood there in the drafty empty lobby, completely at a loss for direction. How did one play this? Ten minutes before, I'd regarded myself as a privileged party, a welcome guest of the management. Perhaps I wouldn't get a large red carpet, merely a small one, but the treatment should be, at minimum, Grade A . . . and suddenly I was being attacked as a small-time Willie Sutton. My humiliation was turning rapidly into righteous wrath. Fists clenched, I peered into the box-office window, where the small, darkish man was back at his labors, laying out pairs of seats for the night's show on a chart.

"Listen," I complained, "what the hell right's he got to talk like that to me? I'm not—"

The box-office man put two fingers to his lips. "He's the boss around here," he murmured. "He can act any way he wants to. Remember that, my friend."

Behind him, the inside box-office door opened, and Mr. Eldredge reappeared. He stared long and hard through the bars at me, as if a criminal whose capture he'd been responsible for had been reprieved by the governor moments before execution. "All right," he said, at last. "They say it's correct in New York. Sam, give Wilk here a couple of seats for tonight."

"Yes*sir*, Mr. Eldredge," said Sam. His last name, I later discovered, was Horwath, and he was as much a Shubert fixture as was his boss. He began filling out a pass blank.

I couldn't resist a parting salvo. "Are you satisfied I'm not a crook now, Mr. Eldredge?" I asked.

The manager pursed his lips. "I'll tell you one thing, Wilk," he said softly. "They can do what they like in New York, but this is *my* theatre to run, and I run it the way I'm supposed to, get it?"

The door to his lair inside slammed shut behind him.

Ever since that first season of free seats, I've understood why it is that some men decide to be drama critics. It's because of that steady claim on two good orchestra chairs, that permanent lease on a small piece of valuable theatrical real estate in Row G. What an exultant feeling . . . to read the signboards of the theatre that bore the one-sheets announcing a new play starring Katharine Cornell in November, followed by a new musical with England's Jack Buchanan, and a week later Maurice Evans in *Richard II*, and to know that, barring any accidental damage at the hands of New Haven motorists, you would be down front for all of those theatrical events! It's a powerful high, believe me.

And if the Shubert curtain was to descend on something less than wonderful—usually well past 11:30 p.m., for premiere try-out performances are always overlength—well, what matter? Something else was due into the theatre within the next week or so. We'd be back. Shubert audiences always come back . . .

Following our first brief lobby skirmish, Sam Horwath and I became quite good friends, and we lapsed into a first-name basis. Sam it was who first taught me commercial theatre body language. If there was a new melodrama coming in next week, a shrug from Sam, a raised eyebrow, or a slight moue—and you knew the word wasn't good. Conversely, if you asked for your regular two seats for Thursday night's S. N. Behrman opening, or for the latest Rodgers and Hart musical, Sam's rolled eyeballs and brief sigh of irritation were readily translatable; that show already had good word of mouth—for his box office to hand over free two perfectly good orchestra seats caused considerable pain.

Sam might communicate, but Mr. Eldredge remained implacable. He would tolerate me, but no more. If he passed me in the lobby during intermissions, he would deign to nod, but should I try to strike up a conversation, he would shoot a glacial stare at me through his pince-nez, answer in a monosyllable, and continue patrolling his domain. Our relationship was as formal as that of hostile diplomats.

Mr. Shubert's brief but magic letter was an incessant open sesame for a whole theatrical season. Needless to say, among my freshman classmates, it provided me with a certain status. If an especially good show was announced for the Shubert, I suddenly found myself inundated by new-found dormitory friends, all casually suggesting that I could use their company downtown on Row G. For a whole year, I was able to dispense largess right through to June. When I returned to New Haven the following September, there was already up on the Shubert boards the announcements of the new season's plays. Pavlovian, I salivated and presented myself at the box office. Sam Horwath shook his head. "Sorry," he said. "It's a new season. This year I don't have any instructions for you."

Disaster! I knew that my slender allowance would never pay for anything here except perhaps one balcony seat; even in 1938, theatregoing was pricy. A full year of freebies downstairs had corrupted me; how was I to kick the habit? Piteously, I asked Horwath what he expected me to do about this. He went inside to consult with his upper echelon. Moments later, the lined face of my grey-haired nemesis appeared at the window. "Write New York and they'll tell you," Eldredge snapped. "It's not *my* decision." *Bang!* went the door to his office.

I wrote Mr. Lee Shubert that afternoon, an obvious bread-and-butter letter which thanked him for a past year of his favors and casually inquired whether 1938–39 would be on the same basis. I waited, fingers crossed. Two or three days later, back came another truncated note from Mr. Jack Morris. "This letter," it read, "is to confirm Mr. Lee Shubert's instructions to the New Haven Shubert box office. Max Wilk is to be a guest of the management until further notice."

What glorious promise was contained in those laconic lines! I marched back down to Sam Horwath and slid the note under the grating to him. His eyebrows went up again. He carried it inside for confirmation. A moment later he returned, heaved a sigh (aha, the show was a good one!), and reached for the pass blank . . . and on we went into another season, with touring George Abbott farces, and plays by Sidney Howard and Maxwell Anderson, new Rodgers and Hart musicals, the Lunts, *On Borrowed Time*, with the great Richard Bennett making his last appearance on a stage . . . bad plays, good plays . . . something different each week.

Every so often my father would call from New York for a bulletin on what play was trying out in New Haven, and if I protested that I wasn't going to waste an evening on some dreadful stinker which had staggered into town on Thursday and probably wouldn't even make it past New Haven before it closed on Saturday night, he would have none of it. "Go see it anyway," he'd insist. "If you want to be a writer, you won't learn anything from the good plays. It's the stinkers that will teach you what *not* to do . . ."

It was in the second season that I had my first brush with Eldredgian discipline. There arrived in town the new Cole Porter–Dorothy and Herb Fields musical, *Leave It to Me!*, which starred William Gaxton, Victor Moore, and the immortal Sophie Tucker. Plus a young lady who came out in the second act and sang a mocking little Porter number called "My Heart Belongs to Daddy." On the spot, Mary Martin made fans out of all the Yalies present on that memorable night.

Gaxton was a family friend of long tenure; ever since *Fifty Million Frenchmen*. So when the show ended, I went backstage to say hello. I was undaunted by the sign above the stage door which sternly announced, "Visitors Are Strictly Forbidden Backstage." The stage doorman was sullen, but I convinced him I wasn't an autograph hunter, and he took in my name. Moments later, I sat in Gaxton's dressing room, basking in a cloud of reflected glory and chatting with that ebullient gent while he removed his Pancake #7. Naturally, his first question was how I'd felt about his performance, but before I could phrase the first superlative, there was a brief knock at the door, and without any further ado it was flung open. We both turned to see Mr. Eldredge, staring in at us like an avenging angel in tweed. "Come on, you!" he ordered. "Can't you read the sign, Wilk? *No visiting!*"

"Wait a minute," protested Gaxton. "This kid is a friend of—"

"Meet him outside somewhere," snapped Eldredge. "I made a rule here and it applies to everybody. I can't have people back here tripping over the scenery—I'm responsible." He reached over and seized my arm. "Come on," he commanded.

"I never heard of such a thing," complained Gaxton, with bravura.

"*Out!*" said Eldredge, guiding me towards the open door.

Humiliated as I was, I refused to lose face completely. "You don't have to pull," I told him. "I was just leaving anyway." I turned and waved goodbye to Gaxton. Then I let Eldredge escort me out of the backstage area.

At the stage door, he pointed his finger at the explicit sign.

"From now on—you obey that!" he warned, and slammed the door shut behind me. It was a scene right out of an old-time melodrama.

I stumbled out through the dark and dirty alley, humiliated and furious. So I'd violated his rule, so what? With typical Yale insouciance, I'd proceeded on the assumption that authority is there only to be flouted. What sort of petty dictator was this old fossil—to hint that I might trip over scenery? Nonsense—I knew my way around backstage. Enough of this tyranny—*à bas* Eldredge!

And yet, he did run the theatre. Life was beautiful here in those two free orchestra seats. Wasn't it worth swallowing my bruised pride, and staying out of his backstage domain?

For a while, at least.

Late in the spring, I tried it again, this time to visit another acquaintance backstage. I didn't get past the stage door; the ubiquitous despot was waiting for me there. "Out!" he commanded. "You're trying to break my rule again."

Out the stage door I went. It was a standoff.

Week after week, the Shubert banquet spread out like a theatrical smorgasbord. Thursday after Thursday, good nights, tedious ones, out-and-out time-wasters, aborting on the spot. When they were great, however, they were memorable. Ethel Merman and Bert Lahr in *DuBarry Was a Lady*. *Twelfth Night* with Helen Hayes and Maurice Evans. The joyful premiere of *The Boys from Syracuse*, and the giddy excitement of Jimmy Durante and Merman clowning around a stage in *Stars in Your Eyes*, and the Gaxton-Moore partnership in *Louisiana Purchase* . . . Wonderful exciting evenings, when our tweed jackets brushed against the sharkskin of Broadway ticket brokers up for an early look-see and the minks of New York ladies up to see Dick and Larry's newest, or to cheer on their pal Buddy DeSylva, or Irving Berlin, and in the back of the theatre it was always standing room only.

One day in October, 1939, my father called to tell me that a new play would be opening in New Haven the following evening, something by a new young playwright named William

Saroyan, titled *The Time of Your Life*. He instructed me to go and see it, and then to go speak afterwards with Eddie Dowling, the producer, who was also starring onstage. Dowling was an old friend, and my father had told him that I was a fan of Saroyan's. Eddie, it seemed, was worried about the play's prospects, and it would be helpful if I'd tell him what I thought.

It was so exhilarating to be told that anyone of Dowling's status would consider my opinion of any value that I brushed aside the problem of going backstage. That was a serious miscalculation.

The play was fine. The scenery was wrong—far too realistic—and some of the actors were unhappily cast, and yet Saroyan's nimble talent shone through the proceedings like a bright beacon. If the New Haven audience was a bit uncomfortable with the play's rambling construction, I couldn't have cared less. I wanted this show to succeed because it was good. That night, its prospects were poor. Happily, however, history proved me right. *The Time of Your Life* went on to win the Pulitzer Prize and to become an American classic.

If I was to speak to Dowling forthwith, I decided to employ a different gambit to avoid the dreaded Eldredge. At the right of the Shubert stage, beneath the tier of boxes, there is a fire door which leads directly backstage. I could use that.

Dowling's dressing room was just inside that door, and his door was open. He was seated in front of the mirror. His face reflected fatigue, uncertainty, perhaps depression. That New Haven audience hadn't been encouraging. I knocked on the inside of the door, and he looked up. Seeing me in the mirror, he smiled. "Jake said you were coming," he said. "What's the verdict, laddy?"

"I loved it," I said, fervently.

He was startled. "Really?" he asked. "You're not kidding me?"

"Why should I kid?" I asked. "It's a wonderful play, and I only wish I'd written it."

He shook his head. "Sure," he said. "Up to tonight, I agreed with you, but this audience—they threw me for a loop. Something's wrong with what we're doing." He waved me to a chair, and I sat down. "Now . . ." he said. "What about that first scene, with the old man who says, 'No foundation, all the way down the line . . .' Think it's too slow, maybe?"

It was a flattering moment for a tyro drama student.

"Well," I said, "I'll tell you . . ."

And got no farther. My arm had been seized from behind, and an all-too-familiar voice was saying, "Get *out* of this dressing room!"

I got to my feet, defensively.

"Say—I'm *talking* to him," Dowling protested. "It's important . . ."

"Meet him somewhere else!" Eldredge insisted. He shook a finger in my face. "You know better than to come in here, Wilk— no excuse. *No excuse!*"

And there was no recourse, not for me, nor for the astounded Dowling. Out I went, with Eldredge scolding me all the way to the stage door. Whatever status I'd derived from being consulted by a leading man ebbed away as the old man warned me, "Just because you get free seats in my theatre doesn't mean you own the place! Keep this up and I'll report it to Mr. Lee himself!"

From that evening on, I was very circumspect around the Shubert. To have the miraculous bounty of free seats vanish was a dire prospect. Who knew if Eldredge would carry out his threat? It wasn't worth the gamble. I never returned to the backstage from which he'd barred me. I never even tried to sneak a smoke in the inner lobby, rather than the outer one where fire laws permitted one. If it was a retreat, defeat had its compensations . . .

With the speed of one of Harry Blackstone's illusions (he was a touring magician who came to the Shubert, too), the next two seasons whipped past, and all of a sudden it was June, it was 1941, and we graduated from Yale.

Over in Europe, England was single-handedly holding off the Nazis. Within days, most of the members of my class had traded in their J. Press clothing for outfits tailored by the armed services. A year or so later, my own draft board embraced me, and off I went to the Army, dropping the B.A. from the end of my name and replacing it with a simple Pvt. up front.

One warm day in September, 1942, I received a three-day pass. I headed in to New York and, like a homing pigeon, made for Times Square. There, I strolled, happily inhaling the sights and echoes and odors of the theatrical district. I went down Shubert Alley, which runs between Forty-fourth and Forty-fifth, and as I passed the Booth Theatre, I heard a voice calling out my name.

I turned. There, standing by the Booth box office, greyer, a bit more stooped, but still eminently dapper, was my old adversary, Mr. Eldredge, smiling benignly on me as he hurried over to seize my hand. "How are you, my boy! Nice to see you again! You're in the Army—good for you!" he said.

The abrupt reversal of attitude floored me. I mumbled something about New Haven, and the Shubert . . . was he still up there? He waved a careless wave. "No, no, I've been transferred. I'm managing the Booth here now," he explained. "We've got a good show—what are you doing tonight? Like to come in and see it?"

"Sure," I said, involuntarily, still bewildered by his cordiality.

"Come and be my guest," he ordered.

He beamed at me through the pince-nez. Had it only been a year since I'd seen him? Somehow, he'd got smaller . . . and had a bit of the old imperiousness ebbed away? "Say," he asked me, fondly, "remember all those shows you used to see up there at my theatre? We used to get the best of them, didn't we?"

Once before, in prep school, I'd encountered a teacher, a small, sharp man, who seemed to gain pleasure out of indulging, before the entire classroom, his acerbic sarcasm at my particular expense. Many nights, my ears still tingling from his barbed thrusts, I would lie awake and plot eternal vengeance on his head. I dreamed of returning to the school and offering the headmaster a huge endowment, with one proviso, that this particular bastard be publicly ousted, at a ceremony over which I could preside.

A few years later, at an alumni gathering, I met my nemesis again. He hurried over, thrust out his hand, and bubbled with lavish praise for my progress in the world. Quite suddenly, this nightmare threat of my youth was gone, dissolved, and in its place stood a small, unkempt man, an obvious stain on his cheap tie, his attitude that of Uriah Heep. I remember feeling cheated. Gone was one of my youthful motivations. He'd deprived me of the zest I'd derived in despising him.

And so, here on Forty-fifth Street, had old Mr. Eldredge.

"Didn't we get the best up there?" he insisted.

"You bet," I conceded. "The best."

At 8:30 that night, I showed up at the Booth with a lady friend. Ushers were chanting, "Curtain going up!" inside, but Mr. Eldredge kept me in the lobby for a good five or six minutes, asking questions about our mutual friends in New Haven (I had no idea he considered them friends), and reminiscing about past hit shows. At last, reluctantly, as the Booth house lights were going down, he pushed us inside to a pair of the best seats down front. "Have a good time," he told me. "Any time you're around here again, come up to the box office and ask for me— I'll take good care of you. After all," he said, patting my shoulder paternally, "*you're* from New Haven."

It was two years later that I got back to the Booth. Mr. Eldredge wasn't inside the box office; the man behind the grille was a stranger, who mentioned that Eldredge had retired. But over at the St. James Theatre, I found my other New Haven friend, Sam Horwath, now the house manager. How was Mr. Eldredge? Sam shook his head, and raised those expressive eyebrows. "Died last year," he told me. "Never liked leaving New Haven. That was really his town, you know . . . not down here. He hated the move . . ."

I went back to the Shubert in the summer of 1948—a little more than a decade since Mr. Lee Shubert had bestowed his largess on me. But this time I was no longer an eager freshman. I had contributed comedy sketches to a new revue, titled *Small Wonder*, and this Tuesday evening we were going to raise the curtain on the show's premiere tryout performance. I left my bag up in the room at the Taft, and hurried next door to the Shubert.

The lobby doors stood wide open; the day was brutal, a steaming Connecticut August heat wave was on, and the Shubert had no air conditioning. Inside, on the stage, the designer was sweating over the hanging of his scenery. In the inner lobby, Gower Champion was running through a last-minute change in one of his choreographic routines. All through the theatre there was that attendant tension, frenzy, and hysteria that goes with Shubert D-days.

I looked for Burt Shevelove, the director. The stage manager told me that he was backstage, waiting for me to bring him some late line changes in one of the sketches.

I walked down the right side of the house, up to that small fire door, opened it, and went up the stone steps to the backstage. On my right was the star's dressing room, the same one where Eddie Dowling and I had conducted our abortive conference, years ago. The door was open; Shevelove was in the midst of a conference with our star, Tom Ewell. He beckoned me in. "Come on in—we've got work to do!" he said.

I suppose I should have felt some small flicker of triumph as I closed the dressing-room door. After all, I was free to come and go anywhere in the Shubert now; I wasn't in on a pass. I was *with* the show.

But there wasn't any glow. The only person at whom I might have been able to flaunt my new status wasn't around that afternoon. Pop Eldredge would never again throw me out through the stage door of the Shubert . . . and for some reason, I resented that.

•••••••••••••••••••••••••

CHAPTER SIX

TITA on Tour

A FRIEND has called this Monday morning to report on a theatrical benefit performance she attended last night at Lincoln Center. An impressive roster of blue-chip performers donated their talent to make the affair a success, and it seems that one of the masters of ceremonies was the affable, saturnine composer, Arthur Schwartz.

Most of these charity affairs are ponderous, peopled by friends and relatives of the organizers, dragooned into dutiful, tax-deductible good works. But not last night. The show was good, and Mr. Schwartz was most entertaining. In the course of the evening, he told quite a few good show business stories, especially one about his fellow composer, Mr. Irving Berlin, and since she knows that I am so involved with all these musical men, my friend insists that she tell me Mr. Schwartz's story instanter . . . and since it cost her so much money last night, I pay respectful attention. "It has to do with the time when Mr. Berlin was making that movie called *This Is the Army*," she says. "He was out on the sound stage and the director had him stand up in front of the cameras and sing his song 'Oh, How I Hate to Get Up in the Morning'—you know how they do that, with a recording of his voice going, and him mouthing the song."

Yes, I know how they do that. And further—

"And anyway, the director gave him his cue, and Mr. Berlin began to do the number, with the record playing, and there were these two stagehands standing there, and one turned to the other and said—"

"Yes, excuse me," I say, interrupting her reportage, "but I

know what he said."

"You do?" she asks, arrested in mid-anecdote.

To prove that I do, I tell her.

"But *you* weren't there last night at Lincoln Center," she says, disappointed and puzzled.

No. Not at Lincoln Center last night when Arthur Schwartz related the anecdote, thirty-odd years after the fact. But I was there on that Burbank sound stage, in 1943, when Mr. Berlin mouthed his classic song to a playback record. I stood a foot away from that long vanished stagehand. Which is why I know exactly what he said . . .

An eerie feeling to be reminded that you were once witness to the birth of an anecdote.

But then, the entire saga of Mr. Berlin's *This Is the Army* seems, after thirty years, legendary. . . . *Tell me, Daddy, how does it feel to be a member of a legend?*

Heads high, shoulders back, eyes front, ramrod straight, we marched down Broadway.

Up ahead—our platoon was bringing up the rear of the unit —the Army band swung with a snappy martial tune. Beneath those helmets were musicians who had sat in with Benny Goodman, others who'd filled Philharmonic chairs. Flags flying, in full military kit, the outfit looked great—especially the first five platoons, who marched with a rhythmic precision that wowed the crowds. To them, it came easily. Before Pearl Harbor, they'd been some of the best hoofers and chorus men in the business. (Master Sergeant Bob Sidney, when drafted, had marched his entire male chorus line out of a Broadway show, *Banjo Eyes*, down to the recruiting station, and enlisted them en masse.)

It was September, 1942. Civilians lined the New York sidewalks as the men of (DEML) *This Is the Army* headed downtown. Kids ran alongside, cheering. Old men waved from windows. Middle-aged women wiped tears from their eyes. "God bless you, boys—go to it!" yelled one greybeard, outside Lindy's Restaurant. "Git over there and give that bastid Hitler hell!"

Out of the side of his mouth, the soldier marching beside me muttered, "I wonder what he'd say if he knew we were only going to attack the National Theatre in Washington?"

As anyone who was lucky enough to get hold of a pair of seats to it will testify, *This Is the Army* was an absolute wipe-out of a hit show—the precisely right sort of entertainment, conceived and produced at precisely the right moment in time.

It was the brainchild of a master showman. Irving Berlin has always sensed exactly what his public wanted, and for seventy-odd years he's been giving it to them, in large doses. *This Is the Army* was shamelessly patriotic, blatantly chauvinistic, often simple-mindedly so. But anyone with the price of a flag can wave it. Berlin sets his to music. From the moment Master Sergeant Milton Rosenstock gave the downbeat to his pit orchestra, and the curtains parted to reveal two hundred massed GIs, singing "This Is the Army, Mr. Jones," until the finale, two hours later, there wasn't a slack second. And when, next-to-closing, the lights went up to reveal the tiny figure of Berlin himself, backed by a line of grey-haired vets from his original World War I show, *Yip, Yip, Yaphank!*, and Berlin stepped downstage to sing his own classic, "Oh, How I Hate to Get Up in the Morning," audiences from New York to Los Angeles stood up too—to cheer him.

All right, we can concede that old 1942–45 war is strictly a has-been, our memories of it already covered with moss. It's most unlikely that anyone will ever revive *This Is the Army*, à la *No, No, Nanette*, even as a high-camp exhibit—although beware . . . practically everything Berlin has ever been associated with turns out to have a mysterious inner strength . . . But if anyone ever does revive *This Is the Army*, he might be able to re-create all those wonderful Berlin numbers—"I Left My Heart at the Stage Door Canteen," "Mandy," et al., that played in *front* of the curtain.

As for what went on backstage? Nobody could ever re-create that.

We were a self-contained military unit, civilians drafted by the Army, miraculously assigned to do the job we all knew best— to entertain. Perhaps we didn't do much actual fighting (what was that old wartime wheeze? "I fought and I fought and I fought —and they *still* drafted me!"), but the tour of a wartime America with Mr. Berlin's show was probably the most surrealistic military

IRVING BERLIN, who, as Jerome Kern once said, ". . . *is* American music."

campaign that never made the history books.

It was a talented cast. Sergeant Ezra Stone, radio's Henry Aldrich, now in his Uncle Sam's khaki; Corporal Burl Ives; Private Henry Jones and Private Anthony Ross, both Broadway leading men; Sergeant Gary Merrill; Corporal "Stump" Cross, ex-half of Stump and Stumpy, the dance team; Sergeant Gene Nelson, née Berg; singers, dancers, comics. Private Julie Oshins, a fugitive from the Borscht Circuit, had struggled for a break for years. When it finally came, success draped him in olive drab and paid him fifty-six dollars a month. He killed the people with his hair-trigger ad-lib throwaway to a bossy sergeant: "Go ahead— break me—make me a civilian!" When critics such as Brooks Atkinson raved over Oshins' debut, he became an overnight star. Julie shrugged it off. "I'm the hottest thing on Broadway tonight, maybe," he said. "But when this damn war is over, I'll be just another unemployed comic in a dark blue suit, wait and see . . ."

Alas, his prediction was only too true . . . *ave atque vale,* Julie.

The Army went into show business the Army way. We were assigned a cadre of officers; neither before nor afterwards has the Pentagon ever coped with such an exotic task force, or the problems attendant on raising money for Army Emergency Relief. What general ever had to work out the logistics of shipping massive scenery and lighting equipment from town to town in freight cars? Or how to handle block-long box-office lines of avid ticket buyers; where to house three hundred GIs in wartime-tight cities from New York to Los Angeles, while at the same time paying each soldier a bare $2.75 per day subsistence. (How about that, Actors Equity?)

For men who'd been accustomed to earning good pay in Broadway shows and in night clubs, this new life was a constant series of adjustments. In an Army camp, each man would have been fed and housed; out in the civilian world, with the audience out front paying top dollar for standing room only, we were traveling GI mendicants. But nobody complained . . . any more than the usual bitching. There was far too much happening, everywhere we went.

Opening night at the National Theatre, in Washington, was

to be an awesome experience. Up to now, the show had been a
smash hit on Broadway for three months—but that was with the
civilian audience. Tonight, for the first time, the cast would be
proving itself to its Regular Army bosses. Very tough critics.
They'd authorized the show.

At 2010 that evening (Army for 8:10), a formidable array
of brass began to filter into our lobby. First came a coterie of staff
captains and majors, discreetly awaiting the call to duty—to
hurry out to the street and open staff-car doors for their superiors.
Lieutenant colonels and full chicken colonels seemed to be
assigned to more important duties, i.e., to provide souvenir programs for generals and their ladies. The one-star generals began
to arrive, carefully checking out seat locations for the big brass.
And then, at last, in came the upper echelons—two- and three-
star wearers, Somervell, Surles, et al. The Vice-President, the
Secretary of War, the Secretary of the Navy, Field Marshal Dill
of the British Army, four-star General H. H. Arnold, admirals,
rear, vice, and full, outnumbered and outjostled . . . and, finally,
the boss himself, General George C. Marshall.

When the last of the brass had hurried his lady inside the
doors, one of the GI ticket takers turned to me and grinned.
"Now," he murmured, "do you know what an ant feels like?"

That night, the audience threw the normally self-assured
cast completely off. "We're laying an egg!" moaned Ezra Stone.
"And with the boss, yet!"

It took some time before the GIs onstage could figure out
why. None of the lower-ranking officers in the house dared to
laugh at the gags thrown from the stage until they noticed if the
nearest brigadier general was laughing. One-star generals checked
their own amusement until two- and three-star generals chuckled.
And those exalted rankers controlled their official response until
they'd noted that the four-star generals down in front were
pleased with the joke. It was truly a chain reaction . . . in
reverse.

Finally, Sergeant Hank Henry, late a star of the Minsky
burlesque circuit and a prime specialist in low comedy and
double takes, made his entrance. Unfazed by his audience, he
bellowed an aside: "This has to be the coldest house I played

since I met my draft board!"

Silence. Then, a second later, General Marshall gave out with a four-star belly laugh. On cue, his staff joined in, and only then did the rest of the house follow. From then on, the show was back on the tracks . . . Talk about facing Clive Barnes?

Several days later, by specific request of the White House, there was a matinee performance given for the man at the very top . . . FDR himself.

Prior to curtain time, the Secret Service searched the National from basement to roof. Machine guns were mounted on the venerable old theatre's roof. The cast, soldiers all, were relieved of the bolts to their GI Springfield rifles. In one scene, Hank Henry, playing the part of an angry mess sergeant as foil to Sergeant Larry Weeks' juggling act, was wont to carry on a meat cleaver and pare his fingernails as he delivered his gags. The Secret Service men took away Hank's meat cleaver. Ever the resourceful comic, Hank substituted a turkey leg as his prop—which was to get him a bigger laugh . . . the first time on record that the Secret Service ever improved a joke.

The theatre was packed with some 1,400 servicemen, the President's invited guests. Crouched in the orchestra pit, facing the audience, were a phalanx of Secret Service men. Not once during the entire matinee did those strong-willed gents ever allow their eyes to wander onto the stage behind them . . .

Our President, his box full of guests, enjoyed himself thoroughly that afternoon, so much so that within a day or two—astoundingly, for one so busy with a global war—he reciprocated . . .

Several of us, now traveling press agents who'd been assigned to stay ahead of the touring show, were in Philadelphia, arranging for the next engagement at the mammoth Mastbaum Theatre. Late one afternoon, our NCO, Sergeant Ben Washer, called from Washington and told us to report back to the main unit immediately. What was up? "You're invited out," said Sergeant Washer, cryptically. "Shine your shoes and wear clean uniforms."

We grabbed drugstore sandwiches at the Philadelphia station, and got a train down to Washington. When we arrived at the National, Sergeant Washer handed us each a small engraved card. Beneath the presidential seal, mine said:

> *President and Mrs. Franklin D. Roosevelt*
> *request the presence of*
> *Pvt. Max Wilk*
> *at midnight supper*
> *The White House   Washington, D.C.*
> *Sept. 28, 1942*

The curtain went down at the National.

In formation, we marched through silent, deserted, pitch-black streets towards a darkened White House.

It was close to midnight before we reached it, went through the gates, and formed a double line at the doors. Secret Service men, very polite, checked our identification, scanned the invitations, and shepherded us into single file. One by one, up the stairs we went, into the main hallway of the White House.

From the head of that long line of GIs a rumor came whipping back. The President was greeting each and every one

AN ARTIFACT of incalculable value, circa 1942.

of the three hundred of us . . . in person!

"Can you imagine a guy as busy as he is—taking the time to shake hands with *me*?" muttered the awestruck GI beside me.

The line snaked upwards. We came to a large drawing room. One by one, we snapped to attention, then marched across the carpet to where the President, in a huge high-backed armchair, sat beaming that famous smile. Next to him stood an aide, murmuring the name of each soldier as we clicked our heels in front of his chair.

President Roosevelt seized my hand and clasped it tightly . . . the President. Not a shadow on the weekly Paramount newsreel, or a photograph from the *Times'* front page. Mr. Roosevelt's deep eyes flashed, and that leonine head seemed even larger than any camera had ever caught it. Charisma? It came out of him in shock waves, as that high, familiar voice said, "Good evening, Private."

I came to attention, mumbled "Good evening, sir," and walked on by . . . and that was all, except that the handclasp, thirty-odd years later, still tingles on mine.

The President soon excused himself and retired—he had a war to take care of tomorrow—but the tireless Mrs. Roosevelt stayed up until the wee hours, acting as our hostess, along with Harry Hopkins and the tall, gaunt Robert E. Sherwood, the Broadway playwright who'd left show business to serve as FDR's speech writer. We were ushered into the state dining room (tables had also been set up in the Green, the Oval, and the Red Rooms), where, in front of our astonished eyes, we found place settings for a sit-down dinner. Soon we were at the tables, and waiters began serving us a full meal . . . cream of tomato soup, chicken salad, tomato stuffed with cream cheese and chives, cake and ice cream, and coffee. (We kept the menus.)

"How're you gonna complain about a mess hall like this?" remarked Private Julie Oshins, between bites.

During the dinner, Mrs. Roosevelt went from room to room, chatting with each of us in turn. That night, cynical Broadway comics, dancers and musicians and technicians, none of them known for their sentimentality, all fell instantly in love with that tall, gracious lady. How could anyone top her opening line?

As she entered our dining room, she snapped, "Don't get up when *I* come into the room, boys—you all know my reputation as a traveler!"

That night, one of our musicians, a diminutive trombonist named Joe Lawrence, had a very special problem. Prior to the arrival of the White House invite, he had, it seemed, made a date with a local young lady for after the show. Summoning up what must have been a massive load of *chutzpah*, he went up to Mrs. Roosevelt and explained his predicament. He didn't wish to stand up the girl—not even for this awesome occasion. And besides, if he had, what girl would have believed his excuse? "It's not that I don't *want* to stick around, you understand, Ma'am," he said, torn by ambivalence. "But it's not exactly polite to *her*, either, you know what I mean?"

"Heavens," said Mrs. Roosevelt, "you're not a prisoner in the White House. I understand completely . . . Do come again soon . . ."

She was still standing by the door as we filed out into the blacked-out streets; smiling cheerfully, she wished us all good night and Godspeed . . . and three hundred GI Cinderella types went back to their respective sculleries.

Which for us of the advance unit was Philadelphia, where precisely at 0800, at the cavernous Mastbaum Theatre, we were due back on the job. We caught the Pennsy milktrain, dozed on its filthy coach seats, and at dawn stumbled out onto the platform of the Thirtieth Street station.

A brace of MPs, their meaty fists twirling batons, .45s hanging from their thick hips, closed in on us. Obviously we were AWOL, perhaps drunk, definitely suspicious characters in our present blear-eyed state. They demanded to see our identification and our Class A passes—if we had them.

As we fumbled in our pockets, involuntarily I snickered. This situation was Runyonesque. Midnight supper at the White House, as guests of the President and his lady, and now, harassment by two uniformed yahoos.

One of the MPs turned his hard eyes on me and glared, warily. "Sojer, whatso funny?" he demanded.

I couldn't resist it. "Would you like to see my invitation to supper at the White House?" I blurted.

He hefted his billy. "You tryinta be funny, sojer?" he rasped.

The world is full of critics.

"Not *me*, sergeant," I told him, meekly.

With the wildly cheering audiences that packed the house each night, the tour was, to borrow from our own Mr. Berlin, blue skies, nothing but. Backstage, life wasn't so glamorous.

Once that curtain fell, we went right back to soldiering. We were so definitely in the public eye, front and center, that it behooved our officers to see that we stayed 107 percent GI at all times. That meant early-morning formations, duty rosters, drill, the whole bit. Each move to a new town meant dismantling the show, packing it into freight cars, sans union help, and unloading and hanging it in the next theatre. Not a slight task, considering the mammoth dimensions of the production. And if there were any free hours left, they were usually spent—willingly enough— entertaining at nearby service hospitals.

The Army classification system had done a fine job of casting Mr. Berlin's show with talent, but when it came to staffing the unit with a military cadre of officers, we were provided a group that would certainly never hear a shot fired in anger. True, our medical officer, Captain Chartock, was a fairly good choice for coping with the problems of three hundred creative types—he was a psychiatrist—but our commanding officer, a major in the pre-war reserves, had very little prior experience in leading troops anywhere. For the past quarter century, he had been a New York police detective. A ponderous gent in his ill-fitting khaki, he traveled everywhere with a riding crop dangling from his hand. Why such an appendage? "He's got lead shot in the handle, for riots!" said one cynic. "Nah," said Julie Oshins. "Watch the tip of the riding crop. He keeps a piece of chalk there—for marking tires!"

Most of the actual daily SOP—Standard Order of Procedure— devolved on the trim shoulders of Lieutenant Marc Daniels. Even though he'd actually gone through the rigors of Infantry OCS at Fort Benning, he'd been a director before the war. He could get the point of one of Hank Henry's ad-libs without having it carefully explained to him by a junior officer . . .

Lieutenant Daniels went by the book, and that included a weekly short-arm inspection. (For the benefit of those unfamiliar with the term, the short arm is Army-ese for a private's privates.) Army medical officers routinely checked each EM's most personal piece of equipment for any sign of infection, and since we were wandering across a country where hordes of male-hungry females clustered outside our stage door each night, Lieutenant Daniels insisted on carrying out the regulations.

But where?

Lacking proper medical facilities, he and Captain Chartock improvised. The clinic was the stage of whatever theatre we were currently playing. One afternoon, it was the bare stage of the Boston Opera House. The drill went like so; the auditorium doors were locked, and a very bright work light was brought down front on the stage. The entire company was assembled in formation. One by one, Master Sergeant Alan Anderson would call the troops front and center. As the first man approached the work light, Captain Chartock, waving a flashlight that would enable him to do a close exam, gave the order. "Unbutton, soldier, and present arm."

As the first GI obeyed, from the rear of the huge theatre there came a muffled female scream . . . then a second . . . then the sudden pound of footsteps up an aisle, and the slam of a fire-exit door!

Undetected, two stagestruck Boston ladies had sneaked into the theatre and had been seated in the darkened auditorium, interested onlookers to what must have seemed a simple Army exercise on the stage.

One still wonders what those two proper Bostonians must have told each other, after that surrealist striptease . . .

There's nothing like being even vaguely associated with a hit show to turn the most normally sane civilian into a raving megalomaniac. In city after city, the audiences roared their approval of Mr. Berlin's revue . . . and by some mysterious process of osmosis, our major began to suspect that he was Flo Ziegfeld, reincarnate. In his new role as showman, he began by collecting documentation. He assigned a group of his office cadre to compile press clippings. But so thorough was the 1942 press and magazine coverage of *This Is the Army* that the major's official Scrapbook Detail soon found itself attempting to cope with a newsprint blizzard. By the end of the New York run, a three-by four-foot scrapbook had been requisitioned through military channels, and most of its pages had already been filled. Each city we played provided more clippings; the dogged GIs went on cutting, pasting, and cussing. The major requisitioned more scrapbooks and assigned Sergeant Pete Feller's carpenters to design and build a special packing case, to ensure their safety for posterity.

He also insisted that his advance men arrange decent facilities and proper hospitality in each town for his unit. That was only proper. But along with his troops, he wished attention to be paid . . . to himself. In whatever town we were to arrive, he instructed that we arrange welcoming ceremonies, a proper parade, and such military hoopla as befitted our (and his) star rank.

In Cleveland, the quality of the military parade that had been organized for TITA's arrival displeased him. It hadn't been big and brassy enough. Lieutenant Daniels called me in Cincinnati and informed me that our CO expected to see a much larger and more impressive display of military might upon the show's arrival, this coming Sunday, and that would be my specific assignment.

But . . . how did one organize a military parade?

"Call up the nearest Army post and demand one!" said Lieutenant Daniels . . . and that was an order.

Sometime during our first weeks in Philadelphia, each of us in the advance publicity unit had received a mimeographed copy of a historic document. Alas, I did not keep mine, but I believe that I can quote from memory to this day what it said.

OFFICE OF THE COMMANDING GENERAL
TO: WHOM IT MAY CONCERN
FROM: THE CHIEF OF STAFF

1. *This Is the Army*, the official soldier show, is an important Army project, its purpose being to raise funds

for Army Emergency Relief and to raise civilian morale.

2. All COs of Army Posts, Camps, and Stations will cooperate to the utmost of their ability with the officers and EM of (DEML) TITA, to ensure the success of this venture.

(Signed) George C. Marshall
General, Commanding

A TRUE COPY

Curt, precise, and Spartan, this official piece of Army paper was possessed of wondrous powers. As we were to discover countless times, it not only served to ward off those omnipresent MPs who prowled every civilian street, but that discreet signature, even in mineograph, carried with it the ne plus ultra in clout value.

A parade, eh?

Somewhat dubiously, I checked with Cincinnati telephone books. The nearest Army post was a permanent training installation, some twenty miles out of town. I dialed the number and told the GI operator that I was the official rep of TITA, and I wished to be put through to his CO forthwith.

With typical Army foot-dragging, he put me through to the post adjutant. He wanted to know what this call was about. But for once I was going to fly high above the red tape. "Sorry," I said crisply, "but I can't inform you of my business, Captain. This is highly confidential and most important. Put the colonel on."

"I'll—ah—put you through to his aide," said the captain, a bit nervous.

After a moment or so, I had a major on the line. Could he help me?

"Not at all," I snapped, beginning to enjoy my mission. "I'm under orders to deal directly with the CO. Now put him on immediately, please!"

Finally, a third voice came on the line, very gung ho, and barked, "This is Cunnel So-and-So. What you want?"

In the pantheon of Army power, a colonel commanding a large post is something of a minor deity unto himself. That

I knew well, but I had the bit in my teeth now, and I was armed with General Marshall's mimeographed missile. "This is Wilk of *This Is the Army,* Colonel," I told him, clipping my words à la early Pat O'Brien, in a service picture. "My unit arrives in town Sunday afternoon, and my CO has instructed me to call you up and request a parade in our honor, from the station to the theatre."

"A parade?" said the colonel. "You . . . want a parade?"

"From you!" I snapped.

"Mmm. Well now. What you'd better do," he mused, shifting gears to cope with this problem, "is to have your CO write a letter requesting his needs, in triplicate, send it through channels up to the general commanding this service command, and then in time it will be bucked down to me—"

"Sorry, Colonel, I haven't time to go through all that," I said, happily. "Now let's discuss what we need for the parade . . ."

"Official channels are official channels!" warned the colonel.

"Right, Colonel," I said. "Now, I have here on my desk a copy of a letter from General George C. Marshall. In it, he specifically *orders* all COs of camps, posts, and stations in the U.S.A. to cooperate fully with my unit. Would you care for me to read it to you, sir?"

I could hear the colonel's heavy breathing some twenty miles away.

"What sort of a parade did you have in mind?" he asked, at last.

"Well now," I said, drunk with power. "Let's just see. We have our own band and a color guard, but I think some equipment would dress it up. How about mechanized troop carriers?"

"How many?" asked the colonel.

"Oh, say half a dozen," I told him. "And toss in some field pieces, and some howitzers—they always look good." I consulted my mental shopping list. "What else have you got lying around the post, Colonel?"

"How about half-tracks?" he suggested, now cowed.

"Good, good, throw them in," I said. "Say, what about tanks? They always make a big hit with the people. Got some?"

"No—this is an Infantry post," said the colonel.

"But you know where to get them, don't you?" I demanded. I had him on the defensive. "I'm sure I might borrow a few from down the road," he conceded, "But I'm not promising—"

"Fine, I'll leave that to you," I said. "Make it four tanks. Two in front, two at the rear. Now, let's see, have we left anything out? Troop carriers, howitzers, field pieces, *and* tanks . . . The train pulls in at 1600 on Sunday, and I expect you'll see to it that everything I've ordered is waiting there at the station, correct?"

Oh, yes indeedy!" said the colonel. "Tell me," he said, very man-to-man." There any chance of—ah—getting a couple of seats to the show, Wilk? I hear it's all sold out, but my wife is dying to go, you know how it is—"

"I'll see what I can do, Colonel," I said, also man-to-man. "And we'll keep in touch with each other about this parade, right? Don't want any little snafus, do we?"

"Right, Captain!" he said. "And how do I reach you?"

I gave him the theatre telephone number. "Oh, and by the way," I said, "don't ask for Captain Wilk, sir. It's *Private* Wilk."

The telephone lines hummed, and there was silence from the other end, as the colonel digested this last piece of information.

"Private," he said, in a strange, high voice, which might have denoted the oncoming first stages of shock. "Right. I'll—ah—see to everything . . . then . . . Private."

"Good show!" I told him. "And I *know* General Marshall would be pleased!"

The parade was a smash.

"*This* is more like it," said the major, seated in the first half-track, riding up the streets of Cincinnati like a triumphant field marshal, at the head of a formidable array of Army equipment. When he dismounted at the theatre, he sent for me. "From now on, Wilkie," he said, "let's have one of these in every town we play!"

I became parade specialist, first class.

We advance men had to cope with the housing problem, as well, and it became trickier as we moved west. Boston was rough, Cincinnati was even rougher, but Detroit offered problems that were ugly. That sprawling industrial city was delighted to have us play two weeks at the huge Fox Theatre, to roar approval

to our company on the wide stage . . . but as for housing the cast
after the curtain fell, we were strangers.

The problem was that we were an integrated military outfit.
Long before the postwar Army brass decided to break down the
old racial barriers, TITA had created its own set of standards.
Within our ranks are a large number of black performers; we
operated on one standard—talent. Even the major abided by our
democracy-in-ranks. He issued strict orders: if all his men were
not invited out to local parties and functions, then the invitation
was refused.

He might turn down free meals, but his GIs still had to
sleep nights after their long day's duty. And the tension in
Detroit, where thousands of southern whites and blacks had
migrated to find employment, was building up by the hour.
Within months, it was to explode into an ugly, full-scale race
riot in the Paradise Valley section. In the fall of 1942, it took
a lot of tramping up and down Detroit streets and arguing with
room clerks and surly managers to secure even a short list of
hotels and rooming houses that would accept our men . . . *all*
our men.

When the list was finally posted backstage, we took pains to
separate the integrated hostelries from the much longer list of
those which insisted on a lily-white policy towards GIs . . . even
in the midst of a war. We'd be damned if we were going to subject our black brothers to that sort of chicken-shit, at the hands
of some mealymouthed room clerk.

The separated list was redundant. En masse, the men
decided to boycott the offending establishments. "I wouldn't set
foot in one of those rotten hotels," cracked one of the EM.

"You're right," said his friend. "They'd take one look at
your bankroll and heave you right out the door."

"Okay, so I'm flat," said the first. "But I've still got my
principles."

Most of the men ended up at service clubs and Y's.

Pity the world; it hasn't yet learned to operate on the same
simple premise that a traveling troupe of three hundred GIs
lived by . . . you take bows together, you take on the world the
same way.

Our final theatrical date was at the old Philharmonic Auditorium, in downtown Los Angeles. It was a truly gala premiere —sans Army brass, but with a procession of Hollywood producers, stars, and performers crowding into the lobby, waiting attendance on Hedda Hopper and Louella; our new boss-to-be, Jack Warner; L. B. Mayer and his retinue . . . famous faces posing for flashguns everywhere. Early on, the major beckoned me over, and pulled me close. "You stand next to me," he ordered.

"What for, sir?" I asked.

Out of the side of his mouth, he said, "I want you to point out the celebrities."

The following morning, he was far from amiable. Somewhere between San Francisco and L.A., that mammoth collection of press notices, photos, human-interest stories, and interviews from all the newspapers and magazines, all of which had been neatly clipped and pasted into the major's scrapbooks (there were now three), had mysteriously disappeared from one of the Southern Pacific baggage cars.

Furious, he ordered a thorough search. "It must've been the German Secret Service," murmured Hank Henry. "They needed some good notices and they pinched ours."

No use. All three books had vanished. There were those disbelievers who still maintain that the major's own Scrapbook Detail, fed to the teeth with that endless daily cutting and pasting, may have itself jettisoned the paper albatross, packing case and all, out of the baggage-car door. And who knows? Perhaps somewhere, along those Southern Pacific tracks, there may still be a lonely track walker who sits up each night in his shack, turning the pages of a huge scrapbook, and vicariously reliving a tour which broke theatrical box-office records from New York to Los Angeles, back in 1942 . . .

But we were far from finished with *This Is the Army*. Saturday night we were finishing our run at the Philharmonic, and Sunday morning we were due to report at Warner Brothers Studio, in Burbank.

We were going to be stars. At fifty-six dollars a month . . .

•••••••••••••••••••••••••

The Battle of
Burbank

OUR TROOP TRAIN pulled into the station. In full field kit, we scrambled down the steps and fell into formation. The band struck up a march, and off we went through the streets of beautiful downtown Burbank. On and on we trudged. The sun was out and it was warm as we marched across the San Fernando Valley. A few housewives gaped as we passed through dusty housing developments, but nobody cheered at the sight of three hundred GIs on the march.

Finally, up ahead, the sprawling complex of dun-colored sound stages, the Warner Brothers Studio, at the foot of busy Cahuenga Pass, came in sight. It has to have been the first time, before or since, that movie stars have ever walked to work . . .

At the studio gates, a thin crowd—passersby, kids on bikes, and a batch of studio stenographers, briefly excused from their desks to pad out the group—applauded as we marched in.

"Cut! Hold it!" yelled a Hungarian accent, from behind the bank of Technicolor cameras. "Looked lousy. Boys, go back—we got to do de whole ting again!"

We had acquired a new commanding officer—Mike Curtiz. The lean Hungarian director would turn out to be a more demanding and critical boss than any drill sergeant, but from *him* we'd accept it without a murmur. Curtiz had a hell of a lot more talent than any officer we'd had to deal with. Nobody had to remind us of his *Yankee Doodle Dandy*, or *Casablanca*, *Captain Blood*, or *Air Force*. Besides, Mike was never dull. Who else

WELCOMED by a cheering throng of eleven, the men of (DEML) *This Is the Army* arrive at Burbank to be immortalized on film.

could mangle the language better than Curtiz, yelling, "Bring on de empty horses!" on a set where his thoughtful prop man had posted a sign which read, "Curtiz Spoken Here." Behind the camera, Mike was utterly single-minded. Old Warner hands love to remember the day when he stood on a hill, filming a scene in which a flight of Army planes was to pass by his cameras, waving his arms at the planes above and ordering, "Go back!"

"Dot's better," said Curtiz, after we'd repeated our march through the Warner gates several more times. "Print dot—and you boys, keep on marching!"

We kept on going, through the vast Warner lot, past all the sound stages, then on through the never-never land of the back lot, with its New York brownstone streets, London alleys, Arab villages, and Western main streets, and, finally, on through an open back gate which led to a deserted suburban street. It was hard to tell whether it was still a movie set. There was nothing in sight.

"That's the fastest career I ever had," muttered a weary EM.

"*Halt!*" yelled Master Sergeant Alan Anderson, and we fell out.

"What the hell is this—some other picture location?" demanded Julie Oshins, staring at our surroundings. "Or did we get drafted again?"

Behind the studio, on a vacant Burbank block (oh, why hadn't any of us the foresight—or the cash—to buy up a few square feet of that undeveloped Southern California sagebrush?), the Warner studio carpenters and electricians had erected a complete, miniature Army field post. Constructed strictly to GI specifications, Camp TITA, as it was named, consisted of thirteen wooden-floored, furnished tents. It also had a shower house, three large latrines, an administration building, a small PX, a telephone exchange of its own, a dispensary to accommodate the good Captain Chartock and his medicines . . . and it also had an extensive drill field.

It looked hot, dusty, and very unappetizing to a crew of GIs who were primarily city boys.

"*This* is Hollywood?" complained Hank Henry.

For the next six months, Camp TITA was to be our first and last permanent HQ, a small military enclave surrounded on all sides by home-front San Fernando Valley residents. There, each morning at 0600, our bugler annoyed our neighbors with reveille. At 1600, we held Retreat, and lowered Old Glory. Weekends, to no admiring crowd whatsoever, we held full-dress parades. Each night, the Charge of Quarters officer posted regular guards over this peculiar post, taking precautions first to remove any ammo from his guards' rifles, lest by accident a stray shot might go through some nearby living-room window. Duties of the guard? To shoo off neighboring kids on bicycles and the potential loving couples who hadn't enough gas to drive up into the hills and wished to use a copse below our parade ground. There was also the pressing problem of keeping unauthorized civilians from using our latrine facilities . . .

Shortly after we were established there, our major, in typical semper paratus style, ordered our crew of carpenters to construct a GI obstacle course, complete with monkey walks, Tarzan swings, scaling walls, and other such rigorous hazards. Two days later, we publicity men brought down a photographer from *Look* magazine, and he photographed four of our huskiest dancers going through the obstacles. "SOLDIERS FIRST—ACTORS LATER!" was the headline on that spread.

All four of the dancers needed extensive medical aid for bruises and lacerations, but that didn't stop our major from going forward. So carried away was he by the possibilities of his vest-pocket training setup that orders were shortly posted on our bulletin board . . . All EM were to report Monday morning at 0900 in fatigues; object, to run the obstacle course, *daily*, from then on.

When word of the major's latest ukase reached Master Sergeant Bob Sidney, our dance director, he was hard at work on a Warner sound stage, rehearsing the opening number of the film for Curtiz' cameras. "It's very simple," he remarked. "We're shooting this number on Tuesday morning. Will you have somebody go ask Mike Curtiz what he wants for the cameras—two hundred dancers, or two hundred cripples?"

The major's oh-so-GI installation was to grow a bumper crop of Burbank weeds.

Claude Binyon had written a screenplay for the film version of *This Is the Army*, one which provided a story of sorts, and all manner of patriotic embellishments were grafted onto our already successful revue. Mr. Berlin rummaged in his formidable trunk and brought forth several vintage World War I songs, and Kate Smith was summoned from New York to sing "God Bless America" in the finale, with a symphonic background and a huge choir. "Name" stars—Warner standbys Joan Leslie, George Tobias, Alan Hale, Charlie Butterworth—took on various fictitious character parts . . . As Jerry Jones, an amiable song-and-dance man named George Murphy; subsequently, he was to quit show business to go into California politics . . . As his son, Lieutenant Johnny Jones, a fresh-looking young Warner contract player who'd recently been called up by the reserves, Second Lieutenant Ronald Reagan, thus making the film the only picture Hollywood has ever released to star a senator and a governor . . . And for added ethnic marquee value, the Army summoned Sergeant Joe Louis, the world heavyweight champion, to play a brief guest shot.

His broad shoulders draped in GI olive drab, the champ soon arrived at Burbank for a six-week tour of duty. From a respectful distance, the Brown Bomber had always been a formidable sight . . . A modern-day fable, a legend—the taciturn puncher with the dynamite fists, who said little, but bored in right to the point with whatever brief statement he did make . . .

Close to, Joe was a complete contradiction. Away from the press, he relaxed. He joked, sang, danced, traded quips, and was constantly "on." Sometimes, even a bit more than any of us needed him to be. But then, as Julie Oshins remarked, "Joe isn't exactly the kind of a guy you say 'Shut up' to."

Countless times each day, always in good humor, Joe would pose for photos and sign autographs; never once did he become irritated, even once when two enthusiastic fans approached him, autograph books at the ready, as he was using the latrine. But let

Mr. Murphy went on to the U.S. Senate. Second Lieutenant Reagan became California's governor but is now at liberty. Gary Merrill, the MP, has announced that he is available for a candidacy in 1976.

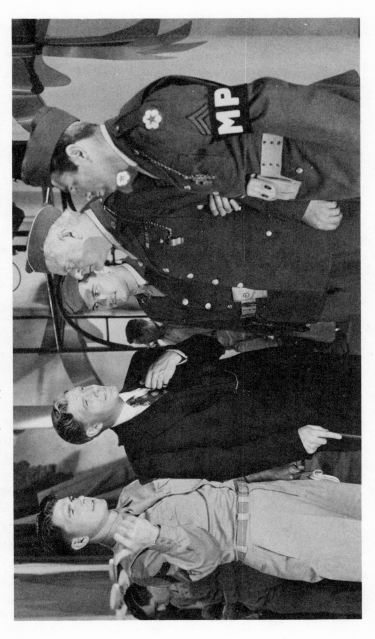

one newsman appear, a hundred yards away, and Joe's radar flipped into operation. The cheerful smile vanished, his lips tightened, his eyes went blank.

What did he think of the war? "We're gonna win this war because we're on God's side." What about fighting Billy Conn, the contender? "Can't consider that now—we've both got us a new boss." And what about after the war—what would be Joe's plans? "We've got us a more important job to do. I worry about the other afterwards."

It was as if he'd been programmed. But thirty seconds after the newsman had departed, Joe would instantly metamorphose back into that singing, dancing joker—our own cheerful Jekyllian Joe.

It was typical of Joe that in years to come, when his Uncle Sam pursued him for all those back taxes he'd never make again, he never once complained. In public, that is. I have a pretty good idea of what he must have said . . . in private.

Even though the brass had provided that elaborate Camp TITA as a home base, by some typical Army miscalculation it proved too small to hold all of us. Ergo, those of us who were fortunate enough to find housing in the area were—reluctantly, of course—permitted to live off the post. Since only the most confirmed masochist would stay on in a sun-baked San Fernando Valley tent, where the days can hit 105 and the nights drop to a frigid 33, and where the rainy season could and did turn our vest-pocket post into a mud flat, we went foraging for creature comforts.

We hitchhiked into Hollywood and trudged through its streets in search of housing. By some minor miracle, four of us found an apartment house where, by pooling our scanty resources, we could make the monthly rent. The landlady was hospitable, patriotic, and besides, her building was strictly rent-controlled. So, at a daily cost of a dollar plus per man, we lived in three rooms. Amazing splendor.

Transportation, however, was something else. Distances in Greater Los Angeles are vast, bus service from Hollywood to Burbank fitful and unreliable. We were due each morning at

To prove my physical prowess to Max of mental prowess — Best Ezra

To Max from Joe Louis

SERGEANT Joe Louis and Sergeant Ezra (Henry Aldrich) Stone, improvising funnies between retakes.

Camp TITA by 0600. At 0530, bleary-eyed, we piled out onto Sunset Boulevard, waiting for some car, driven by a fortunate aircraft-factory hand who had access to precious gas rations, to come by. One of us was stationed out on the street, a pathetic smile on his face, his thumb outstretched, wistfully waiting. In a matter of minutes, a car would emerge from the early dawn-light, screech to a stop as a patriotic civilian responded to the sad tableau. "Hop in, soldier," he'd say, smiling. "Gee, thanks," replied the stake-out. "Just a second . . . would you mind giving my buddies a ride, too?" Before Mr. Civilian could reply, from behind the nearby shrubbery three or four GIs had materialized, trotted over, piled into his back seat like Keystone Kops, and completely inundated his vehicle. "Gee, pal, you're a prince!" we'd chorus, slamming his doors. "Let's get going!"

Eventually, we acquired wheels of our own. People who had cars in 1943 often had no gas for them and were only too happy to get the heap out of the driveway on a rental basis. After a certain amount of haggling with a relative of one of the studio musicians, we came into temporary possession of his car.

Perhaps the description is a trifle optimistic. What we leased was a tiny six-year-old sedan, a misbegotten sardine can on wheels, manufactured in the depths of the Depression by the Willys company. In its own humble way, it was as basic an automotive mistake as would be the as yet undesigned Edsel. Our Willys Americar was an amusing upright, presumptuous little four-door curio that set us back a dollar per day, pre-Hertz. Its under-powered four-cylinder engine popped, hissed, and ticked; with the wind behind us, we could manage at least a dizzying 45. The Willys cornered like a spaced-out rabbit; as we lurched around the curves of Cahuenga Pass, groaning upgrade, our engine gasping and straining, civilian drivers doing a staid 35 passed us. They gaped at the sight of four full-sized GIs trapped in that circus-clown model of a car. Swaying beside me in the front seat, with civilians zipping past, my co-pilot buddy Private Ed Kogan grimly commented one evening, "This company's motto should have been 'Watch the Cars Go By.'"

When it came to rubber, the Willys was a self-contained disaster area. In the space of three months, its threadbare tires blew countless times. Daily, the garage mechanic across the street from the Warner studio took in our latest flat, and shook his head in frustration when a vulcanization of the tube was suggested. "*Can't!*" he protested, finally, holding up a limp ribbon of rubber, already so pockmarked with patches that it resembled a smallpoxed snake. "You're not riding on rubber any more, fellas, you're riding on glue!"

The good Lord must have been watching over children, drunkards, and four GIs in a rented Willys, for we continued to make the daily Burbank run without major disaster, coming in for a landing each morning on a wing, a prayer, and four tissue-thin tires. (The fifth was always over at the gas station, under repair.)

The actual filming of *This Is the Army* began, and when it came to that set of complex daily logistics, it was the Warner production department that took charge, not the Army, and nobody goofed. Not only were all our own three hundred GIs employed, but the studio had hired other, civilian actors, and the many musical numbers were, in typical Hollywood fashion, enlarged to double and triple their size upon the screen. So many actors in uniform were spread all over the studio, in different locations, that our arms were sore from saluting newly arrived officer types. The Warner costume department eventually provided arm bands to differentiate the real GIs from the 4-F actors from Central Casting. From then on, if you saw a colonel with a "W-B" on his arm, you were free to ignore him . . . it was a heady sensation.

On an ordinary shooting day, some of the actors would be making story sequences with Mike Curtiz, singers were over on the recording stage, making music tracks with Ray Heindorf and the studio orchestra, and all over the studio, on vacant sound stages, dancers would be rehearsing numbers. One hot afternoon, a second assistant director appeared on Stage 13, where Bob Sidney was rehearsing a platoon in an intricate routine. "Sergeant," he ordered, "LeRoy Prinz says to bring your men right over to Stage 2 and run through this number so he can see what it looks like."

Leroy Prinz was the contract director whom Hal Wallis,

the producer, had assigned to "supervise" the dances. His actual contribution was little more than to point a battery of cameras in the right direction, and to photograph Sidney's creations. "I'm busy," panted the perspiring Sidney. "Later."

Ten minutes later, the A.D. was back. "Sergeant! Mr. Prinz says that Mr. Curtiz himself will be there in ten minutes—you've got to get your dancers over now!"

"Look, buddy," said Sidney, impatient at the interruption, "we're not ready. Tell them some other time!"

"But Mr. Curtiz is the director!" prodded the A.D. "Nobody keeps *him* waiting."

"*I* do!" said Sidney. "Beat it—I'm busy!"

Short moments later, the studio man was back, near hysteria. "Now listen!" he cried. "Mr. Prinz says to tell you that not only Mike Curtiz but Jack Warner *himself* is going to be on Stage 2, in exactly five minutes, and they want to see you run through this dance routine—or you're in big trouble!"

"*You* listen," said the GI dance director, drawing himself up ramrod straight, cold steel creeping into his normally pleasant tone. "You can tell Miss Prinz—and Miss Curtiz—*and* Miss Warner too—they can go fuck themselves! *I'm* working for Aunt Sam!"

For nearly six months, Private Larry Weeks, a diminutive juggler, had tickled audiences with his plate-tossing act, in our military vaudeville show segment. As a GI on KP duty, he did remarkable things with plates until interrupted by Hank Henry, as the mess sergeant (with the Secret Service turkey-leg prop). Without ever missing a single plate, Weeks had juggled his way across the country, and now, in front of Curtiz' cameras, he was ready to re-create the scene for posterity.

"Action!" called Mike, and Weeks began to juggle. In front of the ominous, glassy eyes of the cameras, with no audience save an impassive crew of grips, something happened to the redoubtable Weeks. His hands began to tremble; he froze. *Crash!* He dropped a plate . . . Cut!

Take Two . . . Weeks began his routine again. A moment or so later, another plate landed on the sound stage floor. Cut!

Take Three . . . Two broken plates . . .

It went on that day, for several hours, with Iron Mike Curtiz keeping his Hungarian temper in close rein, with studio overhead mounting with every wasted take . . . with an entire crew stymied while the hapless Larry Weeks struggled to do his one set of tricks—those same tricks he'd done for months now, faultlessly.

On the twenty-fourth take, he succeeded.

Exhausted, he, Curtiz, and the crew called it quits for the day.

Next morning, as we stood in morning formation, Hank Henry, who had been a horrified spectator of the previous day's debacle, sidled up to me. "Hey, press agent," he said. "I've got a bulletin for Louella Parsons. I heard Warner Brothers just signed Larry Weeks to a seven-year contract—for one picture . . ."

Only one recurrent question kept passing through our ranks . . . when we were finished making this picture, what was to become of DEML *This Is the Army,*—and to us? Down in the latrines, in studio streets, wherever we traveled, rumors kept flashing through the conversation. We were going to tour again. We were going north to the Aleutians. Berlin was writing a sequel to the picture . . .

Each day, there was a new rumor available. Fact was in very short supply.

Late one afternoon, one of my fellow GI press agents, Max Gendel wandered into our temporary office in the Warner publicity department. We'd been quartered there for the filming of the picture, and given a unique assignment—i.e., to keep publicity about the picture out of the papers. The Army quite properly felt there had already been too much space devoted to its traveling DEML group, and a low profile was in order.

My colleague Gendel mentioned that he'd been on the phone with a local press agent who was nagging him for a hot piece of gossip, a "column plant" which he could pass on to another p.a. in New York, something that might end up in Walter Winchell's daily collection of facts/news/jokes/hearsay. Did I have anything?

Nothing of any news value.

He sat staring out at the sunny California scene, grimacing

at the eucalyptus trees. He was strictly a Broadway boy; to him anything north of Forty-ninth Street was the wilderness. "I've got it," he murmured. "I'll make one up. I'll give him an item. When we finish filming, the Pentagon will probably send us overseas to entertain the troops. From shooting film to shooting Nazis—how does that sound?"

Ominous. "Don't send it—not even as a gag," I said.

"How can it hurt?" he protested. "It's a simple 'iffy' item—they don't mean a damn thing. Winchell prints 'em every day. Half his column is full of stuff like that. If it doesn't happen, nobody remembers it . . ."

Despite my cautionary strictures, he left the office and went to a phone.

The musical finale of *This Is the Army* had always been a guaranteed show-stopper. Two hundred GIs in massed formation on the stage, roaring out a Berlin lyric which stated that we would now get this war over and done with, and make sure that we would never have to do it again (in retrospect, a trifle over-optimistic, true, but remember—it was a simplistic war, one in which no programs were needed to explain which were the good guys and which were the bastards).

For Jack Warner and Hal Wallis and Mike Curtiz, however, that finale was too small. They wanted it bigger and better. In Hollywood, those two words were always symbiotic. Thereupon, the production brains went to work, and when they finished dreaming impossible dreams, the finale began to assume gargantuan proportions.

Carpenters moved into Stage 22, the biggest one in the studio, and labored for days to erect a veritable Mount Everest of a set—a forty-foot-high statue of Uncle Sam and a fierce American bald eagle, which towered above banks of steps, ramps, and, down in front, a dozen or so moving stairs. All members of the unit were assigned to finale duty. Some of them were assigned to carry banners representing our brave allies. One of our EM, popular with members of the opposite sex wherever we toured, took a firm stand. "I," he said, "insist upon carrying the banner of the Free French."

Mike Curtiz, the director, decided that the war needed re-staging.

But three hundred men in full military kit, spread out across that monster of a set, couldn't even begin to fill it. We resembled a forlorn pack of olive-drab ants, spread across the face of Mount Rushmore. Curtiz demanded reinforcements. "Ve got to fill up de goddamn Uncle Sam!" he insisted, and from nearby infantry camps the Army requisitioned him several hundred more soldiers.

At 0800 the following morning, a convoy of dusty trucks roared through the studio gates and unloaded at Stage 22. GIs in full field kit, carrying Garand rifles, leaped down. Tough, well-trained dogfaces, they looked around the Warner studio street, gaped at extras in eighteenth-century costume, at beautiful chorus girls headed for other sound stages, and at passing actors. One of them blinked, and turned to a nearby GI—one of ours, an ex-burlesque straight man named Dick Bernie. "Hey, buddy," he asked, "what kind of a fucking Army post *is* this?"

"The craziest," ad-libbed Bernie. He winked. "This," he said confidentially, "is a top-secret base."

"You're crapping me," said the newcomer. "What are all these broads, and them cameras and lights? Looks like some fucking movie studio to me."

"That," confided Bernie, "is the beauty of it. Camouflage, see? You're going to go inside this sound stage, and you'll even get to fool around in front of some cameras. Don't kid yourself—strictly dummies." He winked again, and pointed downwards. "Down there. *That's* where it's at, buddy."

"*What* is?" asked the bewildered infantryman.

"Shhh," cautioned Bernie. "Going full blast," he whispered. "Aircraft factory."

The GI digested that military secret. Then he nodded. "But . . . what the hell are *we* here for?" he demanded.

"For God's sake, don't ask that," said Bernie, and glanced about to make sure they couldn't be overheard. "Top secret," he whispered. "Remember . . . loose lips sink ships . . ."

After days of intense, grueling rehearsal, the number was ready for the cameras. The sound stage was lit by hundreds of kliegs, and Curtiz climbed aboard the dolly which soared him

The **FINALE** of World War II, as brought to you by *les frères* Warner.

to the upper altitudes of 22. "Action!" he yelled, on went the playback music, and up there on the set, which they now filled, six hundred marching men mouthed Berlin's lyrics. Bayonets at the ready, flags flying, they tramped grimly on the moving stairs, marching towards the cameras. It was the kind of shot that would make Busby Berkeley green with envy, a splashy extravagance in Technicolored splendor. It took two days of soaring back and forth up there with his cameras before a satisfied Curtiz finally yelled, "Cut! I tink dot's a good vun . . ."

The kliegs went out, the doors opened, and the imported GIs from the nearby camps were released from their peculiar assignment. As they piled out of their waiting trucks on the studio street, that gullible GI came up to Dick Bernie. "Lissen," he said urgently, "if you hadna told me what's down below us . . . I coulda sworn we were up there making a fucking movie!"

"Beautiful, isn't it?" Bernie winked. "That's exactly what they want the Axis to believe. Get it?"

"Oh, yeah," said the dogface. "*Yeah.*"

And still shaking his head, he climbed aboard the waiting Army truck, and headed back to the world of reality.

My press-agent colleague Gendel rushed up to me on a studio street, his face ashen. He thrust a newspaper clipping at me. "Read *that*." he said, his fingers trembling.

It was Winchell's *Daily Mirror* column, mailed from New York. Circled in red crayon was a short item: "Pentagon biggies report to Yr. Correspondent that right after the filming of *This Is the Army's* flicker version, the entire cast heads for the nearest foxhole. From shooting film to shooting Nasties. Goodbye and God bless, fellas . . ."

"We're going *overseas!*" groaned my friend. "There it is—see? Straight from the Pentagon!"

"Ah, it's just another Winchell item, " I said.

"The hell it is!" he insisted. "Winchell always gets the straight goods—right from the horse's mouth!" He mopped his forehead.

"Which in this case is *you!*" I said. "You idiot—that's your *own* fake column plant—don't you recognize it?"

He stopped moaning long enough to stare at the clipping. "You made it up and sent it out yourself. Your pal in New York obviously passed it on to Winchell!" I insisted. "You're terrified of your own rumor!"

He clapped a hand to his brow. "Of course!" he cried. "Now I remember!" Relieved, he burst into hysterical laughter.

A second later, he stopped and stared at me. "That's no help," he moaned. "We're going to have to go overseas."

"Why?" I demanded.

"Because we can't afford to get Walter Winchell sore at us!" he said.

For several months now, down at his HQ in that Burbank field, our fearless leader, the major, had been coping with a mounting sense of frustration. Gone were the cheering crowds which had greeted his triumphant entrance in all those cities we'd played, vanished were the happy audiences who'd packed the theatres, and where were all those lovely local matrons who'd so royally entertained him and his troops? Here in Hollywood, he'd expected to be treated with a certain amount of respect, to be fawned on, and invited to a gay round of parties on the fabled Bel Air circuit . . . And what had happened?

Nothing. The once galloping major was now slowed down to a dull walker. Down at Camp TITA, his office phone barely ever rang. Each morning, he would arrive in his command jeep, expectantly waiting for the message that Mr. Warner wanted him for dinner tonight, a simple sit-down for twelve, perhaps . . . or that Marian Davies expected him out at her Santa Monica beach house for the weekend. Or would he join L. B. at the front table at Ciro's for supper and the show tonight?

Nobody called. The major couldn't realize the truth. In Hollywood, he had fallen victim to the old adage *Today you're a headline; tomorrow they use the paper to wrap fish.*

He took to brooding, down in his makeshift command post on that rocky Camp TITA field, with its weedy obstacle course and its parade ground where, once a week, he presided over a full-dress Retreat ceremony sans audience. Fairly soon now, his show business career would be finished; the unit would be disbanded, and he would certainly be transferred to some other far more mundane command, away from the public eye. A supply depot in Indiana, perhaps, or some windswept recruiting depot in Nebraska . . .

A few blocks away, the bright lights of Hollywood twinkled seductively; the high life of Beverly Hills society, even in wartime, went on, without him. The major decided to fling down the gauntlet, smack in their teeth. If he hadn't made it into their living rooms, then, damn it, they'd have to come when he called them to *his* . . .

He organized a mass picnic in nearby Griffith Park, and in his capacity as CO of our outfit, he issued invitations to a formidable roster of celebrities. Upon intensive consultation with his public relations men, he developed quite a guest list. Gary Cooper and Ingrid Bergman, who were filming *Saratoga Trunk* across the street from our own sound stage. Bette Davis, Errol Flynn, John Garfield, Cary Grant, who was making *Destination Tokyo*, Bogart—the entire roster of top Warner stars went into his circle of the favored few. He invited Mike Curtiz, Hal Wallis, both of the West Coast–based Warner brothers, Jack L. and Harry M., as well as Louella Parsons, Jimmy Fidler, Hedda Hopper, Sheilah Graham, all the prominent press people. "They will come," he announced, with the grandeur that went along with his command. "They *have* to attend. They have been asked, haven't they?"

The invitations went out, somewhat ominously worded, "You are invited and expected to attend." And the major proceeded to requisition supplies sufficient to entertain his guests in the style to which they were accustomed. Beer, sandwiches, hard-to-find hot dogs and hamburger, even some liquor for the VIPs. And then he put his cadre to work to arrange all the details of what promised to be a gala affair, worthy of Hollywood's most ultra . . .

Meanwhile, Curtiz was winding up his final sequences. One memorable afternoon, he prepared to shoot our next-to-closing high spot—Mr. Berlin himself, singing his famous "Oh, How I Hate to Get Up in the Morning."

"All right. Irveen, now ve make de shot," he called, and the songwriter-producer, neatly dressed in his 1918 uniform, stepped before the cameras.

From a nearby loudspeaker, a recording of Mr. B.'s high, reedy voice (it was the late Joe Frisco who once described it "You have to hug him to hear him") began, the words and melody of his old World War I classic echoing through the sound stage. Synchronizing his lips to the playback, the little man with those hundreds of melodies in his head stood there and mouthed the lyrics.

A few feet away, I stood beside two studio carpenters, whose work had been suspended while Curtiz made the shot. In the middle of Mr. Berlin's second chorus, one carpenter turned to his buddy. "Y'know something?" he murmured. "If the guy who wrote that song ever heard this guy sing it, he'd turn over in his grave."

The moment that Curtiz yelled, "Cut! Ve print dot!" I ran back to the publicity offices and tapped out the story. Next morning, it was out on the Associated Press wire. The New York *Times* ran it on page 1, in a small box. Ever since then, it has been reprinted countless times, and it's become a Berlin legend.

It was my first exclusive . . .

Came the Saturday of the major's lavish Griffith Park shindig. We piled into Army transport and arrived, in our GI best, at the scene of the picnic, on the dot called for. Our band sat out in the bright sunlight, the musicians jamming away at jazzed-up versions of our score, as we and our female companions wandered back and forth on the green fields, sipping the major's beer and gorging on his delicacies. He himself, immaculate in his dress uniform, his riding crop at the ready, stood by the entrance to the picnic grounds, waiting to greet Gary and Ingrid, Bogey and Bette, Jack L. and Hal B. and Louella and Hedda.

Time passed. We went on enjoying ourselves. A few minor Hollywood newsmen, ever ready to eat and drink on the cuff, showed up. Some minor studio functionaries appeared. Mike Curtiz dropped by to say a brief hello, and then excused himself; he had to go back to the cutting rooms. But as for any of the other celebrities? The major obviously didn't know his Hollywood. Nobody else showed . . .

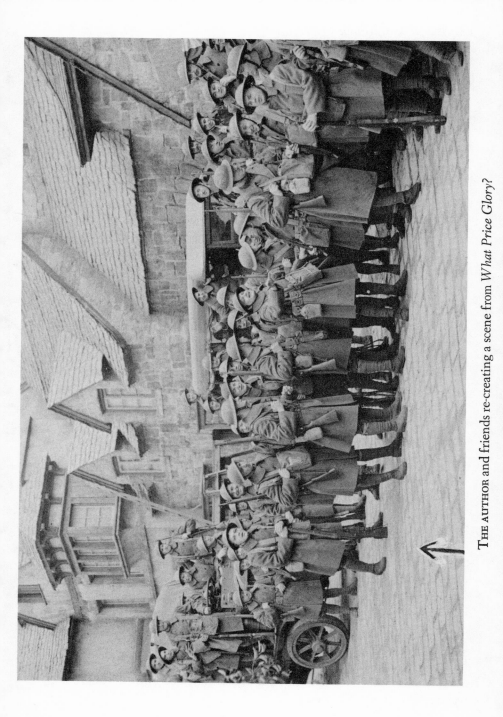

The author and friends re-creating a scene from *What Price Glory?*

In the words of our own Private Louis DeMilhau, who had come to show business from a family that possessed some social standing, "Two Popes have I seen in my day—but not one damn Warner brother!"

We put on a good show of enjoying the major's hospitality. But for him it must have been a bitter put down of a day. He hadn't seen the handwriting on his GI canvas tent wall . . . the *mene-mene-tekel* that Julie Oshins had seen so clearly, much earlier . . . our brief tour of duty as stars was over.

The film was being edited, dubbed, and scored. It was due to open in New York at the Hollywood Theatre early in the summer—on July 4th, natch. We of the press department—my hysterical confrere included—were assigned to continue with our work, to beat the official Army drums on behalf of the picture and thereby to raise more money for Army Emergency Relief. As for the rest of the unit, there were no more rumors; official orders had finally come through. The troupe would be split in half. One hundred and fifty-odd EM would be sent on an extensive overseas tour, along with Mr. Berlin, to give performances of the show in theatres, camps, foxholes and trenches, and hospitals all over the world. That troupe would sail to England, travel down to North Africa, into Italy, and then go on out to the Pacific . . . a heroic assignment. The remaining EM were to be dispersed to suitable duties at other Army posts, camps, and stations.

Came the day of our final formation, at good old camp TITA, behind the Warner studio. In contrast to the excitement we had generated on Broadway, on Michigan Boulevard, on main streets all over the country, this ceremony was quiet, utterly without any hoopla. Our band played, we fell in, and marched across the parade ground, neatly, smartly as always . . . dancers always drill with precision. Our audience, which consisted of several small Burbank boys and one or two local dogs, applauded.

We stood at attention as the bugler blew Retreat. Down from the flagpole came our colors, and were neatly folded and handed over to the Officer of the Day. The major stood there and took the final salute himself. After all, he was the ranking officer . . .

"Compan*ee* . . . fall out!" bellowed Lieutenant Daniels.

We went to our tents to collect our barracks bags, and headed for our new assignments. (DEML) TITA, the most unique task force ever created by the Pentagon, was officially redundant.

Several days later, before my departure for New York, I hitchhiked out to Burbank, to say goodbye to some of our civilian confreres of the Warner press department. The creaky little Willys, with its five chewing-gum-patched tires, had long since been returned to its owner's driveway . . . where it could now quietly rust into decent disuse.

After lunch, I took a final stroll through the Warner lot, and out the back gate, to take one last look at the diminutive, comic-opera Camp TITA, that Ruritanian domain where the major had ruled his troops for the past six months.

There was nothing on the field.

The camp had vanished. As quickly as it had been erected, within twenty-four hours of our final formation, Warner construction crews had moved out there, and removed every building and tent from the field. Lock, stock, latrine . . . and obstacle course—every stick of lumber had been returned to the studio shop, whence it had sprung. There was a war on, and wood and nails and hardware and plumbing fixtures were too scarce to leave out there for any scavenger . . .

Not a trace remained of the place where three hundred citizen-soldiers had drilled, bitched, joked, slept off hangovers in the canvas tents, shot craps in the tiny latrines . . . and mounted guard each night with empty rifles.

Travel past that field today, and it won't be there.

All you will see, beneath the San Fernando Valley smog, are a dozen or so ranch-type bungalows, complete with two-car garages, air-conditioning, and back-yard swimming pools. Not even a plaque stands in one of those back yards, to say "*This Is the Army* camped here."

But then, as Hank Henry might have said, "Hell, that was what we were fighting for, wasn't it? To get out!"

CHAPTER EIGHT

•••••••••••••••••••••••••••

The Flying Typers

OVER THE RADIO comes a news bulletin. President Richard M. Nixon has announced that as his bequest to the nation's tax-payers, he is presenting us, at some time in the future, the large western White House which he enjoys as his home in San Clemente, California . . .

San Clemente? It was once a quiet beach town, reached by the coast highway, and known mainly for the fact that Ben Hecht had a home down there. When I first saw that pleasant little settlement of one-story houses, it was 1944. There was a war on, and the most reliable means of travel was by hitchhiking along the two-lane road that ran down from Laguna Beach. The highway ran along the bluffs which overlook the beautiful sands below, and the early Spanish settlers named that stretch of beach San Onofre. A few miles away was the huge Marine base, Camp Pendleton, where thousands of crew-cut young gyrenes trained for Pacific battles on Tarawa, Okinawa . . . and all the rest of those bloody island fortresses that they were to wrest from the Japanese . . .

Nowadays, Californians drive down the coast on a broad freeway towards San Diego and Mexico, zipping past Pendleton in their Toyotas and their Mazdas and their Subarus, all of which have been shipped by boat to California from Japan, where they have been assembled in factories by hard-working Japanese. Three decades ago, the fathers of those Japanese workers were our sworn enemies, and I, who now drive a Datsun, wore an Air Force uniform . . .

And down on San Onofre Beach, near San Clemente, some of us were engaged in the most exotic sort of military effort that any general ever devised. Equipped with lights, cameras, and sound equipment, we GIs from the First Motion Picture Unit (AAF) at Culver City were busy taking San Onofre Beach . . . for an Air Force training film.

But we weren't stars; we were strictly supporting players. Our star couldn't even speak; it beeped and blipped, and stayed under wraps at all times because it was Top Secret . . . And our star had no name—only initials. PR-B-7 (Portable Radar).

And in the process of making PR-B-7 a star, we almost drowned . . .

Oh well, that's show business.

We stood at attention. Our CO paced behind his desk. He was a trim military figure; his uniform had been tailored at Jerry Rothschild's Beverly Hills haberdashery, his mustache bristled, and he carried a riding crop which he flicked back and forth as he spoke to us, his troops.

"Now, listen to me, men," he said to us, through clenched teeth. "There's a war on. Men are out there in tanks—in foxholes—flying through flak in B-17s. You guys are just goddamn lucky that you're not out there with them—instead of doing this cushy job here in Culver City. Now, I don't want any more goldbricking down there in that Writers' Building, get me? Nobody's going to get away with this shit—missing formations and ducking out of fatigue details. Just remember—I was a writer too—and I know all your tricks. From now on, I want you at your desks by seven-thirty . . ." He glared at us, eyes narrowed. "And I want to hear every goddamn one of those typewriters in the building going—and *not* on scripts of your own . . . You bastards stick to Air Force scripts, get me? Or you can expect a transfer out to Guadalcanal—where you ought to be! *Dismissed!*"

Silently, we filed out of his office. We headed down the studio street to the plywood and tar-paper GI structure that served as the Writers' Building of the First Motion Picture Unit (AAF), Culver City, California, far, far behind the combat zones . . .

As we walked down the street, out of earshot of the COs, one of my colleagues spoke out of the side of his mouth. "He's a rotten officer . . . and he was a rotten writer," he said. "I ought to know. I had to rewrite two of the bastard's scripts at RKO!"

Don't drive out Washington Boulevard in Culver City to look for the old Hal Roach Studios where FMPU flourished, three decades ago. The plant is gone, torn down, vanished along with most of Hollywood's evanescent artifacts. There's a new supermarket there on the site.

Occasionally, on the screen, if you're watching an early Roach two-reeler, you can catch a glimpse of his tiny back lot, with its street on which comedians tossed pies and committed comic mayhem. When the Air Force took the place over in 1942, Roach had given up filming; GIs moved in, cleaned out the accumulated dirt, re-equipped the plant, and stationed MPs at the gate to keep the civilians out. For the next three years, it was officially known as FMPU (AAF)—Culver City.

It was also less reverently referred to as Fort Roach . . . and its troops as the Flying Typers, the Culver City Commandos, or the fearless veterans of the CBI (Culver City, Burbank, and Inglewood).

None of us asked the Air Force to assign us to filmmaking. It was all General H. H. Arnold's idea. He wanted a film studio of his own, and he got one, and when it was staffed, the Table of Organization consisted of a rare mix of West Point ramrod types and backwoods country boys assigned to be its military cadre, alongside neurotic film writers in uniform, temperamental actors called into service, autocratic directors assigned to Fort Roach, dozens of the best studio technicians, all working for GI pay.

During its short stay in Culver City, FMPU was the scene of daily insanities that no satirist could have improvised. Throw together a random collection of filmmakers, subject them to rigid GI discipline, and the ensuing chemical reaction would have to produce comedy situations far wilder than anything ever filmed by our absentee landlord, Mr. Roach, in the days when his studio was devoted to Our Gang, Charlie Chase, and Laurel and Hardy.

And yet, this hasty improvisation, this random, raffish assemblage of a military unit, served General Arnold well. From 1942 to early 1946, the studio turned out hundreds of reels of first-rate training films, propaganda shorts, even full-length features. FMPU organized and trained combat camera crews that flew all over the world to film the war from above and beyond. Its capable art department devised techniques in camouflage that concealed vital California aircraft factories from enemy eyes; an animation department pioneered in a new style of clever educational films. Directors and editors turned out film documentaries, such as Colonel William Wyler's *Memphis Belle,* which can still be studied today as lasting examples of the art.

Its roster contained names to make a film producer drool with avarice. Among the officers and EM were such familiar marquee standbys as Lieutenant William Holden, Alan Ladd (he was famous for his custom-tailored private's uniform with its cunningly padded shoulders), Edmond O'Brien, Barry Nelson, Kent Smith, Van Heflin, Arthur Kennedy, and George Montgomery, all of whom labored long and hard in front of Air Force cameras, operated by some of the most prestigious technicians in IATSE. The CO was, for a time, Colonel Paul Mantz, a hardflying aviator whose thrilling stunt work is still visible in many of the greatest air films ever made, all the way from *Only Angels Have Wings* down to his swan song, *The Flight of the Phoenix.* For his adjutant, Mantz had Captain Ronald Reagan, late of the Warner Brothers stock company. Directors? Besides Wyler, there were others like William Keighley, Robert Sinclair, and Bernard Vorhaus; and down in that little old ramshackle Writers' Building were a whole platoon of talents—Ben Maddow, Harold Medford, Norman Krasna, Jerry Chodorov, Guy Trosper, Edward Anhalt, and Nedrick Young—all of them jammed into cubicles, tapping out scripts on their GI typewriters, all of them booked into this assignment for the duration and six months by their agent, Uncle Sam.

Many of FMPU's personnel went overseas. More of us did not. Rear-echelon duty had its drawbacks. Among one's friends

Film Men of the Air Force

Their job is to make the training and combat films that
help pilots to understand planes and fighting tactics.

and neighbors, one's continual presence in Culver City could cause raised eyebrows.

One of our number, a quiet, noncombatant type, inadvertently dramatized our plight as non-heroes. Early one Friday morning, he was called in by his CO and told to collect sufficient equipment for a weekend assignment doing research on a project out at an air base in nearby San Bernardino. By noon, he'd departed. Nothing more was heard of him until late Monday afternoon, when he returned to our midst, somewhat haggard and unshaven.

Where had he been since Friday?

"Oh, they flew me out to the Pacific," he told us. "Got into a little trouble out there. Japs attacked our B-17. Wounded one of our waist gunners, so I grabbed his gun and got in a few rounds. I think maybe I got a Zero," he added, modestly, and then he went home.

He'd obviously been down on Central Avenue, drinking. Who could believe such a lunatic story?

The fact that it was absolutely true surfaced when he received a citation several weeks later. We believed him . . . but how about his friends and neighbors out in San Fernando Valley? The fact that they never believed him was typical of our improbable status as civilian-soldiers.

His weekend at war later served one of our own, Lieutenant Sy Gomberg, who used it as the basis of a screen story which he sold to Fox, and which became the basis of one of John Ford's rare comedies, *When Willie Comes Marching Home.*

Life on an Air Force post dedicated to the making of training films might often be frustrating, but it was never dull. One grey California morning, Private Sam Locke, a fellow writer, was seated in the cubicle we shared, wrestling with his latest assignment; he was working on some nuts-and-bolts venture that dealt with proper field sanitation. My current magnum opus was a series of one-minute propaganda films which would serve to recruit skilled labor to work in northeastern ball-bearing factories. It was a peculiar way to help win the war . . . but orders were orders.

A staff sergeant from the upstairs GI production office stuck his head into our office. "*You,* and *you,*" he said, pointing at us. "Up—and get down to the Costume Department. You're assigned to Captain Sinclair's project—Metro Back Lot 2. Get moving!"

In vain we protested that we had vital assignments, that we weren't actors, and that what we were doing was far more important than what he proposed. The NCO was unimpressed by our glib response—an order was an order—we were to get moving.

Reluctantly, Locke and I downed our L. C. Smiths and obeyed.

Down at the Costume Department, both of us were measured, and then we were handed uniforms.

Government issue, yes, but these were German issue . . . and not khaki. They were that nasty field grey so beloved of the Prussians.

We stared at the offensive outfits, complete with belts, daggers, even the coal-scuttle helmet. Mutely, they stood for Hitler, the SS, the Gestapo . . . everything we were fighting to erase. Simultaneously, we rebelled. We wouldn't wear these uniforms. "Put them on—that's an order!" yelled the NCO. "And get into the truck outside—the captain's waiting for your bodies!"

Even more reluctantly, we obeyed. Shortly thereafter, two somewhat nervous writer types, now attired in German uniforms, were being driven through the quiet back streets of Culver City, headed for Metro's huge back lot. When our driver stopped at a busy intersection for a stop light, the normally placid Culver City ladies on the street stared up at us in the rear of the Army six-by-six. They did a double take . . . what was this? Two Nazi prisoners of war being transported to some desert prison camp? One old lady waved her fist at us and yelled, "Dirty German bastids!"

"Hanging's too good for 'em!" chimed in her companion, a young mother wheeling a baby carriage. Soon we had a whole platoon of angry burghers cursing at us . . .

It was the sort of nightmare that induced spontaneous reaction, and since we had both been assigned to be actors for

the day, act we would. Both Locke and I responded with a series
of angry imitative Low Dutch curses of our own, straight out
of a remembered Weber and Fields vaudeville routine. That
really got the hoi polloi fired up. They started towards us—and
there probably would have been an ugly Ox-Bow Incident right
there on that Culver City street, save for the traffic light's changing to green. As it was, they chased our truck for a few hundred
feet, yelling threats . . .

Shortly thereafter, we were safely dumped on the set. A
huge MGM German castle set was the background for the
scene we were to star in; the film was a feature-length training
film called *Resisting Enemy Interrogation.* Written by Sergeant
Harold Medford, it would depict the fate of an Air Force B-17
crew which had been shot down over Germany. The prisoners
were thereupon put through a clever program of subtle German
interrogation which would separate the most well-meaning,
tight-lipped American flier from his military knowledge.

The director, Captain Robert B. Sinclair, tall and diffident,
was a Metro alumnus; before coming to Hollywood, he had been
well known for his directorial work on such "smart" stage
comedies as Philip Barry's *The Philadelphia Story.* Now it was
his job to shepherd a GI crew and a cast that included Edmond
O'Brien and Arthur Kennedy through the complicated script.
In this sequence, in a long shot, the American prisoners were
being marched through the gates of the castle, now a German
prison camp.

Sinclair querulously inspected us. The assistant director explained that we were the two men sent over from FMPU as
per his request.

"What did I want them for?" asked Sinclair.

"The two German guards, sir," said his assistant.

Sinclair stared long and hard at both of us. "They don't
look very much like German guards to *me,*" he murmured.

"Yes, but sir, they're in a long shot," said the assistant, hopefully.

"Oh, all right," sighed Sinclair. Obviously, this was far removed from the time when Metro's casting department could instantly provide him with gilt-edged $150-per-day bit players at the snap of his fingers . . . From the look on his face, it was clear that to him we were strictly Victory casting . . .

Five minutes later, both of us had been armed with prop rifles and were standing in position by the castle's main gate, seventy feet or so from Sinclair's cameras and actors.

He peered through the camera finder, then stepped back. With an imperious wave of his hand, he issued an order to his assistant. Then the second assistant came running up to me. "Hey, Private," he said, "Captain Sinclair says take off your glasses!"

"Why?" I asked, confused.

"Because the camera picks up the glass flashes," he said, as if to a small boy. "*Off!*"

"I can't," I told him.

"Why not?" he asked.

"Because without my glasses I can't *see*," I explained.

My eyesight has never been good. Sans my glasses, it's negligible. In order to get into the Army, I'd had to beg . . . a quixotic act I was to regret in the next three and a half years.

The assistant trotted back to Captain Sinclair. There was another murmured consultation, and then a few seconds later he was back. "He says you don't need to see," he told me. "Off!"

Reluctantly, I removed my glasses and tucked them safely into my German uniform pocket. I focused on the cameras far away; in the distance the bright lights were a vivid blur.

"All right now, when the prisoners are marched through the gate, I want you two guards to snap to attention," called Sinclair. "Action!"

How he expected us to *see* them come through the gate I didn't have time to ask; in the distance a group began to move towards us, a large blur . . .

I squinted at it to make out whether or not it was close enough. I blinked. I stared. I couldn't make out a damn thing, or whether it was time to give my starring performance . . .

"Snap to!" hissed Locke, desperately.

As we snapped to, my rifle clattered against my thick German boot.

A large group of figures were approaching our gate—Kennedy, Eddie O'Brien, Barry Nelson, all captured GIs.

O'Brien was peering at me. "Sonofabitch, you're cross-eyed," he remarked, and we all burst out laughing.

"Cut!" yelled Sinclair. What had caused the breakup? No one told him. "Do it *again*," he said, annoyed.

The group came striding up towards us. Again, we snapped to.

As the blur they made on my vision loomed up, I heard Locke say under his breath, "*Bitte*—Americanische actors—could ve please have ein autograph?"

The laughter ruined another take.

From seventy feet away, Captain Sinclair wanted to know what the hell was so funny. It was a simple shot and he wanted to get on with it. Damn it—there was a war on!

I was blind, but uncowed. Mutiny brewed in the ranks. As the cameras whirred for the third take, and the mass of prisoners moved towards us, we went into our snap-to routine. This time, it was my turn. In my very best Bela Lugosi Transylvanian accent, I murmured, "Velcome to de castle of my ancestors."

It was four takes later before Sinclair was satisfied and I was allowed to put on my glasses. I'd made my film debut—but when they ran the first rough cut of Captain Sinclair's epic, there was nothing left of me. I'd ended up on a GI cutting-room floor. . . . I should have known better than to fuck around on *his* set . . .

Quite a few of the EM stationed at Fort Roach, as well as their officers, had homes and/or family in the area nearby, and were permitted to live there, rather than stay in our official barracks. That piece of so-called housing consisted of a rapidly decaying barnlike structure near Culver City which had during the '20s housed a school for troublemaking juveniles called the Pacific Military Academy. (Of which a frend of mine, an alumnus, grimly quipped that the school's official motto might well have been "Built on a Bluff—and Run on the Same Principle.")

So those barracks housed our MPs, and the other unfortunates from the rest of the United States who were unable to find willing friends, relatives, or mistresses nearby. Living off-post meant that officers and EM could skip reveille, but damn little else. To commute in gasless wartime Southern California, whose broad boulevards were pleasantly free of cars, took constant ingenuity; travel to and fro meant car-pooling in old jalopies, antique motorcycles, hitchhiking, or, in the case of energetic homebodies like Private Kent Smith, a daily bicycle ride to and from Brentwood. The morning rush through the Fort Roach gates resembled the arrival in Washington of Coxey's Army. By 0730 of the dawn's early fog, the entire post complement had to be at work, whether it be filming on sound stages or on location, or in the various technical departments.

Private Arthur Kennedy made dozens of training films which involved his arrival each morning on the set with his day's lines memorized. Since his words were not the product of some scriptwriter's imagination but highly technical instructions that dealt with intricate Air Force devices and their workings, his actor's training was invaluable. It enabled him to adapt to crises. On one memorable shooting day, Kennedy was on a location, freezing in an Air Force life raft, for a film which dealt with survival techniques for air crews. The cameras were ready to roll, and Kennedy prepared to deliver some three minutes' worth of complicated instructions on a piece of new equipment.

The GI technical consultant on the film interrupted the director, waving a sheaf of paper. He'd just heard from Washington; there had been changes made in the workings of the device Kennedy was to describe. Here were the two new paragraphs, as amended, just arrived off the teletype. The director thrust the pages into Kennedy's hand. He sat there at 0830, bobbing up and down in his life raft, while the crew waited for him to memorize three new minutes' worth. "Okay," he said, after studying the pages. "Let's go." And without blowing a single technical detail, he made the shot in one take.

"How the hell did you do that?" asked his admiring director.

"Easy," said Kennedy, as he climbed out of the life raft. "I'd d-do anything to get out of this floating ice box . . ."

If Kennedy wasn't working on a specific film, which was rare, he could always be seen prowling the streets and lawns of Fort Roach with a rake in his hand. Years later, I asked him how he'd enjoyed being post gardener. He stared at me. "What made you think I was gardening?" he asked.

"That rake," I said. "It was your standard piece of equipment."

"Oh, that," he said. "I kept it stored in a broom closet, and whenever I was off a picture, I took it out and carried it around. Any sergeant who was looking for warm bodies for a fatigue detail automatically assumed from my rake that I already had a job . . ."

Second Lieutenant Edward Anhalt was not only busy writing scripts for Air Force training films, but his superior officers also assigned him the unenviable job of supply officer for various post departments. There was a certain amount of GI procedure that had to be followed through proper channels whenever props and equipment were requisitioned. Most of this work entailed Anhalt's official signature on GI forms—in quadruplicate.

"I signed for a hell of a lot of equipment," he remembered years after the fact. "Blackmailed into it by senior officers who threatened to ship me off to Alaska if I didn't. I managed to account for most of the stuff by keeping my ears open for air crashes. When a B-17 would go down off Catalina, it always unaccountably had two of our moviolas on it . . . But one of the items I signed for was larger than any of that technical stuff. It was a genuine German Messerschmitt fighter, flown into Scotland under radar by two defecting *Luftwaffe* men. We used it in some training film, and then I forgot about it . . .

"The end of the war came. Along about 1955, I was called on the phone at my home by a Colonel Grauman . . ."

" 'Of the feet-in-the-concrete Graumans?' I asked.

" 'No,' he responded. 'Of the military intelligence Graumans.'

"It seems I owed the U.S. Air Force about $175,000, to

THIS PICTURE, a surrealist exhibit from the propaganda mills of World War II, was conceived and executed in bygone days when creative minds did not need LSD to come up with far-out ideas.

cover the cost of one German Messerschmitt fighter, which I'd signed for, back in 1944."

Eventually, a frantic Anhalt was able to locate the missing airplane, for which, by signing those forms eleven years previously, he was still quite legally responsible. "With the help of a brigand of my acquaintance," he says, "I finally located the thing. It was stored on the back lot at Metro, where for all these years it had been serving as a mock-up for pictures. Well, after all, where else would you stash a hot Messerschmitt?"

Private Sam Locke received orders from the head of the script department, Captain Robert Carson (the author of *I Wanted Wings, A Star Is Born*, etc.), to proceed to a remote supply base up north and to do research for a two-reel training film that would deal with the problems of transshipping equipment overseas. The title of this thrilling epic of the type known as a "nuts-and-bolts" was to be *Packaging and Corrosion*.

Locke reported to the CO of the supply base, and spent three long days down in GI warehouses, familiarizing himself with such exotic subjects as the proper method of applying steel strapping to wooden crates, the wrapping techniques for heavy machine tools that were to be sent off to jungles, deserts, and mountainous areas, and the uses of greases and cosmoline in coating said equipment for protection against salt water and the elements. Then he returned to the CO's office to report that he was well steeped in the subject.

"Have you got all the information you'll need for the script, Private?" asked the officer.

"Yes, sir; absolutely, sir!" said Locke.

"Good!" said the colonel, a true ramrod. He seized Locke's hand and shook it firmly. "Now, Private," he instructed, "you go out there and give 'em hell!"

The Air Force was a law unto itself. When, back in 1942, General H. H. Arnold, its commander, decided he wanted his arm of the service to have its own film unit, rather than to rely on the Signal Corps, he moved full speed ahead. Through a mutual friend, Bill Guthrie, who was one of Jack Warner's studio managers, Arnold established contact with Warner. Eventually,

Warner put on a natty uniform, assumed the rank of lieutenant colonel, and went to work to provide Arnold with staff, technicians, and a studio. As a sort of executive producer of this whole operation, General Arnold was treated with double the usual quota of respect by his Culver City troops. In Hollywood, rank has always had its privileges . . .

One evening, Arnold, on an inspection tour, was entertained by Warner at his home. After dinner, Warner showed his high-ranking boss the Warner "blow-up" reel, a hilarious assemblage of out-takes, scenes of Bette Davis blowing her lines, Basil Rathbone trying on endless helmets for *Robin Hood,* Bogart, Edward G. Robinson, Muni, et al., all filmed in moments of inadvertent anger, shots that had misfired—out-takes that had been clipped and made into twelve minutes' worth of private jokes . . .

Arnold must have enjoyed that reel enormously, for the next day he called Colonel Owen Crump, then the CO at Fort Roach, and asked if it would be possible to see whatever reel of out-takes had been amassed at *his* studio. He thought it would be pleasant to run it down at the Pentagon, to amuse his hard-working colleagues. When might he have it in Washington?

There was no such reel available, but Crump knew better than to explain that to a four-star general. He promised the reel forthwith.

The following morning at 730, all other work was suspended in the Writers' Building while the troops went to work on a top-secret assignment. Objective: comedy blow-ups.

Captain Norman Krasna, Lieutenant Jerome Chodorov, Captain Edwin Gilbert, EMs Irving Wallace, Harold Medford, Nedrick Young, an array of writing talent which in peacetime would have commanded a five-figure weekly salary, rushed out impromptu gag scenes, and then turned them over to equally skilled GI directors and actors, for filming.

The GI technicians worked all night, and the following day, on various sound stages, the actors were called in, to work on tightly closed sets . . . Captain Ronald Reagan, as an Air Force general, briefed bomber crews on their next mission. "Our target for tonight, gentlemen, is *this,*" he growled, and pointed to a

nearby wall map. On cue, the map rolled up; there on the wall
was revealed the full-length picture of a pinup girl . . . George
Montgomery and an ingénue drove up to the gates of an air
base, to bid each other a tearful farewell as he departed for parts
overseas. One last cigarette? Montgomery pulled out his lighter,
flicked it, flicked it . . . flicked it . . . and finally exploded in a
frustrated curse . . . In the cockpit of a two-place trainer, with
a process screen behind it, Barry Nelson gave flying instructions
to a rookie. High above the earth they soared . . . until behind
them, in front of that process screen of fluffy clouds, two GI
technicians appeared, tiptoeing across the set, carrying a ladder.
. . . In the midst of a lecture on the use of a new-model Air
Force life jacket, Kent Smith inadvertently tripped the device
that would inflate it—the equipment instantly ballooned with
CO_2, pinning Smith against the wall . . .

There were several other rather elementary gags, and for a
finale, a shot of a staff officer, played by Edmond O'Brien, delivering a hard-as-nails pep talk to his troops. "From here on in,
this outfit has got to operate strictly GI!" he roared, pounding
his desk. Then he turned and picked up his cap; as he wheeled
away from the cameras, the cap, three sizes too large, came down
over his face.

The next day, Major Warren Low and his cutters labored to
put together this elemental collection of carefully scripted gags,
always retaining the inadvertent quality that had been so carefully injected by the post's top directors. Then off went the
FMPU out-take reel to the Pentagon.

Where it met with great success in Arnold's screening
room. If it wasn't quite as star-studded as Warner's reel, that
didn't bother the Air Force brass. They relaxed with it, secure
in the knowledge that the Signal Corps had never collected anything so hilarious . . . and for a few hours there, the old Roach
spirit pervaded FMPU.

But most of the time, what was being filmed on those sound
stages was far from amusing. Much of the material was enormously important, and quite often strictly top secret. For weeks,
a special-effects crew labored to re-create a vast miniature of the

coast of Japan. Above the hundred-foot-by-hundred-foot model, which reproduced every town and village, factory, harbor, road, and rail line, cameras ranged, slowly filming the terrain below as if from the angle of a B-29 navigator. Then a narration was added, which described the topography the eye was seeing, and when the film was complete, it would give bombing crews the exact sight of what they might expect when they flew off to begin bombing Japan. *Target Tokyo* was shipped off to our Pacific bases, and with it B-29 crews were given a vivid and unique training course for their future successful operations against vital targets.

FMPU combat crews, self-contained with cameras, sound equipment, and developing and printing tanks, were trained and shipped overseas to join each of the fifteen Air Force commands. Wherever there was action, a crew was filming.

There was also humor. Without it, survival was difficult. In far-off India, with the Air Force, Charlie Lederer and George Oppenheimer served as field officers with the FMPU crew. Waggish Lederer seized the opportunity to invest in a full-sized native elephant. He even had stationery printed locally to advertise his new venture; mail began to arrive in the Writers' Department under a letterhead sedately announcing, "THE LEDERER ELEPHANT CO., New Delhi."

It was also in India that Lederer achieved legendary status. One evening, he was entertained by a British lady, the wife of one of the local brass. In her living room, she began to deliver a rather inebriated diatribe against international Jewry. Lederer sat by quietly, politely controlling his temper. Finally, even his patience had worn thin, and he stood up and strolled across the room, to stand by a glass cabinet containing valuable porcelains. "Tell me, Madam," he inquired, "do you know any Jews personally?"

"Certainly not," said the British grand dame.

"And therefore you don't really have anything against the Jews yourself, do you?" sweetly asked Lederer.

"No-o, I don't believe so," she replied.

"Well," said Lederer, leaning against her cabinet and giving it and its contents a push which sent the whole affair crashing to the floor, "you do *now*."

Second Lieutenant Stanley Rubin was assigned to make a film dealing with the bombing techniques used by the B-29, an absolutely top-secret project. He and his crew were ultimately ordered out to a remote training base in the wilds of Nebraska. One miserably cold morning, Rubin was escorted to an even more remote set of hangars, some miles away, passed through MPs armed with submachine guns, led behind walls that were guarded with radar devices, and finally taken inside a vast hangar. There he encountered a colonel, who was about to discuss a new project, a B-29 raid with the code name of "Gimmick."

Rubin presented his orders to the officer. The colonel stared at them, and then at him. "Lieutenant," he said, softly, "you're in the wrong place. Now get out of here and return to your proper base, and I want you to forget from this moment that you ever walked in here. Or that you ever saw me, or spoke to me. As far as this place is concerned, you were never here. It doesn't exist. Is that understood?"

The confused Rubin nodded. Snapped a salute, turned, and left.

Months later, the radio in our office blurted forth the incredible news that the United States possessed an atomic bomb, and that Air Force B-29s had dropped the first one on Hiroshima. The lead plane, the *Enola Gay,* had been in command of a Colonel Paul W. Tibbets, Jr.

Dead-white, Rubin jumped up from his desk, clapped his hand to his forehead. "My God!" he exclaimed. "*That's* what was going on in that place!"

Shaken, he eventually explained the story to us. "The colonel was Tibbets" he said, hoarsely.

For nearly a year, he had been the repository of the war's most closely guarded secret.

But what about San Clemente, which saga could be titled The Taking of San Onofre Beach"?

Once again, that whimsical GI casting department plucked

me from my typewriter and assigned me once again to perform
in front of the camera. It couldn't have been my triumph in the
role of a German guard in Sinclair's picture . . . but whatever
it was, I found myself in a new venture, a two-reel training film
that was to be shot on location. We were sent down to Camp
Pendleton, from which post we could proceed each day to the
nearby San Onofre beach, to shoot the scenes . . .

We drove into Camp Pendleton in our trucks with a certain
amount of nervousness. Who hadn't heard of the legendary
Marines, those single-minded fighting men who lived, ate,
slept, and fought in a world apart? All of us had seen enough
John Wayne pictures to know exactly how rugged the gyrenes
were; how would they react to this unit of limited-service Flying
Typers who'd never heard a shot fired in anger?

Our trucks parked by the proper huts. Over on one nearby
field, the voice of a tough gunnery sergeant could be heard
clearly, as he chanted, "This fucking rifle is Model M-fucking-
One, and was adopted by the Corps in nineteen-fucking-forty-
one!"

We piled out of the trucks and began unloading cameras and
equipment. Soon we were surrounded by a group of curious
Marines, who eyed us with quiet interest. All one had to do was
to scan their impassive faces to know what they were probably
thinking about us . . . *goldbricks/goof-offs/typical rear-echelon
slackers* . . .

"You guys from Hollah-wood?" drawled one Oklahoma
voice.

We nodded.

"No shit," said another. "From the pictures?"

We nodded again. Behind us, there was a buzz as they
took that in.

"Jee-sus!" said a third, with undisguised admiration. "Can
we get your fucking auto-graphs?"

We were celebrities. Everywhere we went, we were followed by young Marines, none of them over twenty or so, but
already hardened veterans home from Guadalcanal and other
terrible battles. And the constant questions we were confronted

with had nothing to do with the war—that nobody talked about. We were from Hollywood, so we must know the answers . . . Did Rita Hayworth really put out? . . . How about Veronica Lake—was she an okay babe, or as weird as she looked? . . . And were Betty Grable's knockers for real?

One evening, at chow, which at Pendleton was served in two Marine mess kits, and which was good, albeit somewhat like a tossed salad of four courses, I sat with a tall youth. He queried me in a deep Texas drawl. Did I know a certain bar on Hollywood Boulevard? The reason was that he and his buddy had been up there last week, on a pass, and the goddamned bartender had cheated him and his buddy . . . "But ah took care of him yesterday," he said, between mouthfuls. "Went down to our armory, stole me a hand grenade, see? Hitchhiked up to L.A., went back to that there place where they cheated my buddy and me, went into the back to the crapper, pulled the pin on that there hand grenade, dropped it right in the goddamned crapper, and walked out, whistling." He shook his head with quiet satisfaction. "Ought to teach them not to cheat me and my buddy again, don't you think?"

"Oh, yes indeed," I agreed, shaken.

It was at that precise moment that I became convinced that with the Marines at the ready, we would win the war in the Pacific . . .

Our location was on a beautiful wild stretch of San Onofre Beach, and in the film it was supposed to represent a South Pacific island, on which an observation plane had crashed during battle. Later on, the script called for a crew of radar technicians (they were us) to land on that beach, carrying a Portable Radar Unit PR-B-7, set it up, and guide the rescuers at sea to the downed plane. It may have been a strictly B-picture plot, but then, we were out to win a war, not the Academy Award . . .

With the efficiency bred of years in Hollywood studios, our technicians and prop men weren't relying on picking up a wreck locally; they had brought their own—a vintage Air Force transport which had been trucked down from Culver City in parts and reassembled on the beach location.

Next morning, we were ready for action. The morning sun came out, the technicians removed the tarpaulin from the wrecked plane, and the Captain, our director, a Warner Brothers veteran of pressure-cooker-type B-picture schedules who was raring to make film, set up the morning's first shot.

Just as he yelled "Action!" two Naval Air Patrol planes out of San Diego roared by, on their hourly routine flight up and down the coastline. They dived low, swooping down on us, the sound of their engines effectively ruining the take. As they disappeared across the horizon, the director angrily shook his fist. "And don't come back!" he commanded.

He got in one shot, but fifteen minutes later, as he started another, there was the sound of sirens coming towards us. Down the beach road, racing hell-for-leather, came two police cars, an ambulance, and a fire engine, all converging on our crew. "Where's that wrecked plane?" demanded a panting fire chief, as his men began to unreel their hoses. "Navy reports a crash!"

"It's a prop!" yelled the captain. "Now get the hell out of here and let me make some film, will you?"

Eventually, the local authorities withdrew. The captain lined up another shot. As the actors began to go through their lines, the sound of airplane engines coming at us filtered through the mikes. Flying low, another pair of Navy patrol planes zoomed over, turned, and circled our site, then roared off . . .

"Action?" said the captain, hopefully.

He managed to get in another setup before more sirens shattered the necessary silence. A parade of Navy jeeps and pickup trucks roared down the road, led by a gung-ho crew of SeaBees in battle dress who piled out and came running towards us. "Somebody reported a downed plane!" yelled their chief petty officer.

"Go on home and build a bridge!" yelled back our captain.

The Seabee CPO examined our downed plane, the cameras, the lights, and the sound equipment. "Say, you guys making some goddamn movie?" he asked, at last.

"Not the way you're interrupting us!" said the captain.

The Navy reported our downed plane twice more that day,

and we were reached by two more rescue parties. The captain's blood pressure mounted dangerously . . . until, finally, a harassed communications center somewhere in San Diego got through the message to all coastal patrols that the wreck on San Onofre Beach was strictly home-grown, out of Culver City, belonging to the goddamned Air Force.

"Christ!" complained the captain. "We never had this trouble when we were making Torchy Blane pictures!"

The following morning, we arrived at the beach in full field kit. A large LST was drawn up, waiting for us. "Today we shoot the actual landing," announced our road-company Mike Curtiz, as he supervised the installation of cameras on the rear of the formidable LST that the Navy had loaned us for the day. "Now, we're going out there and turn around and come in, and when we hit the beach, you guys will jump out with the equipment and run up off the ramp, get it?"

Obviously, the actual equipment, an intricate new radar set, wasn't to be risked on the set. We, however, were expendable. The crew piled plywood cartons aboard the LST deck, and each of us was assigned his particular box to carry off the ramp. It would be very easy to accomplish, the captain assured us— the cartons didn't weigh much . . . "As soon as you feel the keel hit the sand, the ramp goes down, and out you go. One man runs to the left, the other to the right—that's to avoid enemy fire— get it? And don't stop running until I yell 'Cut!' "

We piled into the hold of the LST and set sail for a point on the placid blue Pacific a half mile or so from shore. Behind us, the captain and his camera crew crouched over their cameras, ready to go . . . and then, just at the moment when the LST had stopped and was ready to head in for our big scene, the sun disappeared behind a bank of dull grey California cloud.

"*Hold it!*" commanded the captain. We'd have to sit there and wait for the sun; there was no artificial lighting available.

There we crouched, at the ready, in the dank hold of the LST . . . waiting for the sun.

Later, I was to discover that what happened out there to us

was endemic to the passangers on any LST. Flat-bottomed boats when moving forward are stable enough. Sitting motionless on water, however, they assume the characteristics of a cork in a bathtub; the slightest touch of a wave causes them to bob up and down, to sway back and forth. In a matter of moments, we unfortunates down in that airless hold became queasy . . . en masse. Queasiness led to nausea led to *mal de mer* . . . half a mile off the Pacific coast. On the D-day landings at Normandy beach, GIs suffered from the same complaint—but their anguish was in a good cause . . . it wasn't induced by a power-mad Captain Queeg who wanted proper contrast on a long shot.

Half an interminable hour or so later, the sun emerged. By now, most of us were pale and limp. We'd long since lost our breakfast down in that floating torture chamber.

"Action!" yelled the captain.

Below us, the engines rumbled, and the LST began to move in towards that blessed shoreline, running at top speed. Crouched at the ready, we braced ourselves for our big landing scene. Behind us, the cameras whirred . . .

On and on we plowed. Behind that huge ramp, we couldn't see a damn thing . . . *Thump!* The keel hit sand. *Whang!* Down went the ramp door into the water. "*Go!*" yelled the captain behind us, and off we dashed, down the ramp of the LST. Not onto sand, however—but into water six feet deep!

What the bastard *hadn't* told us was that an LST with such a heavy load would run aground twenty feet sooner than ordinarily—something any ten-year-old Sea Scout would have known!

Dragged down by plywood cartons and field equipment, packs, rifles, cartridge belts—and that GI stuff—we floundered underwater, making desperately for shore through the breakers.

Gasping for breath, we finally made it onto shore, spluttering, drenched . . . with all those damned plywood cartons bobbing up and down behind us in the surf.

"Ruined!" yelled the captain. "The whole shot stinks! Have to do the whole thing again—from the top!"

A squad of bedraggled GIs stood there on the beach, staring

silently at him from beneath dripping helmets, pure hatred in every eye.

He stared back. None of us spoke. None of us trusted ourselves to. After all, cursing an officer was a court-martial offense—even at Fort Roach.

"On second thought," he said, "maybe we can cut *away* from the actual landing . . . and—ah—get a reverse angle . . . mmm?"

"A very good idea," said his assistant. "Smart thinking, sir."

Our trucks pulled into Camp Pendleton late that afternoon and dumped us, weary, wet, and near mutiny. As we toweled ourselves dry in the Marine hut we'd been assigned, there was a knock on the door and a young gyrene peered in.

"Hey, you guys in there," he drawled, thrusting a long hunting knife at us, "anybody want to take a chance on this here knaf? Ah'm a little short, so ah'm holding my own raffle . . ."

The prize was a wickedly gleaming eight-inch bladed beauty, easily capable of killing.

"I don't want a knife, thanks," I said, politely.

Next to me was a fellow veteran of today's landing, George O'Hanlon. "Oh yes you do," he said. "We *all* do."

The young Marine sold six chances in our hut.

Luckily for the captain, none of us won the knife.

Two days later, we were home at FMPU, hardened veterans of a portable-radar landing, back at our sedentary scriptwriting.

Somewhere deep in the Army Air Force film archives, it still must be stored, a two-reeler that is out of date technically but definitely a film curio. I can think of at least one film buff who'd be happy to screen it, so he could finally demonstrate to his sons what he actually did during the war.

It may never be cited by *Cahiers du cinema*, but that picture will always remain a cinematic landmark to those of us who came near drowning in order to get it all on film.

CHAPTER NINE

••••••••••••••••••••••••••

Shambles

This morning, a very good friend calls. She's a dedicated theatre-goer, and last night she went thirty miles north to the opening tryout performance of a new play.

As they always do at news of an opening night, my ears perk up. How did it go?

Not well. The audience was restless, and some of them did not return for the second act. She's a very intelligent lady, well read, and today she is honestly perturbed. "*You*'re in the business," she says. "*You* must know. It was so obviously bad. How do these things happen? How do rational people get themselves mixed up in such terrible flops?"

Is that a hypothetical question, or does she want a rational answer?

She wants a rational answer.

From me? "Sorry," I tell her. "There isn't one."

She takes umbrage. She believes I'm being fatuous.

I only wish it were so.

"If I had the rational answer for you," I sigh, "I'd be a very rich man, wouldn't I?"

She hangs up, convinced, I'm sure, that I'm hiding some basic truth, some professional tricks of the trade from her.

Dear lady, when it comes to flops, there are none. Around a flop, there's only scar tissue.

You haven't really lived until you've died . . . somewhere out of town with a flop show of your own.

It was that native American wit, Mr. Abe Burrows, who once quipped, to the music of Irving Berlin:

"Yesterday they told you you would not go far.
Last night you opened
And they were right."

Abe was making a great gag out of *Angst*—and like all such jokes, his contains an ultimate truth. It applies primarily to nightmarish opening nights. Until you've been through one of your own, you're a tyro, a hanger-on, a civilian with dreams of glory. It's when that curtain comes down and the audience—or what's left of it—starts up the aisle with blood in its eye, looking for revenge . . . looking for *you* . . . that, my boy, is where they separate the amateurs from the pros, that's the night you'll have your own private theatrical rite of passage . . . That's the bloodletting that leaves you wan and nauseated and forces you to decide right then and there whether or not you're going to stick with this *farkakteh* business or go into advertising . . . or (if you're lucky enough to be female) to marry that rich stockbroker from Scarsdale . . .

You bet it's a nightmare. Old Franzie Kafka never dreamed up anything to top it. There you are, naked to your enemies in the lobby, over there's your nervous knot of friends and agents, plus a few loyal relatives, pity in their eyes, all standing by, making sporadic small talk in the midst of whatever paying customers are still around . . . and you can hear that angry matron over there as she stamps out and says to her friend, "Well, who ever thought *this* would make a show?"

Good question. And what's the answer?

We *all* did, madam.

One of us sat down at his typewriter long months ago and typed "Act One, Scene One" on a piece of paper, and then his agent passed the next hundred pages around to various producers until she found one who would spend eight or nine months locating some otherwise perfectly sane citizens to open up their checkbooks and underwrite the venture . . . Actors and actresses came in for readings, signed contracts, rehearsed for long hours in a loft with the director, and then everybody got onto a train and left New York and came out here to the hinterlands . . . and at 8:40 the house lights went down, the curtain went up, and *wham, bam* . . . the shit hit the fan.

Better, madam, you should ask *why* we all did it. For that there is an answer.

In two short words. Self-delusion.

That poor, benighted bum in tweeds who started it all, he figured he was writing the next Pulitzer Prize winner. The director seriously assumes he's the new Elia Kazan, the producer was dreaming of ways to hide his profits from the IRS . . . and as for all those hapless actors and actresses who were trapped up there on the stage . . . well, they have to be the purest example available of driven dreamers. From that first day of rehearsal, they've all firmly believed that this show has to be the next *My Fair Lady*. The leading lady knew in her gut that she was about to assume Julie Andrews' tiara . . . all of them, down to the bit player with the smallest part, had visions of their own TV series dancing in their head. Fantasists, every last one of them, and since it's a free country, there they are up there, making exits and entrances into that brightly lit lion's den, single-minded Christians from Actors Equity, who will wait for applause that never comes. To watch them, you'd never believe anything was wrong, that they're trapped in a disaster, that this three-act slaughter of the innocents, or this limp musical non-comedy, is a particular sort of torture that would have made Mr. Torquemada chortle with delight.

Actors are remarkable for another gift they seem to possess. They don't know what went wrong. Chances are, they never will. The late great musical director, Robert Emmett Dolan, once related a story about one of his many musical tryouts. The show's leading man was William Gaxton. Gaxton crossed Boston Common one afternoon and spied the creative crew, producer, composer, librettist, lyricist, all slouched out there on a park bench, grieving over and pondering their sick second act. The following morning, Gaxton came to see Dolan. "Bobby," he said, "I saw all the guys out there yesterday trying to figure things out. It's that damn second act that worries everybody, right?"

"Right," said Dolan, wearily.

"Well, don't worry about it any longer," said Gaxton, an ebullient gent. "I was up all night thinking, and you know something? At five o'clock this morning, the answer came to me— I've got it!"

Dolan waited patiently for the revelation.

"You know that second-act scene where I make my entrance?" asked Gaxton, afire with inspiration. "Think about that, Bobby. It's absolutely wrong. I come out wearing my dark blue suit—right? Well, it should be *grey!*"

Early on, I was a witness to minor theatrical shambles. Once, at the very first tryout of *On Borrowed Time*, in New Haven, the leading man, Richard Bennett, lost his lines in the middle of the first act, and spent the remainder of the evening wandering about the scenery, missing cues and audibly complaining about the quality of the local stagehands. It was a harrowing sight. Once, in a summer-stock production, I watched in horror as the leading lady came out in a performance of *Her Cardboard Lover* and began to reel off her third-act speeches in the midst of the first act. That night, her two leading men turned grey-haired sans make-up.

The first major shambles I recall took place at that same Shubert in New Haven, in 1940. One never forgets such a time and place. This one involved a revue titled—somewhat optimistically—*All in Fun*, and it starred Phil Baker, Imogene Coca, and the great tap dancer, Bill Robinson. The production was complete with a large cast of other solid performers . . . Ben Lessy, Jerry Lester, singers and dancers. The curtain went up at 8:40, and this misbegotten affair began with a decent enough opening number. (The program should have warned us up front when we read the note "THE ORDER OF THE SHOW TONIGHT MAY VARY.") From that point on, it was all downhill. This haphazard conglomeration of half-rehearsed skits, songs, and ballets went on and on and on. Dances followed comedy, followed stand-up routines by comics, interminably. At one point, a valiant couple came out and sang a ballad called "It's a Big, Wide, Wonderful

World" and then disappeared. There was a confused ballet called
"That Man and Woman Thing," and, finally, poor Bill Robinson
came out dressed in a Grecian costume to do a duet with Miss
Coca which was called "You're the Prettiest Piece in Greece."
And God bless the man, he made it sound halfway decent . . .

By midnight, the thing was still going on, well past anyone's
bedtime. Through their Pancake #7, the performers perspired,
but they carried on their appointed rounds with more skits, more
dances, more songs, in no particular order. Their eyes became as
glazed as ours. The entire affair became an endurance contest
. . . who would last longer—they, or us?

Finally, the bearbaiting up on the Shubert stage wound
down to an abrupt conclusion. A haggard Phil Baker came
through the curtains to stare at the numbed spectators. "Folks,"
he croaked, "it's almost one o'clock. We haven't got a finale
prepared. Would you all mind going *home?*"

Silently, we filed out.

The show eventually limped out of New Haven, reeled to
Boston, then staggered into New York, where it lingered for a
few days, and then died a merciful death. All that remains of it
today is the late John Rox's lovely ballad, "It's a Big, Wide,
Wonderful World" . . . and the memories of it that those of us
who suffered through that Shubert shambles will always retain.

Nearly ten years later, my own personal shambles took place.
Not at the New Haven Shubert, where the lobby has so often run
red with intermission blood that for a time the management
considered a carpet in burgundy in order to match the stains left
behind by anguished producers and authors . . .

No, my first bomb was to misfire in the City of Brotherly
Love, Philadelphia, and in involved an abortive musical revue
titled *Curtain Going Up.* A clever young comedy writer named
George Axelrod had formed a loose collaboration with me; the
two of us had achieved a certain measure of success in 1948
by writing sketches for the successful Broadway revue *Small
Wonder*, a deft little show which Burt Shevelove had created,
and which ran on Broadway for seven or eight months with Tom
Ewell as its star. Subsequently, George and I had contributed to

weekly TV variety shows, and we had concocted a two-act mini-revue for a smart New York restaurant, the Versailles. All of these ventures had filled us with a certain heady sense of false confidence; here we were, two functioning sketch writers taking in a steady amount of weekly income. We had acquired a small reputation among various producers around NBC and CBS as being somewhat zany but clever chaps who had the youthful stamina to meet those inexorable weekly deadlines by which live television frenetically existed. We were willing to put up with impossible rehearsal schedules and the neuroses of un-certain comedians who could pitch out eleven pages of a script without warning and angrily scream for completely new material by nine tomorrow morning. And we were too young and eager ever to concede that anything was impossible.

That euphoric naïveté was our first Achilles' heel. To para-phrase old man Alexander Pope (a retired scribbler capable of getting off a few nifties of his own), a little success is a dangerous thing.

When the pie that was to hit us in the face surfaced, it was disguised as a lucrative Broadway venture. A young performer, short on experience but long on cash, was to star. Miss Hazan (all names from here on will be changed to protect the guilty) came from a famous show business family. For many years, her father had been a superstar. Perhaps Freud could explain why Hazan *père* seemed to be eager to underwrite a full-scale musical revue in which his daughter would at last have the proper show-case for her limited ability as a mimic, comedienne, and/or pro-ducer . . . Whatever was his problem, she became ours. She had seen our Versailles show and adored it, and shortly afterwards we had signed contracts with her to create the show in which she—and we—were to knock old Broadway for a loop.

Miss Hazan came equipped with a partner. He was a knowl-edgeable, witty chap named Felix. For years, he had made a decent living by staging night-club acts for fading Hollywood stars who were desperately trying to revive a career, putting on summer shows in Borscht Belt mountain hotels, and creating little revues which played little theatres for little runs. The secret of Felix's success was not his talent, which was minor, but his gift of language, which was major. He talked a marvelous show.

When he had finished describing his concepts, it was a dazzling prospect—Noel Coward reborn . . . jolly comedy sequences played against clever songs and dances . . . our satiric thrusts firmly embedded in a fast-paced, knockout show. "Put us all together, we simply have to be a smash!" Felix cried, and George and I, a pair of rabbits hypnotized by this jovial cobra, heartily agreed. By the end of three weeks, we had emerged from our office with four or five serviceable sketches, and off we went . . . pell-mell into the Valley of Death . . . the one in which Caine's Warehouse is the final stop.

We should have seen the second set of warning smoke signals that portended massacre, but down the valley we rode, ignoring the fact that none of the major comics Miss Hazan and Felix approached for their new show were sufficiently taken by their project to sign on. And with good reason. Miss Hazan would have to be co-star. And in this hard-nosed business, what seasoned trouper would be willing to join hands with her and her interminable imitations of Tallulah, Bea Lillie, Greta Garbo, and Judy Garland?

Eventually, she was to settle for, not second bananas, but third bananas, a couple of struggling out-of-work comics who needed her almost as much as she needed them. Then the cast began rehearsals.

Daily, we attended. The group that Felix had assembled seemed attractive enough, but not exactly brimming with talent. One little blond lady, part of the ensemble of singers, was soon awarded two solos, one in the first act, one in the second. She had a high, reedy voice which consistently flatted. It began to grate. Could we please dispense with her services? No, we could not. Why not? Because she was extremely talented! For days the argument continued. No matter how we protested, Felix was implacable. Miss Smith and her two solos would remain. We should stick to our side of the street, which was comedy, and leave the major problems to him. *He* was in charge.

We retired to rehearse the sketches with the comics, and

thus we committed the third mistake—one of omission. We paid little attention to the rest of the show which Felix was devising. We didn't see the ballets his choreographer was preparing, misbegotten little charades, pathetically unrealized by a mini-troupe of five dancers. We didn't hear the songs as they emerged from his rehearsals . . . and if we had, we might have recognized the truth—that this show was a potential flop. Not a big one, to be sure, but a certain wipe-out.

That conditional word "might" is all-important. At that point in time, neither George nor I was rational enough to admit failure. *Our* stuff was funny—wasn't it? Ego dictated rashness; let the rest of the show be second-rate—*we*'d carry the load—*we*'d make that eighty-yard run for touchdown, solo . . . it was all going to be up to *us!*

We held our first run-through, in a bare rehearsal hall. Mrs. Hazan, the mother of our lady producer, suddenly appeared. Mr. Hazan was ill out in California. Stone-faced, the formidable mother sat through the two hours' worth of rehearsal. When the last of Felix's gay little numbers had been performed, Felix beamed at her. And how had she enjoyed their little venture so far?

Mrs. Hazan stood up, grimly took her daughter by the arm, and walked her a few feet away. Then, after a whispered consultation, in a loud, angry voice she was clearly heard to say, "The bastards stole your father's money!"

Miss Hazan pressed on regardless. Despite a warning from Al Goldin, the business manager she and Felix had retained, to the effect that this venture was somewhat undercapitalized and was already leaking at the seams, she persisted. We had our booking in Philadelphia; we would open on schedule. It was expected of anyone named Hazan . . . *Avanti!*

Gradually, we became aware of a certain schizoid pattern that lurked within Miss Hazan. She was far from a stupid girl; in fact, she was very bright. She could sit in the back of the darkened theatre as we watched rehearsals up there on the stage, and when we pointed out errors and omissions, pieces of inept staging by Felix, and obvious dull spots in the show, she wore her producer hat well. She was not only with us, she was ahead of us.

When we got to *her* scenes, however, off went her producer hat, and on went *le chapeau de l'artiste*. Change the merest word of one of her imitations? Forget it! They were tried and true. Restage her comedy routine? Add to her comedy material? Forget it! Eliminate perhaps one of those embarrassing imitations? ". . . What are you trying to do—*destroy me?*" raged our would-be grande dame.

There, in essence, was the most dreadful problem, the trap which was to prove lethal. Our producer was a lovely young lady playing Mr. Hyde and Dr. Jekyll . . . and *that* was no imitation.

We did our final run-through and arrived in Philadelphia. Al Goldin made sure that George and I and our typewriters were well housed in the old Ritz Hotel, on Broad Street. We hurried to the Forrest Theatre and watched as Felix and his frantic production crew saw to it that the show was hung. Our first dress rehearsal with scenery and costumes was the usual all-night madhouse. Missed cues, sets that did not function, sketches that hung up there, limp and unfunny, and some very obvious old hangups. I.e. That little blond singer with those two numbers, Miss Smith, was flatter than ever. Our leading lady, Miss Hazan— she wasn't getting any better, either. As opening night approached, she missed cues, fluffed her lines, and the tension was beginning to tell on her.

But none of that seemed to bother Felix. The major problem he seemed to be addressing himself to was our opening number. With his cast onstage in pale blue trench coats, happily singing the opening song that hopefully told everyone that the most beautiful words in the whole wide world were not "I Love You" but "Curtain Going Up" . . . Felix was most unhappy. When we approached him about possible changes and cuts in other places, he was distant. "Something must be done about the opening!" he insisted. "Those trench coats are ghastly!"

Both of our wives arrived in Philadelphia for the opening. By some coincidence of time and passion, both ladies were *enceinte*. We took them out to dinner, fortified ourselves with considerable drink at the Last Supper, and proceeded to the theatre.

The curtain rose as scheduled, and the cast came out in those trench coats and sang to the audience, and the Philadelphia people sat there, watchfully waiting. Number after number moved onto the Forrest stage, to be met by smatterings of applause. Sketches that had seemed hilarious to us back then encountered waves of sullen silence. On went the evening, with an occasional piece of material striking a certain fitful glow of warmth. Miss Smith flatted gaily away in both of her solos. Miss Hazan, to put it mildly, laid several large eggs. By 11 P.M., the curtain mercifully began to descend on the reassembled ensemble onstage. They sang their jolly finale as if nothing untoward had happened. The Philadelphia audience came slowly, ominously, up the aisle towards the back of the house where George and I and our sympathetic wives had repaired for safety.

"Maybe the worst show I ever saw," said one lady, showing teeth through sneering lips. "I want my money back."

"Yeah," said her escort. "Where did the people who put on this dog ever get the idea that it was any good?"

We stood aside to let them pass. Neither George nor I would venture to speak to each other. We were inundated by further waves of hostile theatregoers. That night, the City of Brotherly Love seemed to be overflowing with hatred—and it was all focused on us.

Behind us, on a set of stairs leading to the balcony, sat Felix and his assistant. As angry theatregoers clambered down around them, muttering imprecations, we heard Felix saying to his assistant, "Now, here are the notes for the changes. In the first act, in that opening, we simply must do something about those goddamned trench coats!"

George turned to me. "Buddy," he said, "we are in trouble."

"Deep trouble," I agreed.

Both of our wives sighed in anguish. George patted his wife and glanced at her protruding waist. "Don't worry, dear," he said. "Prolonged exposure to failure can't have any effect on the kid, I'm sure of it!"

It was the last joke either of us was to make for quite some time, either up on the Forrest stage or in the ensuing mad scenes which were to be played around us for the next few frenzied days.

At 2 A.M., we were all of us, the entire hapless production crew, in a hotel suite at the Ritz, fighting over changes. They were impossible to decide on; the choreographer was insistent that his dance sequences had been misproduced and refused to change a single jeté. The composers and lyricists—of whom there were many, since this was a collected revue—were equally insistent that nobody fool around with a single note of any number. Felix was insistent that once the trench coats had been replaced, the running order would straighten itself out, and Miss Hazan hysterically refused to change a word of any of her less-than-successful imitations. It was the scenery behind her which was wrong, wrong, wrong! The designer fought back like a maddened tiger. In one corner, Al Goldin continued to shake his head sadly, while in the center of the suite, arguments, bitchy recriminations, and angry insults filled the night, as bruised egos found their tongues.

Separately and in tandem, George and I fought back amid the confusion, attempting to bring some faint semblance of order out of this catered-by-room-service chaos. Time after time, we hurled ourselves into the fray, demanding major surgery, only to be tossed back by angry dervishes who were dedicated to protecting their own private turf.

After one such useless foray, I dropped back, exhausted, onto the floor, to find a small, undistinguished gent in a business suit seated beside me down there. Him I hadn't noticed previously. I shook my head angrily and said, "This is a goddamned madhouse!"

"Yeah," he said. "You know what this show needs? It needs a boss."

"You're absolutely right!" I told him. I jumped up, and grabbed Felix. "Listen to that man over there!" I insisted. "He knows what's wrong—we need a boss! Now, who's it going to be? How about *him* taking over?"

"Shh!" Felix cautioned me.

I persisted. Eventually, he dragged me out to the hall. "Do you know *who* that *is?*" he demanded. "That's Johnny Belaggio!" "Who the hell is he?" I asked. "Whoever he is, he's right! Let's listen to him!"

"Will you shut up?" whispered Felix. "He's from the Mafia!"

"I don't care if he's Lucky Luciano!" I said. "He's *right!*"

Then I did a bleary double take. "Hey," I said. "What the hell *is* he doing here at our production meeting?"

"He's a backer!" whispered Felix.

"How did *he* come to be a backer?" I asked, confused.

"He's a good friend of one of our girls!" he said, starting back inside the hotel suite.

Two and two suddenly made four . . .

I grabbed Felix. "*Miss Smith?*" I demanded.

Felix nodded.

"*Now* I get it!" I said. "But she sings *flat!*"

"For ten thousand dollars, I'd let her sing hymns!" said Felix.

We made a few changes. We rewrote sketches. We added material. We cut. (None of Miss Hazan's material, needless to say.) As the week labored on, the show began to respond, in a queer, limp sort of fashion, to our various transfusions. We told ourselves that it was getting better. Of course it was; we had nowhere to go but up.

Felix's trench coats were replaced. Some of the really dreadful material was jettisoned. George and I stayed in the hotel suite, hacking away at revisions, hurrying pages down to the theatre for rehearsals, then returning for some sleep and more work.

But the color in the patient's cheeks was caused by fever. Our sad little venture was floundering. As fast as we patched up one wound, another appeared. And medication was difficult to apply; whichever way we turned, we encountered personal jealousy, intrigue, recriminations, and plain old-fashioned bitchery. Felix fell to sulking in his room and refusing to come out. Miss Hazan kept on desperately calling various friends in New York and Los Angeles to come and bail her out with new songs and suggestions. Her friends appeared at various performances and stood in the lobby stony-faced during intermission;

when the curtain fell, they had vanished, back on the first train available.

By the middle of the second week of our run, business had fallen off to such a point that we were playing the show to audiences almost as sparse as the number of Equity members onstage . . .

One morning, George and I awoke to the realization that we had no cash on hand. Since by rule of Dramatist Guild contract, we were due a per diem for each day we worked out of town, we assumed Al Goldin had perhaps forgotten to come up with the necessary cash. We hurried down to his suite to secure an infusion of money.

Al was sympathetic to our plight, but claimed he was in a poor position to help out. From his rapidly thinning bankroll, he peeled off fifty dollars and gave it to us. "This is for your going-home money," he said. "Don't spend it. As for your per diem . . ." He sighed. "We just don't have it in the box office, fellas . . ."

No cash? How did he expect us to survive?

He patted us fondly, paternalistically. "Stay in the hotel," he instructed. "Charge all your meals here. Then, when you leave, I'll sign the bills, and they'll let you out. Use the cash for the train."

Was it that bad?

He smiled wearily. "Worse," he said.

Carefully dividing the cash between us, we returned to the hotel, and to the last few pieces of desperation writing that waited to be put through the typewriter. Both of us had seen the famous farce *Room Service*—now, remarkably, we were to star in it. From then on, we had room-service meals three times a day, complete with drinks for both of us. In between food breaks, we'd repair to the theatre and survey the latest valiant attempt of our cast, then return to the Ritz and try to figure out ways of getting the waiter to bring whisky up by the bottle, rather than by individual drinks. Late one evening, George turned to me. "I'm cold," he complained. "Do you think I could call room service and order an overcoat?"

The following night, after the show, Miss Hazan rapped on

the door. She closed the door behind her and collapsed on the couch. "Listen, fellas," she said, "you two guys are the only pros in this whole damn disaster of a show . . . and you're the only ones I can talk to. Now can we spend a few minutes discussing what we're going to do from here on in?"

It was Producer Hazan talking now, for the next half hour. Quietly and soberly, she outlined what was wrong with the show. What were the weak spots, what were the few strong ones. (They happened to include a brilliant musical number called "Lizzie Borden," by Michael Brown, which later became the high spot of Leonard Sillman's *New Faces of 1952*, as well as a clever sketch by Mel Brooks, "Of Fathers and Sons," which was also to be in Sillman's show, and there were also two lovely songs by Irvin Graham which were to survive the holocaust.)

"Now," said Miss Producer Hazan, "here's what I think is our only solution. We close this show Saturday, pull out the best material, re-routine it, *without* Felix, find ourselves a new director, and the three of us will stage this show as a Las Vegas deal. I've already called one of the guys out there—he's an old pal—and he's willing to underwrite everything, *if* we do it that way."

Goodbye to Felix—hello to professional production. It sounded very sensible and possible. Two drowning sketch writers had suddenly been tossed a very tangible life preserver.

Eagerly, we clutched at it. We began to discuss an entirely new concept, one that *had* to work! In the midst of the planning, George said, "You'll take over the scene with the psychiatrist— you can do that instead of your imitations, and—"

Miss Hazan's producer mask fell away, and she turned on him with fury in her performer eyes.

"What do you *mean* I won't be doing my imitations?" she cried. "For Christ's sake, that's the whole reason we're going to Vegas—to *showcase my act!*"

Al Goldin's fifty dollars got us back to New York on Saturday evening. There seemed to be no point in waiting around for the funeral services in Philadelphia. Each of us carried a mouthwash bottle filled with the room-service shots of bourbon and

Scotch we had charged to the hotel bill. If we were going to spend Saturday evening *en famille*, drinking to forget, the least we could do was to bring home our own bottle. It seemed only fair. Besides, our wives had probably finished off everything potable in the house while waiting for us to return from our triumphant Philadelphia tryout.

It is twenty-odd years later, and George and I have separately gone on to our own various projects. We're still good friends, but whenever we meet, to reminisce about the past, somehow the subject of our two weeks in Philadelphia with Felix and Miss Hazan never comes up. It's still too painful a memory to laugh about it.

Miss Hazan? She's happily married, and the mother of her own family now. She's long since retired from show business . . . but I am certain that after a few martinis, were you to ask her, she'd tell you that she still believes she could have made it . . . if only she'd had the proper auspices. And some decent rewriting . . .

As for Felix, wherever he is, I'm certain that he still believes that the whole problem in Philadelphia was those goddamned opening-scene trench coats.

As a matter of fact, when it comes right down to it, those sketches George and I wrote were miserably cast, and I'm almost certain that with a little rewriting, a decent director, and a couple of really clever comics playing them, we could take them out of town and . . .

•••••••••••••••••••••••••••••

Two Leading Ladies
and One Dog

FACE IT. Most of us who sit down to the typewriter and start to unburden ourselves of our past history are strictly I-droppers. Beneath all the philosophic musings, the accumulated gags, and remembered history which prove that we are now in our anecdotage, we are all of us like that fat man of the legend—inside, there's an ego, fighting to get out.

One day at lunch with some publishers, the name of a famous actress came up in our conversation; it seemed that she was about to present the world with her memoirs, and someone asked the editor if he was interested. "Yes, I could be," he said, "if I could be sure she'd tell *all*."

Well, that sort of a mea-culpa book is impossible to come by, especially if it's an actor or an actress talking. Even producers or directors have a tough time letting it all hang out there for the world to see. And we writers are no less fallible. Once, twenty years ago, George Axelrod and I provided sketches for a weekly television hour on CBS. It was a backbreaking schedule, and we grew to loathe one of our leads, an utterly talentless man who had a knack for turning funny lines into lulls. In self-defense, we scouted around and found an eager young chap who wanted to break into the business so desperately that he was more than willing, for a hundred dollars per week, to spend three or four days working with our Mr. No-Talent. All of us subsequently moved on to other work. Four or five years ago, that same fellow we hired delivered himself of his autobiography. If you read it carefully, you will discover that way back in 1949 he started writing an hour television show on CBS, and since he needed help, he went out and found two young writers who needed a job desperately. Their names were George Axelrod and Max Wilk, and he is proud of the fact that he gave us our start . . .

It doesn't even help when a book is prefaced with that innocent little phrase "as told to." No matter how fervently one's Boswell comes charging in to dig out the truth, the whole truth, and nothing but, etc., etc., his subject's ego is inevitably a far tougher editor than the fastest blue-pencil in the publishing house. And about as reliable . . .

Another time, I spent a few months of hard labor with the late Gertrude Berg, on a TV series which starred her and that urbane gentleman, Sir Cedric Hardwicke. When the writers— and we were all pretty talented in that echelon—delivered a new script to the star, that lady would read it through, nod sagely, and say, "Not bad, boys . . . but now—if you don't mind—I'll take it home and tonight I'll put a few raisins in the cake . . ."

So, herewith, a few raisins for this ego-cake.

And Did You Once See Tallulah Plain?

It was Christmas Eve in Baltimore, in 1941, and—as a stagehand at the old Maryland Theatre was to recall for me— there was a lot of backstage tension surrounding the current attraction. Said play was a new drama by the legendary Clifford Odets, entitled *Clash by Night,* and it starred the legendary Miss Tallulah Bankhead; the producer was the legendary Billy Rose. By the time the play had reached Baltimore, to try out at the legendary Maryland, Miss Bankhead had decided that she was unhappy with her role, with the director, with her cast, with the author and his revisions, and especially with her producer, the diminutive and equally flamboyant lyricist, art lover, stock-market wizard, and theatre owner, Mr. Rose.

So explosive were the various egos involved that Miss Bankhead issued an ultimatum: she would continue with her performance on one condition; namely, that her sworn (and the lady was fairly proficient at swearing) enemy, Mr. Rose, must confine his physical presence strictly to the front of the house. Backstage would be her domain, and the stage door was the new Mason-Dixon Line.

Around 8 P.M., before the performance, Rose decided to make *le beau geste*, and to mend fences on this Yuletide Eve with his leading lady. Into no man's land backstage he ventured, equipped with a bouquet of flowers he planned to present to the lady, and made his way to her dressing room and tapped timidly on the door. When she called from inside, "Who is it?" Rose pushed open the door and peered in behind his flowers.

"Merry Christmas, Miss Bankhead?" he suggested.

Tallulah glared at the intruder. Then she raised an imperious finger. "*Out!*" she cried. "You get out of here—you dwarf Scrooge!"

A year or so later, I found myself working every week at very close quarters with Miss Bankhead. After the demise of the Odets play, the great lady, in need of steady employment, signed a contract with the Biow Company, an advertising agency which represented Philip Morris cigarettes, to perform once a week in a radio show called "Johnny Presents." In those simpler, precancer days, to sell cigarettes was a perfectly respectable and profitable endeavor, so each week, on Tuesday nights, under the direction of Charles Martin, a producer-writer, Miss Bankhead would perform in an eleven-minute playlet. Sometimes it was an original script, written by Martin, sometimes an adaptation of a short story, or a condensed one-act play. Whatever the subject matter, be it comedy or drama, it was designed for only one purpose; to star Tallulah . . . and to sell a few cigarettes as well.

Those were the thriving days of radio drama. All morning and afternoon, the quarter-hour soap operas reigned supreme, five days a week, fifty-two weeks a year, and then at 5 P.M. the kiddy-hour shows. In the evening, there were literally dozens of half-hour dramatic shows which emanated from Radio City and the various network studios in Chicago and Los Angeles.

My employer, Charles Martin, an ebullient impresario, operated on an intensive treadmill. Sundays and Mondays he wrote. Tuesdays he rehearsed and directed Miss Bankhead, and Tuesday night she went on. Wednesdays he locked himself in his office with a secretary and worked on a half-hour show called "The Philip Morris Playhouse," which on Friday nights presented movie stars in truncated versions of current films. By Sunday, he was again prepared to attack Tuesday's show. To survive for any length of time around Charlie Martin and that frenetic stopwatch operation, one needed considerable energy, a rich vein of masochism, and a cast-iron stomach.

Charlie had a considerable flair for the dramatic, which extended down to the actual studio production of his radio shows. Half an hour before air time, he would insist on changing to his dinner jacket, and the ensuing ritual consisted of his thereupon making an entrance and taking a bow (while the studio audience, led by a stage manager, dutifully applauded), and the Charlie would present his cast one by one to the yokels. During the actual radio broadcast, Charlie would stand at a dais, his script pages spread out before him, and direct his actors. Needless to say (although perhaps after all these years in which generations have grown up sans radio drama, it *is* needed), such "direction" as Charlie provided was totally superfluous. The radio actors of that era took their cues and read their lines from their scripts, they all knew to the second what was required of them, and they needed Charlie's hand signals as much as they required a sixth toe. But the studio audience out in the theatre was impressed.

One memorable evening, Charlie and his florid ritual came a great cropper, at the hands of his old friend Orson Welles. Welles and he had done many radio shows in the '30s on a local station. Whenever Welles needed ready cash, which was often, he would have his agent notify Charlie that such was case, and Charlie would thereupon star the great Welles in some dramatic half hour. One that was always good for revival was Lucille Fletcher's suspense thriller, *The Hitchhiker*. That day's work paid handsomely, and Orson, his wallet stuffed, could move back to his theatrical ventures. One Friday evening, after a day's rehearsal, Charlie, in dinner jacket, made his customary entrance. The announcer, Nelson Case, intoned his name. Charlie took his bow and, two minutes or so before air time, spread out his script on the dais. Then he dramatically waved out his actors, who came on, one by one, to take their bows. As per ritual, Orson, the star, remained backstage until last, and then he finally appeared.

Ray Bloch, the conductor, raised his baton. The red light went on, the Philip Morris theme began, and Nelson Case gave the introduction. Orson stepped up to the mike . . . and the script fell out of his hand. Thirty-eight pages of manuscript fluttered to the studio floor. Aghast, Charlie gaped at his scriptless star. Frantically, he dropped to his knees and scrambled to try and pick up the pages, to restore them to some sort of order so that Orson might proceed with his leading role. It was a moment of high panic—out there millions of radio listeners were waiting, and there was no script!

"Act One," intoned Case, and before the frantic Martin could wave at him to hold it, to vamp, to stall, Case continued to describe the scene in the play . . . Behind Charlie, who was still scrambling on the studio floor, Welles casually produced a second script from his inside pocket, walked over to the mike, and, exactly on cue, began to play his part . . .

When Tallulah moved into the Philip Morris–Charlie Martin axis, we were at war. For many years, she had starred in London, and had always considered London her second home. When her friend Winston Churchill announced that someday, somehow, the Allies would open a second front, and that this was a time of great sacrifice, Tallulah decided that she would back him up. She would make *her* sacrifice along with her British friends, and she announced publicly to Messrs. Winchell, Lyons, Louis Sobol, and all the rest of the Broadway boys that she would henceforth refuse to indulge in strong drink until the Allies landed on European soil. She took a sort of patriotic pledge . . .

Which caused her to resort to other stimulants. Early Tuesday mornings, accompanied by her agent from the William

Morris, the great lady would arrive at our small Radio City rehearsal studio, draped in a mink that had seen better days, her eyes half shut, her voice a frog-croak. She would collapse in a chair and sit there waiting, blinking at the outside world, waiting for her breakfast. Said meal consisted of a paper cup full of Coca-Cola, in which Tallulah would decant a half inch of spirits of ammonia. This peculiar potion would be tossed off at one gulp, after which our star would begin to raise her eyelids and prepare for battle. "All right, darlings," she would groan, "what piece of nonsense are we playing *this* week?"

A deferential secretary would present the script to her. "Who am I?" Tallulah would inquire, and when given the name of her character, she would pick up a pencil, and begin to turn the script pages, scanning the speeches. Each time she found her character's name, she would underline it. When she had finished, she returned to page 1, and silently began to count her lines. All she wished to discover was whether the sum total of her speeches was greater than that of any other actor in the piece. Should, by some accident of logistics, her leading man have almost as many speeches as she did, Tallulah would permit Charlie to hold the first rough reading, after which she would wave him over for a short consultation. While the other actors went out for a coffee break, Tallulah would leaf through the script. "It's a little heavy *here*, darling," she would remark, ever so casually. Out went one of the leading man's speeches . . . "And *here*, don't you think we could take a tiny cut and get on with it faster?" Her pencil stabbed at the leading man's solo monologue . . . and then, later on, at his moment of high passion. "Isn't that better now?" she'd ask. "I guess you're right, Tallulah," Charlie would concede. He knew who was the star of his show. "You're damned right I'm right, darling," said Tallulah, and called for a second Coca-Cola . . . And by the time the actors had filed back into the studio for the beginning of actual rehearsals, the cuts were handed out, and nobody came near our leading lady in emphasis . . .

On and on through the day she would work, sans any visible intake of food whatsoever, her energy absolutely incredible and her capacity for detail amazing. By noontime, she was her usual gregarious self, exchanging jokes with technicians, discussing the news of the day, the baseball scene—her undying passion—and commenting on any subject that emerged anywhere in the studio. Around one-thirty, we would repair to a restaurant for some food; usually we went downstairs to Toots Shor's Fifty-first Street watering hole. There Tallulah sat with us, but she staunchly refused to eat anything solid. She might nibble on a bread stick, perhaps, but more often she used it as a baton with which to make her conversational points. One day, we nagged at her until she finally agreed to sip a bowl of Shor's famous leek-and-potato soup. Complaining bitterly, she drank several mouthfuls and then dropped her spoon. "It's so damned *rich!*" she insisted, and would touch no more. For the rest of that afternoon, she claimed she'd been poisoned. "I'm *dying*, darlings," she moaned, clutching her abdomen. "Why did you make me eat that ghastly soup?"

At five, she would return to her hotel apartment, and by seven-thirty she was back at the studio. But this was no haggard lady in a tatty mink. When she made her evening entrance, it was Tallulah, *star*. Her gown was expensively chic, her long hair flowed in carefully combed waves, she glittered, she glowed, all that famous magnetism of hers poured out—in the words of the Broadway boys—like Gang Busters. And when Nelson Case announced her to the studio audience, she came striding out with all the style of the grande dame who knew who she was . . . and she took her preliminary bow with all the regal aplomb that befitted a lady of her status in the theatre.

By eleven, when we'd done the show twice—once for the East Coast and then the "repeat" for California and all points west—Tallulah was just beginning to warm up. We would be asked back to her suite at the Ambassador for a midnight snack, and for a marathon Bankhead monologue. As we sat in her living room, she would wander up and down the room, talking nonstop about her daddy and her uncle, those two famous Alabama politicos; we listened to her stories of the early days in London and the ghastly days at Paramount, her love for Mr. Roosevelt, her insights into politics (which were usually quite shrewd), and her characterizations of various important people of the day, most of whom she knew *intimately*, darling . . .

When we left, at the end of a twenty-odd-hour day, we were all exhausted. Tallulah was invariably still flying . . . and on nothing that any of us could see, save that Coca-Cola . . .

One evening, she invited Charlie up for a script conference and a chat, and he, naïvely assuming that it was to be just that, insisted that I come along with him to take notes. Tallulah met us at the door. *"Darling!"* she said, as Charlie entered. Then she saw me, and there came a decided frost into her voice. "What did *he* come for?" she demanded.

"For a script conference, isn't that what you wanted?" asked Charlie.

"Oh yes, I did say something about that, didn't I?" said Tallulah.

We sat there, discussing the script, and then she inquired if we'd had any dinner. Neither of us had, so she called up room service and ordered food. But nothing for her. "I am not hungry," she said. "I let you poison me once with soup—never again!"

The food came, and we sat down to eat. Tallulah blinked wearily and for the first time confessed that she was somewhat tired . . . would we mind if she went inside and took a short nap?

We ate the room-service repast while Tallulah rested inside.

That night was the first time that New York was to undergo a practice blackout, a fact that had been duly announced in the papers and for which the city was prepared. We were in the midst of coffee when, suddenly, every light in the hotel suite went out.

From the darkened bedroom, a few yards away, there came a wild scream. "My God!" yelled Tallulah. *"I've gone blind!"*

Both of us had to spend five minutes inside her bedroom, leading her to the window to show her the grim, darkened skyline of Manhattan, with not a single light to be seen, before she was convinced that it was the entire city that had gone dark . . . and not her eyes.

The very last time I saw Tallulah was one sunny afternoon in Westport, when she came to pay her respects to her great and good friend, the late Dick Maney, the gentleman who had served her well as biographer. It was three decades after those days in

It is 11 a.m. in an NBC rehearsal studio, circa 1942. Miss Bankhead, her Coke bottle at the ready, is almost ready to stop commenting on the ghastly quality of this week's script, and to get down to the ghastly business of rehearsing it. The brunt of her comments is being borne by Charles Martin (his back to the camera). *Left to right*: the author; Charlie Cantor, of "Duffy's Tavern"; Betty Mandeville, of the advertising agency; Will Geer, now of "The Waltons"; Frank Readick; and Morgan Farley. The woman at the extreme right served a brief tour of duty as production secretary, but being an old-fashioned type, withered under a barrage of Bankhead profanities, and left for the relative peace and quiet of the WACs. To this day, she prefers to remain anonymous.

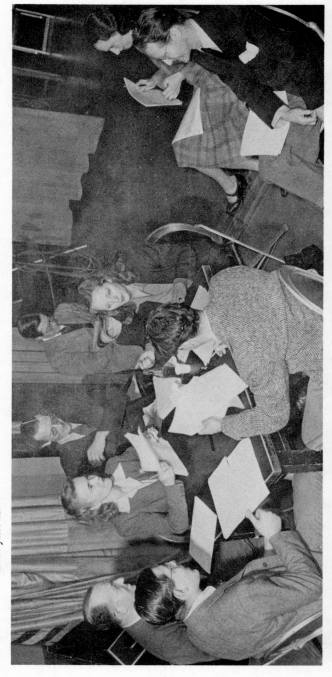

Radio City, thirty years in which Tallulah had made films, been back on Broadway, had her own NBC radio show, toured in summer stock. Her years had been filled with many more triumphant, and not-so-triumphant, entrances and exits. Perhaps she hadn't eaten much food, perhaps she'd gone back to drinking after her dear friend Winston opened the second front . . . perhaps all those days and nights of driving herself full speed ahead had finally begun to wear away at that energy-packed frame. The human body, even that of a leading lady, can withstand just so much . . .

So the Tallulah who walked into the Maney living room, her arm held firmly by her gentleman friend, was somewhat frail . . . a shadow of that beautiful Alabama belle who'd been drawn by Augustus John, who loved to stand on her head at parties, who'd held center stage for all those years . . .

But if she was frail, she stood very erect, and she was chic, and even though she wasn't out to make an entrance that afternoon, when she entered everyone in the room turned around. And if it's a cliché to report that a hush fell over that small crowd, then so be it. Most times cliché expressions are precise because they tell it the way it precisely happened. Tallulah walked into that room, and we all knew a star had entered, darling . . .

Ah, but Tallulah would never let anything that dealt with her go out on such a sombre note. She subscribed to the truth that whatever the scene is, no matter what the climax, the damn thing needs a good solid exit line. Preferably a good laugh.

Something like the story she loved to tell us about Mrs. Patrick Campbell, the great actress, who once opened in London in a less-than-great play. The notices were poor, and the next day, at lunch, one of her actress friends came over to Mrs. Pat's table at the Ivy. "My dear," cooed the lady, "an absolute *tour de force!*"

"*Forced to tour!*" snapped Mrs. Pat.

Bogey's Baby's Harvey

Chicago may be a toddling town, but in the winter of 1944 the railroad stations were packed with people trying to toddle off somewhere else. Space on any day coach meant waiting in long lines, and Pullman berths on sleepers out of Union Station or La Salle Street were worth their space in gold . . . or sirloin . . . or cigarettes, gas, and/or other precious commodities.

This traveler was a GI bound for Los Angeles, equipped with the usual sheaf of Army travel orders, requisitions, and meal orders which called for the railroad to serve whatever food might be in the dining car to the traveling soldier—fifty cents' worth for breakfast, a dollar for lunch, and a dollar and a half for dinner. Such sums didn't buy much nourishment, and those travel requisitions couldn't produce space on a train west. Everything was booked up solid. Since my orders stated specifically that I was to produce my body in California three days hence, on pain of court-martial, I had a problem.

The U.S. Cavalry appeared, in the form of a publicity lady named Lucia Perrigo, who was an old acquaintance from the Warner Brothers Chicago office. It seemed I was precisely the person she needed . . . I was? Yes! We both had a problem, and I could solve hers for her. Would I consider riding the Santa Fe Chief from Chicago to Los Angeles, leaving this afternoon? Through intricate machinations known only to herself, she had pried a valid ticket from the Santa Fe calling for one first-class Pullman berth to L.A., and it could be mine . . . *provided* . . . I repaid the favor with one small gesture. I.e., would I consider escorting a small dog to California and delivering said animal to one of the reigning Warner stars, Humphrey Bogart?

Miss Perrigo had a deal before she'd finished making the offer. I've always liked dogs, I was a Bogart fan years before he was fashionable, and the prospect of sleeping between clean Pullman sheets and eating Fred Harvey food for forty-odd hours, while being whisked across the country first-class style, as well as avoiding court-martial for being AWOL, was miraculous. A two-thousand-mile jaunt with a star waiting at the other end? Miss Perrigo had bought herself a boy . . .

The royal canine consort was delivered to Union Station that afternoon, complete with a custom wooden carry-kennel. He was a purebred boxer puppy, raised by author Louis Bromfield up north in Wisconsin, and he was being sent to Bogart by Bromfield as a wedding present to the star and his new bride, the ex–Miss Bacall.

In a simple ceremony, he was turned over to me on the platform; a cheerful tan puppy with thick legs who leaped happily all over me, nibbled my hand, and frolicked aboard the sleeping car which stood waiting for us. The Santa Fe had been alerted to his presence; officially he was to sleep in his kennel in the baggage car by night, but during the day he was to be permitted visiting privileges in my accommodations . . . he was, after all, the property of a celebrity. Even in wartime, the Santa Fe knew how to pay homage to stars . . .

So lavish was the railroad hospitality that I found myself cum dog and kennel being ushered into the most opulent of all Pullman facilities, a full compartment, in which it seemed I had been assigned the second berth.

But we were not alone. Seated inside the compartment was a middle-aged, ruddy-faced very Annapolis naval officer. The gold on his arm added up to commander. He wore steel glasses, and his eyes behind them were not friendly. He stared at the Pfc who had barged into his inner sanctum, equipped with a musette bag, a suitcase, a portable kennel, and a cheerful boxer puppy. "Soldier," he said softly, "you've got the wrong quarters. The day coaches are up forward."

Behind me, the Pullman conductor cleared his throat. "Sorry, Commander," he said. "This here soldier has the second berth. You two are sharing."

The commander glared at me, and blinked at the pup as if he had suddenly been projected into a nightmare. "To where?" he demanded, finally.

"To Los Angeles, sir," I said, setting down my belongings.

"With this dog?" he asked.

"Yes indeed," said the conductor. "He'll sleep in the baggage car, but we don't mind if he visits in the compartment, long as you two spread a lot of newspaper around."

The puppy was attempting to lick the commander's hand. The commander gritted his teeth and jerked away his hand. He

picked up his copy of the Chicago *Tribune* and hid his face behind it. "Je*sus*," I heard him mutter.

We pulled out of Chicago and headed west. Between the
two of us there was a conspicuous silence. I dutifully spread
newspaper all over the compartment floor, and the puppy dined
off scraps from the Fred Harvey car. He rested inside the compartment while the affable steward saw to it that I had a delicious
Chief dinner, and even accepted my inadequate meal requisition
in payment. Across the aisle in the dining car, the commander sat
and glowered at the sight of this enlisted man enjoying a first-
class dinner. Then he left.

When I came back to the compartment, the puppy was
engaged in a tug-of-war with the commander, who was cursing
and trying to retrieve his bedroom slipper. I separated the pup
from his improvised teething ring, carried him and kennel up to
the baggage car, and left him to sleep there. In our compartment, the commander had ostentatiously retired, leaving me to
spruce up our quarters.

Early next morning, there was a ten-minute stop. I took
the pup out of his kennel, and we strolled up and down the
quiet tracks. He joyously explored the smorgasbord of scent
available at the end of his leash. I bought two local newspapers;
one for reading, the other for spreading. Back aboard, I spread the
sheets around our quarters while the commander watched me.
"You plan to keep him here all day?" he asked, as the puppy
romped about.

"Oh, I'll keep him on this side of the compartment," I said.
"That is, if you don't mind, sir."

The commander obviously did mind. Considerably. But in
this tiny piece of Pullman property, rank did not have its
privileges. He tried to read. The puppy kept sniffing his ankles.
He moved his feet. The puppy strove to leap on his lap. The
commander brushed him off. The puppy attempted to kiss him.
The commander, his cheeks pink with rage, got up, put on his
hat, and stamped out, headed for the club car.

For most of that day, the pup and I rode in solitary splendor.

Whenever the Chief stopped to take on coal, or water, we stepped out for a brief stroll and another orgy of sniffing . . . sans commander.

He did not return until dinnertime, when he prepared himself to go stand in line for a seat in the diner. That was for plebeians; the steward had reserved me a place at 8 P.M. Meanwhile, I was enjoying a nip of fine Scotch from a pint the steward had sold me, at railroad prices. I offered the commander a drink.

He glared at the bottle. Obviously, he expected me to be swilling beer; what was I doing with an officer-type drink . . . one which he assuredly would have enjoyed? The puppy lunged at him, aiming his tongue at the commander's hand. *"No!"* he said, and backed away. He might have enjoyed my Scotch, but he was no dog-lover.

When I came into the dining car at eight, and was ushered to my waiting place at table, the commander was just being seated across the aisle. *He'd* had to wait in line while *I* had a reserved place? It was a tough one to swallow. He was obviously due to have indigestion . . .

Later that night, somewhere in New Mexico, the commander's ordeal ended. He got off the Chief. I peered through the window and saw a Navy car waiting for him at the deserted station. A driver whisked him away. Why the Navy chose to assign him to some base in that remote land-locked station must remain an official secret. But I'm certain that there were many nights when he sat at the bar in the Officers' Quarters and mused bitterly on the sardonic fate that threw him together with a lowly Pfc, to share a first-class compartment on the Chief with an obnoxious puppy who insisted on licking his hand, gnawing at his shoes, and decorating his berth with fond little mementos . . . with no regard whatsoever for rank, damn it!

The Santa Fe always used Pasadena as the quiet getting-off place for celebrities and film executives who wished to depart the Chief without having to run the gantlet of the downtown Los Angeles Union Station. Back in Chicago, Lucia Perrigo had instructed me to do the same. Bogart would be waiting at Pasadena for me and for his dog.

I stepped off into the clear, smogless California sunshine, and dumped the kennel, the pup, and all my belongings onto the platform. A hero's welcome awaited me here in Pasadena, at least . . . But nobody was there. No waiting limousine, no Bogart, no Mrs. Bogart . . . no one at all. Behind me, the conductor yelled, "All aboard!"

What was I to do?

Out of the station loped a Santa Fe agent, waving to me. Was I Private Wilk? He had a message for me. "Mr. Bogart says to go down to Union Station—he'll meet you there!"

Somewhat let down, I clambered back aboard, and the Chief rolled through the downtown Los Angeles flatlands until we pulled into Union Station.

That huge building was packed with wartime crowds: soldiers and sailors and Marines all headed somewhere, their wives and families meeting them, seeing them off; tired travelers sleeping on waiting-room benches; kids running back and forth; babies weeping . . . a milling mob scene worthy of a David Selznick spectacle.

But no Bogart. Nowhere . . .

As I paced up and down, musette bag slung on my shoulder, a suitcase in one hand, a kenneled puppy in the other, I was obviously a unique exhibit. After all, how many GIs go off or come home from the wars equipped with pedigreed boxer puppies? Little kids followed me about, poking their fingers through the barred door of the kennel. Old ladies peered inside the kennel and clucked admonishingly at me for being so cruel to the animal. "Listen, lady," I told one such angry harpy, "he's traveling better than you and I are!"

And still no Bogart.

Finally, I went to the phone and called his number, also provided me by the thoughtful Miss Perrigo back in Chicago. "Oh . . . hi there, Wilk," rasped a familiar voice, the same one I'd heard on the sound track of many Warner melodramas. "Couldn't get down so early this morning. Hop in a cab and come on up here—we'll have lunch."

Cabs weren't easy to locate, but finally I got one, and an hour or so later, up on North Kings Road, above the Strip, I was deposited with my belongings and the kennel outside Bogart's home. I rang the front doorbell. The end was finally in sight.

Not quite. Eventually, a tiny window in the front door opened, and a high, querulous voice inquired, "What do *you* want?"

"I'm the guy who's supposed to deliver a dog to Mr. Bogart," I said, wearily.

"Are you *expected?*" asked the voice, hostile.

"I better be," I said, now equally hostile. "I've come two thousand goddamned miles and nobody met me in Pasadena, and—"

"Well, you just *wait* out there," said the voice, now suspicious. "I don't know anything about it."

"Listen, damn you!" I cried. "I'm not some door-to-door dog salesman—"

The front door was thrown open, and Bogart stood there, shaking his head at the thin Filipino butler who'd been cross-examining me. "Ah, cut it out, Charles," he rasped. "The kid's been through enough without taking any more crap from *you.*"

Exactly the sort of speech you'd expect from Humphrey Bogart.

The Filipino retired, obviously miffed.

Bogart shook my hand. In his other hand was a large glass pitcher, glistening frostily. "Have a martini, pal," he said. "You've earned it."

And *that* was the definitive Bogart-type welcome.

The puppy rambled happily through his new home as Bogart led me out to the terrace, which overlooked the city. We sat down. "Sorry about the lack of a proper welcoming committee," he said, affably, "but Baby and I had a kind of rough night over at Mark Hellinger's, celebrating. She's still upstairs recovering; I hope you understand, kid. The spirit was willing, but we just couldn't make it, kid."

He was smallish, relaxed, and charming, not at all like Sam Spade or Philip Marlowe, or any of the assorted hoods which the Warners had type-cast him as with such box-office success. But it took a while before I ventured to call him any-thing but Mr. Bogart . . .

Lunch was a long and wet one. Mrs. Bogart eventually ap-peared, forced herself to take a medicinal drink, and met her new puppy. The two of them took to each other immediately. While we ate, he explored the tiny terraced garden of his new home.

Bogart seemed to be in the midst of one of his customary battles with Jack Warner. A film script had been assigned to him which he felt was less than adequate. Officially, that is. "It's a game I play," he confided. "I tell him I don't want to do it, and Jack yells and screams, and then he gets somebody in to do some rewrites, while I go on suspension for a couple of weeks. Then I agree to do it. I have to play it this way—it's the only way I can get a vacation out of the bastard. See, he's got no stars around until the war's over, and he's been working my ass off."

The puppy dashed over, leaped up on Bogey's lap, and began to gnaw at a tempting button. "He's a nice pooch," he said. "Was it a tough trip?"

"No," I said. "Very comfortable. Any time you want an-other dog delivered, please call me."

Bogey chuckled at the sight of the dog, now licking Baby. "No," he said, finally. "I kind of think he'll be enough. But thanks anyway."

Late that afternoon, I reported for duty at my post. One of my meal tickets was still unused, the one which would have provided me with a dollar's worth of lunch. "You can have it," I told the sergeant on duty. "I didn't need it. Somebody gave me lunch."

"Yeah? Who?" asked the sergeant.

"If I told you Humphrey Bogart, would you believe me?" I asked.

"You drunk?" he inquired.

"No," I said. "Not now. But I *was* . . ."

One night, almost ten years later, I was a guest at a Beverly Hills party given by my old friend George Axelrod. It was a traditionally opulent wingding, complete with an orchestra, a

Does this picture really need a caption? The later Sam Spade and friends in a later *Maltese Falcon*. SPENCER BERGER COLLECTION

catered meal from Romanoff's, a tent under which guests could dance, and a mob of greats and near-greats right out of Hedda Hopper's column. One of the ladies present was the recently widowed Miss Bacall, and later we found ourselves on a sofa together, listening to Jule Styne play the score for a new show he was about to produce in New York.

As the music wafted over us, I leaned over to the lady and said, "Pardon me for interrupting, but I'd really like to know—how's your dog?"

She blinked at me. "My dog?"

"That little boxer puppy who was delivered to you by a soldier during the war," I persisted.

Miss Bacall stared at me.

"*You?*" she asked, at last. I nodded.

"Harvey," she said. "*My Harvey!*"

Quite suddenly, her eyes were wet. "He died last month!" she said. "Bogey and I loved him so damn much . . . Now they're both gone!"

Later, the two of us drank to Harvey, in Romanoff's best champagne.

Bogey wasn't there to join us, but I'm sure he'd have agreed on the toast. To Harvey—a first-class dog, all the way . . .

Yassoo, Melinaki!

She received me stretched out on a chaise longue, her brown-blond hair falling carelessly over sharp eyes as she explained what she expected from me. "You must give the world a true picture of what a great country we are, and why, even though we are small, we are strong. Answer me, Mox," she queried. "What are you? Are you Cath-lic? Prot-es-tant? Are you Jewish? What?" And when I told her, she clapped happily. "Good, good! It is perfect that you are Jewish! The Jews and the Greeks—we are brothers. That is what I always tell Dassin—the two of us together, we can withstand the world!"

She glowed, she glowered, she pouted, she sang, her moods changing by the second. She was the magnetic eye of a noisy hurricane of guests, relatives, visitors, and friends, all of them whirling happily around her in the huge suite she and Jules Dassin were occupying at the George V, in the golden 16th Arrondissement.

That elegant hostelry's cuisine may have been haute enough for other quests; not Melina. Down the hall in a tiny kitchen, she had installed her own loyal cook, and all afternoon the spicy aromas of various Greek dishes wafted through the elegant George V salon, high above the sporadic human traffic that ebbed and flowed, paying court to Melinaki.

We spent two or three intense days in that brouhaha of a living room, both of us engaged in a cram course, I the pupil, she the teacher, the subject, Greece . . . Hellas, her native land, which she adored with a consuming passion. "The poorest man on the street—the cabdriver—the boy with the fresh koulouri bread—all are my friends! When I walk down the street, they look and call, '*Yassoo*, Melinaki—*kali spera!*' Because they like me and I like them—all of them! That is what makes us Greeks!" she told me . . . and I was to find out later, when I finally came to walk down crowded Athens streets with her, that she wasn't exaggerating.

As a matter of fact, most of what she told me during those days in Paris was truth; she was most anxious that the script I was to write for the television show she was to do about Greece would be absolutely authentic, and she took great pains to give me as much authentic grounding in the subject as she could . . .

Of course there was hyperbole. But most of it dealt with the glittering supporting cast she intended to supply for "Melina Mercouri's Greece," which was to be produced for a spring showing on American TV. Any and all Greeks, be they actors, composers, politicos, tycoons . . . "If *I* ask them, they will appear," she promised. "Let us say we discuss the paradox of Greece," she proposed. "We will say that we Greeks invented democracy, we are still a democracy—but we have a king! Paradox—a Greek word! Then we will have a scene in which King Constantine—he is a very sweet man—he will explain what he is doing there in his palace."

Would the King actually be willing to appear? "Of course,

Mox! Can he say no when his Melinaki asks?" We would have
an original poem by George Seferis, the Nobel Prize winner.
Original music from Theodorakis, Hadjidakis—"I adore them
both! Maybe Onassis will tell us about business—you know we
have a saying, 'If a Greek has no head for business, then he
must be a Turk!' "

And we must discuss religion. "Greek Orthodox is a lovely
religion!" she told me. "Very friendly. Understand—our Jesus is
the kind of Jesus who is there for you to talk to—to cry with—
to comfort you. Even if you get mad and curse Him—He smiles
at you, because He understands we love him. So when we talk
about that, we will have a scene with Archbishop Makarios. *I
will ask him*—he won't say no . . ."

Melina's nonstop stream of information, anecdote, and
promises was often diverted. Once, a lean young lawyer, just in
from Athens, loped into the suite, embraced her amid welcoming
cries, and spent the next hour delivering complicated bulletins on who was doing what and to whom and with whom in
their faraway capital. Later, at lunch, a middle-aged lady swathed
in furs made an appearance, and promptly collapsed in noisy
tears. Melina took her into the next room, and for the next half
hour, from behind closed doors, came the sounds of weeping
and voices raised in excited imprecation. When Melina finally
explained, she first exacted a promise that I must tell absolutely
no one. "This is a scan*dale!* That woman is a great star—my
great friend. It is all out of a Greek tragedy, this! Her lover, a
young boy whom she plucked from the gutter to be an actor,
he has left her and is about to marry a young woman—an absolute nobody, a nothing! Some ninny with blond hair who is the
darling of Greek films . . . po po *po!*" Melina's fingers played
with her worry beads; her eyes filled with tears. "How can men
be so cruel?"

It was a hypothetical question. We moved on. Wherever
Melina journeyed, for side trips to the hairdresser, or to the
boulevard for some fresh air, we were enveloped in clouds of
drama, comedy . . . whimsy. In the midst of a dissertation on the
prostitutes of Piraeus, all of whom had become her friends while

she made *Never on Sunday,* she would break off to chat with our waiter, whose sad eyes had drawn her to plumb his home life . . . or to play a game with a small French boy at a street corner, who would stare, wide-eyed, at the elegant lady kneeling down to chuck him beneath his chin. When we returned to the suite, it was time for music. Melina would put on one of her records and sing a duet with herself. "You must *listen* to my songs, Mox," she would insist. "It is not merely for pleasure—they tell a story. I will translate for you—I must—because you cannot learn Greek, you know," she warned. "It is a most complicated language. It is like going into a deep forest—you can get in, but you will never come out . . ."

Seventy-two-odd hours of this exotic Berlitz-type culture shock cum cooking and gossip and fact left me feeling somewhat like a Strasbourg goose who has been overstuffed too quickly. She was intuitive about my insecurities. "You will be all right, Mox," she told me. "It is a big job to tell everyone all about Greece in one tiny little television hour, of course. But you are a bright man. What you now need is to go to Greece and spend a couple of weeks there with my friends. I will see to it that you are equipped with Greek eyes and Greek ears—and then you will write your Melinaki a marvelous show!" We had a tearful parting at the door of her suite. Inside, the guests were arguing, the cook was preparing more heady dishes, and a new friend from Athens, laden with fresh bulletins, had arrived. Melina embraced me. "You will meet me in Athens with a clear mind—now go. *Create!*"

Athens was interesting. Sight-seeing was informative. Guidebooks were factual. But sans our leading lady, the scene was much like the first act of a play, in which the exposition has to be dispensed before the star makes her entrance. One could jot down ideas, half-formed possible scenes . . . collect notes . . . and await her arrival.

Two weeks later, she was installed in a Hilton Hotel suite, surrounded by cook, relatives, Dassin, and a welcoming coterie of Athenians who jammed her quarters, played music, sang, ate, chatted, and kept her occupied from noon until 3 A.M., when she finally managed to get some sleep. Again, she took over my education. We wandered through Athens streets. Everywhere we went, they waved at Melinaki—and she joyfully waved back. We went to restaurants and sampled her favorite native dishes. Chefs would emerge from their kitchens to bow and smile, then disappear to bring forth personally her chosen delicacies. Policemen held back traffic so that we might cross in safety. If we went to a club—be it large or small, wherever—the orchestra would immediately switch to "Never on Sunday" and sooner or later Melinaki would have to get up and sing for her adoring fans . . .

"*This* Sunday we will see a typical Greek event!" she announced. "It must be part of the show! Athens is playing Piraeus at the football stadium. You will see something you have never seen before!"

A camera crew and sound technicians arrived at the stadium early that morning. There were already long lines of football fans lined up, struggling to get seats for this historic match. Cordons of burly Athens police piled out of vans and took their places in protective human phalanxes everywhere in the vast stadium. Fist fights broke out at ticket windows and at the gates; it seemed that a resourceful gang had counterfeited tickets and sold them all over Greece. Those unfortunates who had been gulled were angrily trying to force their way past implacable authority. Everywhere were huge, happy crowds; they packed the roofs of nearby apartment houses and buildings. High above the stadium, all the way up Mount Lycabettus in the distance, the mountain was black with people who strained to get a distant view of the game.

"And *this* is just for football!" Melina chortled, as a cordon of straining police forced open a path for us to enter the stadium.

When she and her party of friends, relatives, and hangers-on took their seats, a low rumble began around them. As the crowd recognized her, there came a huge roar that lasted for minutes. "*Yassoo*, Melinaki!" they yelled. "*Yassoo!*" she yelled back. "Po po po! They love me—and *I* love them!" She stood up and waved to the mass of twenty thousand countrymen. "*This!*" she said to me. "This is what we must have on the television—this is truly Greece!"

Eventually, the game got under way, the two hated rivals, Athens and Piraeus, battling it out on the field—with dozens of minor factional battles taking place for the next two hours in the stands.

We left the stadium exhausted. The film coverage would provide us with about ninety seconds of usable film, far better for "Wide World of Sports," perhaps. We still had no script, and the shooting date was approaching, a fact which our producer was beginning to remind us of daily.

Melina turned pragmatic. She provided me with the Greek eyes and ears, and soon he was working with me in a Grand Bretagne Hotel suite. The fact that Iakovos Cambanellis, a first-rate Greek playwright, did not speak English made our collaboration somewhat sporadic. Lindsay and Crouse, Hecht and MacArthur, Kaufman and Hart we were not. Daily, we strove in pidgin French to build some sort of bridge between his extensive knowledge of all things Greek and my ability to translate some of it, adapt it, and prepare it for American nighttime TV.

There were meetings with Melina at which she thrust a series of must-dos at us. We must go to the island of Crete and capture the excitement and color of a typical Cretan wedding. We must go to Mount Olympus and show the world the majesty of that awe-inspiring home of the ancient Greek gods. We must go down to Piraeus and film the boats and the harbor—and we must certainly visit Lesbos, Rhodes, as many islands as possible. And we must not forget those scenes with the King, with Makarios, with George Seferis, and the music of the composers who would write for us . . . and then there must be bouzouki . . . "But remember, always," Melina would insist. "The show must have only one star—Greece—my beloved Greece!"

Walking back through the quiet Athens streets from a midnight conference, Iakovos and I came to a meeting of the minds that almost needed no language. "The star—*ce n'est pas Greece*," I said. "The star—*c'est tous le temps—Melina*."

"Ah—*bien sûr!*" agreed Iakovos.

Even in pidgin French, we both knew the score.

We hammered out a preliminary outline—pages over which there could be arguments. Somebody has to put it down on paper for everyone else to tear apart; that is a TV writer's first function.

I stood in the center of Melina's suite; behind me, an anxious producer with deadlines hanging over his head, Damoclean style. (Greek simile, and therefore very apt.) Lounging on the sofa, her eyes narrowed, Melina played with her worry beads and concentrated on my presentation. The opening had her on Mount Olympus—where else?—and then a series of scenes took her through museums, music, dancing, a bit of comedy, and had the obligatory visits with the King, with Makarios, et cetera.

When it was done, she nodded. Masterly . . . marvelous. Everything was beautiful! *But* . . .

The ending. It seemed a bit . . . how could she put it? . . . weak, compared to the rest. "My Julie has been thinking about that," she confided. "He has an amusing idea—you will adore it!" It seemed there was a lovely Greek song, an ode to the city, "Athena." We sat and listened to it, and the music washed over us.

How would it be if Melina were to get on top of a Greek taxicab, singing "Athena," and as she rode through the streets, down from the Acropolis, all the way to the harbor, crowds of Athenians, thousands of them, would greet her by joining her in a mass chorus? A wide-screen love duet, one Jeanette Mac-Donald, ten thousand or so Nelson Eddys!

"Isn't that a formidable idea?" cried Melina, her sharp eyes misted with tears at the vision of her and the city expressing their mutual passion.

I glanced at our producer. He forced a limp smile.

"Beautiful," he said. "Ah . . . but who's going to pay for all those people to sing?"

"Pay?" said Melina, scornfully. *"Pay?* Why should anyone *pay* Athenians to make love to their Melinaki?"

"They may be in love, but they'll have to get paid!" he insisted.

"What a crude remark!" she said.

"That's not exactly what he means," I said, attempting to smooth over the gaffe. "We'd have to organize the crowd, and spend a couple of days shooting the mob, and pre-record, and there are all those logistics—"

"What—logistics?" demanded Melina.

"Greek word," I said. "Roughly translates into money."

"You argue about cost when we are discussing spectacle?" moaned our star. "Po po po!" She waved her worry beads at me. "You cannot be harassed by such trivia! When Dassin and I made *Never on Sunday*, we had no money—but we had enthusiasm—and passion! That is how we triumphed!" She seized the producer and brought him close. "It is a Greek characteristic. We survive in adversity. Trust us—and together we will make a great television document, believe me!"

The producer called me later in our hotel suite. He had totted up the prospective costs of all the various scenes called for in the outline. "According to our production manager's first rough estimate," he announced, "we're already bankrupt."

It was open season for suggestions, but somebody had to get out a script, so we closed the hotel-suite door and fell to, the blind leading the blinder. We wrote for several long days . . .

Down the hall, the producer and his production manager paced, waiting for pages. They had a brutally tight schedule to meet; we were in wintertime Athens, when the weather is often overcast and grey, and that alone would make for a tricky shooting schedule. Then there were locations to be scouted, actors to be cast, local bureaucrats to consult, dozens of subsidiary problems. As fast as we finished script pages, off they went to be copied, studied, and broken down for costs.

It's every TV writer's finest hour. And his hairiest. He's under the gun . . . temporarily indispensable. Later on, ex post facto, there will be abuse, argument, accusation . . . but for now that pyramid of pages is his . . . as long as his invention (and his typewriter ribbon) holds out.

When I managed to get through a phone call to London, to re-establish contact with my wife, she inquired how I was enjoying my sight-seeing in Athens. For four days, I hadn't been out of the hotel. "For all I've seen lately," I complained, "I might as well be in Athens, Georgia."

Late that afternoon came a call from Melina, inviting me to

join her and Dassin at dinner. No business . . . no script . . .
merely a social gathering. "Mox, you work so hard—you need
therapy!" she cooed. "Therapy—also a Greek word!"

Greek dining always takes place quite late, but on this
particular night we did not even rendezvous until ten-thirty.
Then, in a fleet of cars, Melina and Dassin led their caravan
some distance out of the city to a small rural taverna, high in the
hills, far off the customary tourist route. There, in a large dining
room with beamed ceilings and a huge fireplace, at a long table,
was a private party of guests, assembled to celebrate the host's
name-fete. Every Greek male is named after a saint, and celebrates
his saint's birthday with a festive occasion. We were welcomed by
our host, an affable gentleman who was high up in Olympic
Airlines, and offered fine Scotch, champagne, and caviar. There
were many toasts, we drank and ate, drank more toasts, and all
was relaxed and polite. As we dined, a group of musicians appeared and began to serenade us. "Never on Sunday," of course
. . .

And then, as if signaling the start of the show, Dassin stood
up, grabbed the rustic wooden chair he'd been sitting on, and
hurled it into the blazing fireplace. Everyone cheered and applauded. The musicians struck up a dance, and Dassin led Melina
in a wild step. Chairs were pushed back, and soon we were all
dancing, improvising steps in time to that shrill, exciting music.

Then began the breaking of dishes. Glasses flew through the
air. Everybody let go.

Melina had told me, "You know there are very few psy-
chiatrists in Greece, Mox—even though it *is* a Greek word. We
don't need them. If a Greek has troubles, he stands up and
breaks glasses and dances his unhappiness out of his system."

If I'd been dubious, the next few hours changed my mind
and proved her point. The room was full of happy people,
clasping each other and embracing, weaving madly back and
forth; around us the waiters and the cooks whistled and stamped,
jovial spectators, enjoying the sight of the room being de-
stroyed . . .

Dassin accidentally cut his forehead on a piece of flying
crockery. He wrapped his head in a napkin. Immediately, in an

effort to make him feel their brother, all the other men did the same. For some reason, our host turned his suit jacket inside out, and all of us, his guests, copied his new style, dancing, singing, and systematically destroying crockery. I spotted one lone remaining chair, and I was seized with an overpowering impulse to burn it, à la Dassin. I picked it up and moved towards the roaring fire. One of the guests, a quiet matron, shook her head. "Do not burn that," she chided. "Suppose someone needs to sit?"

I hesitated. Her husband danced by. "Pay no attention to the women," he said. "Burn the chair!"

I took aim, threw it into the fireplace, and watched the flames consume it. At the time, it seemed wonderfully satisfying. Dassin danced by, grabbed me by the arm, and as we danced off, treading through broken crockery, he yelled, "This is what Greece is all about! Now do you get it? Get *this* into the script!"

On and on we reveled. Somewhere along the way, Mr. Onassis had shown up to celebrate, and he joined in, and Melina sang, in ensemble and solo, and from nowhere a batch of photographers appeared to snap pictures of the revels. Their layouts of the proceedings were to appear in the European magazines which specialize in documenting the affairs of the rich and famous . . .

How we ended up at an Athens bouzouki joint I am still unclear about, but by five that morning we were all downtown, dozens of us . . . Melina, Dassin, Onassis, some survivors from the taverna, still celebrating out on the tiny dance floor, in the center of a happy mob of Athenians, to the accompaniment of cheers, whistles, popping balloons, breaking glasses and crockery. I was out on the dance floor, purged of the past week's hang-ups and frustrations, and if I didn't look exactly like Gene Kelly, so what? I tried to tell Melina that she was right, and to tell M. Dassin that he was a great script consultant . . . but somehow the sentences came out garbled . . . so I gave up and went on dancing.

Exhausted, but euphoric (Greek word), I slept most of the day.

That afternoon, the local AP man called. He'd heard there'd been a small party the night before; had I been present, and if

so, what had it been like? He'd had a report that Mr. Onassis
had cheerfully paid a bill for $600 worth of broken crockery
at the bouzouki place. "I never saw anything like it in my life,"
I told him, truthfully, and went back to sleep.

He proceeded to file the story on the AP wire, complete
with my quote. The London newspapers picked it up.

"I thought," said my wife, a bit distant, the next time we
spoke, "that you hadn't been out of the hotel for four days."

"Oh, I finally did go out," I admitted. "For dinner."

Melina sat and scanned the various newspapers, including
the New York *Times,* which had mildly scolded her for breaking
$600 worth of dishes and glassware. "What are they complaining
about?" she demanded. "I have been out to dinner in New York
when that much money would not even cover the check! At
least we *enjoyed* ourselves—and so did everyone else in the
place . . . po po *po!"*

Finally the script was done. It contained all the obligatory
scenes with Mount Olympus, with the King, with Makarios, with
Seferis, and with all the original music by her favorite composers. As for that huge finale, with Melina riding through the
entire city of Athens, we'd tactfully managed to sidetrack that
typically MGM type musical spectacle by countering it with a
quiet, impressive scene that would involve the more reliable
(and less expensive) background of the Acropolis. That we
knew we could get on film . . .

Melina sat and read the pages of the finished script, stopping
every so often to ask what a word meant, or why we'd made
certain changes in the structure. Most of the changes were calculated to enable our newly arrived British director to come in
reasonably on schedule, so our ensuing arguments were based
less on creative thrust than on pragmatism.

When she came to the final scenes, in which she spoke
quietly and softly to the audience about what her Greece meant
to her, and to her countrymen, she read the lines aloud, and then
she put down the script. Her bright eyes were brimming with
tears. "You are a good student, Mox," she said. "I have taught
you something about Greece, eh?"

THREE A.M. in Athens, and the crockery and glassware are about to be broken by Melina and Ari.

"*Efaristo,* teacher," I said.

"Listen to him—he speaks Greek like a native!" She laughed. Then she turned to the director. "Now, my dear," she said, "*now* we will make a great show, yes?"

Melina's fervently optimistic (also Greek word) prediction of what was to ensue was a bit wishful. As a Cassandra, Melina suffered from the normal thespian ailment—overenthusiasm.

The King did not appear on her show to explain Greek democracy; he sent polite words that he was sympathetic, but unfortunately affairs of state kept him too occupied to accommodate our shooting schedule. Archbishop Makarios was also absent. He preferred to remain on Cyprus, rather than to fly to Athens for a day's shooting. He would, however, greet us when we came to him. Since our budget did not provide sufficient funds for such a hegira, we had to do without his presence as well. All that expensive film we'd shot at the Athens football stadium ended up as forty seconds' worth of background. And as for the poet, George Seferis, who she had promised us would provide us with an original ode—he sent word through intermediaries that he was leaving Greece to take up permanent residence in Paris. Even the original songs weren't forthcoming. Mr. Theodorakis was far too busy, alas, with politics to go to his piano.

Then the director went to work, and even the ancient gods were frowning on their Melinaki. When the camera crew and technicians drove several hundred miles up to Mount Olympus, to make scenes in that legendary spot, it began to snow, and continued to do so for the next two valuable and expensive days. "You promised me that the weather in January would be *perfect!*" cried the anguished producer.

"One does not argue with the gods," said Melina, and changed the subject.

Somehow or other, as the old British saying goes, by sheer dint, an hour or so of film was made by an unflappable director and a hard-working Greek crew. In the face of the hostile weather, which at one memorable point forced the director to shoot a scene in the rain with Melina in close-up, standing beneath two umbrellas unseen by the camera, there was enough serviceable film for a cutter to assemble in Rome.

The television deadline would be met, but with only days to spare. The writing job was done long since; I went home. No more Melina, no more intensive arguments and midnight script conferences; life became relatively quiet and structured again.

We met again in Rome, a month or so later, on a beautiful soft primavera morning. The city was resplendent in that lovely warm spring light as Melina jumped out of a taxi and ducked into our recording studio to spend several hours with us, completing the voice-over narration. She had taken a day off from preparing a film which she and Dassin were about to make in Madrid, and she was tense and tired from the early-morning flight. When we sat in the projection room and watched the cutter's rough assemblage, she blinked warily at herself on the screen.

At the end, the lights in the tiny room flickered on.

Well, had we done right by her Greece?

Melina groaned. "Never mind Greece!" she said. "Greece will survive. But me—the camera is my sworn enemy. *I* look *terrible!*"

Once again, she was wrong. It wasn't the calm eye of our camera which would prove to be her enemy. Rather, it was a cabal of military men, the so-called "Colonels"—who decided that Greece, that same country which Melina loves with such a blind passion, could do without her, Julie . . . her friends, her cook, anyone who subscribed to her "corrupt ideology" (also a Greek word).

But if there's one lesson I retain from her cram course, it involves survival. She, and the Greeks, outlasted *them,* too.

And when returned to Athens, in 1974, they finally did play out that happy finale which Dassin suggested—Melina driving through the streets, singing to the people . . . and all the newly freed citizens of Athens joyfully singing back.

Another case of life imitating MGM, right, Melinaki?

•••••••••••••••••••••••••

A Covey of Comics

COMEDY WRITERS are by nature dour. Cynical, subject to depression (well earned), and not at all funny in your living room. Why should we be? Ask a ballet dancer to dinner; do you expect him to do a few entrechats over cocktails? Very few comedy writers are Avon ladies who pass out free samples.

There are a few I know who are genuine wits, and who enjoy being witty. One of them is my friend Hal Kanter, who is capable of knocking off a nifty ad-lib, three thousand miles away over a phone. We were talking one evening—after the rates changed—and I mentioned that I wouldn't be going to Japan as planned on an assignment. The deal had fallen through, and Tokyo and NBC would have to struggle along without me. "Oh, I knew that," instantly drawled Hal. "Sessue Hayakawa just walked past the house, weeping . . ."

But if comedy writers down in those cornfields in which we labor are a dour lot, let it be said that they are usually sane. The same does not apply for their masters . . . those Simon Legrees for whom the weekly script is argued over, fought and bled for . . . the comedians.

Several of us jokesmiths, itinerant specialists in situation comedy, veterans of years in the arena, were whooping it up at a San Fernando Valley saloon, and while we ate and drank a therapeutic ulcer-inducing lunch and exchanged amiable insults, we also swapped horror stories.

Not about Bela Lugosi, or Frankenstein, Godzilla, or any other such controllable monsters, but about major loonies—the comics for whom we'd all worked at one time slot or another.

And beneath our turtlenecks, we all had the scars to prove it . . . as well as the legends.

That famous singer-comic who, in a massive fit of pique over a batch of jokes he'd been supplied which he didn't cherish, yanked a huge roll of bills out of his pocket to prove his supremacy and yelled, "There—I got a million dollars out of being funny! What the hell do *you* have?" To which his writer, on his way out the studio door, replied, "*I* got a million friends."

Or that demure lady comedienne we knew, who for years and years unblushingly accepted awards for writing her own scripts, all the while keeping not one but two ghost-writers at work, each one unaware of the existence of the other, as they labored in separate hotel rooms.

That diminutive burlesque comic who'd hit the TV big time in the '50s, got his own show, and announced to everyone, "The first fifty years of this century belong to Chaplin—for the next fifty years it's *me!*" Someday he will merit a paragraph in one of Richard Lamparski's "Whatever Became Of?" Or that other monster ego who, when brought a page of jokes by his assembled hired hands, would sit and read them, all the while announcing, "Funny. *Not* funny. *Not* funny. *Not* funny . . ." as he ticked them off like Danton editing a list of victims. Or the famous super-star, who for years has refused to rehearse, claiming that nothing his writers had ever given him on paper was more than a basic set of notes, from which he improvised. "Nobody *writes* for the Great One," he bellows. "The Great One makes it up out of his own head . . ."

Monsters all, and yet, as we all agreed, funny.

But why, tell us why, was it that every comic has to be such a bastard?

"I can think of one who isn't," said a writer, as if challenged. He mentioned an amiable, charming guy, who'd had his own show for years, who was literate and pleasant, and got along fine with his writers.

"Yeah, you're right," growled one of the others at table. "He is a nice guy . . . but then, I don't think he's very funny, do you?"

Sadly, the proposer agreed.

So if you're masochistic enough to want to work for comedians, you better begin with that premise. If they have a talent to amuse, of whatever size, then they have bigger warts than we civilians.

If they don't start out with bigger warts, they develop them along the way. They have to. Warts grow with that nightmare job of going out on a stage and standing there and making an audience laugh, night after night.

Being successful in that unique line of work requires some sort of unique talent. Very few comedians I've ever known had talent for anything else. Their interpersonal relationships are usually a bouquet of neuroses. Their home life is a soap-opera psychodrama. Between them and their writers exists a constant love-hate; the writer watches somebody else up there getting the laugh (or ruining the joke), while the comic's ego won't allow him to admit that somebody back there is helping him be great. It's a hypertense ball game, and being a great comedian involves an exquisite set of skills. Telling the joke, timing a bit of physical business, holding your expression for just the exact hairsbreadth beat that will induce the maximum laugh— it involves the sort of craft that is as delicate as making a watch. That's where the analogy ends. Have you ever seen a Swiss watchmaker get up in front of a couple of thousand customers and get laughs . . . even from non-Swiss?

If all this reference to humor, comics, and jokes has led anybody to expect an analysis of what is funny, one of those ponderous tracts which attempt to isolate laughter as if it were a disease and to search for the microbes that induce it, this is not the place. (Go pick up a copy of Dr. Sigmund Freud's *Wit and Its Relation to the Unconscious,* Modern Library, 1938; it doesn't do much to clarify what makes anything funny, but the good doctor assembled quite a few of the best Middle European jokes of his time, making him the first intellectual Joe Miller.)

There's no real wisdom to be imparted here . . . for the best you can manage, if you've worked with comedians for almost thirty years, is a few pragmatic rules, usually handed down in backstage dressing rooms, or in smoke-filled conferences. Sayings that run: *Get on, get laughs, get off and leave 'em hungry/always let the audience know what you're going to do ahead of time/ never play a comedy sketch in front of anything except a neutral background/*et cetera.

All we got, boss, is pragmatics. Plus scars . . .

Start with the difference between comedians and comics. Shall we quote from the late Ed Wynn, who wore silly costumes, giggled and lisped, and may have forgotten more about comedy than any eight other performers can remember? "A comedian," said Ed, "is a man who says funny things. A comic, however, is a man who says things *funny.*"

Another of Ed's strictures was "Make friends with the audience. If you go out there and they hate you, they'll hate you for the rest of the show . . . so if you spend your first couple of minutes making them like you, or feel sorry for you, or think you're just plain nuts—from then on they'll accept anything from you." Ed kept his audiences as his friends for over six decades. The curtain would go up on an empty stage. At the top of a flight of bare steps Ed would appear, unrolling carpet, which he'd carefully tack to the steps until the red carpet was all prepared for his performers. He'd look up at the audience and ask, "I athk you—would Katharine Cornell do this?" From then on, he was home free.

Offstage, even with all that success behind him, Ed was human; nervous, uncertain, jealous. If you tried to supply him with a joke—as we were trying to do back in 1950, when a crew of us were writing an hour television show for him on NBC—his little eyes would narrow, the joviality would drop from his expression, he would put his fingers together in front of his face, and softly tell you, "Okay—go ahead." And while you launched into your so-called comedy creation, Ed would softly whistle some tuneless little song, Foxy Grandpa challenging you to make him laugh.

It was an unnerving experience. Any joke that could survive Ed's gauntlet had to be a great one. He liked them simple. E.g.,

"There's so much inflation lately that pumpernickel is now pumperdime." (Don't knock it—it got a huge laugh.) Ed also liked inventions. They'd been his stock in trade for years. Seaman Jacobs came up with one—a shoe with a tiny lawn mower attached to its toe. That was for people who didn't want to let grass grow under their feet. Ed bought it . . . first, of course, reminding us that he'd used something like that back in 1927, in a different way. At the end of a day, you left Ed convinced that he'd invented practically everything funny . . . which he probably had.

As Ed grew older, however, he mellowed, like some fine rare Château Rothschild. He changed his style, an enormous undertaking for a clown in his seventies—and yet, not so difficult when you consider that comedy is separated from tragedy by the thinnest of lines. Ed became full time what he had been part time all his life—an actor. And a brilliant one. He put away the funny hats and played it for real, and captured a new audience.

One night, he stopped by Hal Kanter's house for a New Year's party, one which consisted mostly of comedy writers and their patient wives. Ed appeared around midnight, and was greeted with affection. He had a beautiful blond lady with him whom he proceeded to introduce. "She's Mrs. Martin," he said. "And she's very beautiful, and she's also very, very rich."

Leo Solomon, a hardened veteran of years with Ed, turned around from the bar. "Well, Ed, it's a cinch you wouldn't take her out if she got laughs," he snapped. The room fell down. Ed laughed harder than anyone. By that stage of his life, he was secure enough to stand by and let someone else get a laugh . . . once.

Even though Ed had always worked with inventions and hats and funny shoes and outlandish props, he was a compleat artist when it came to telling jokes. To watch him was to learn the art from a master. He would pantomime the actions of each character, he would build his exposition with the care of a draftsman making a blueprint, he paused at exactly the right moments, and when he came to the punch line, you'd been treated to a mini–three-act play.

WHEN YOU HEAR anyone say, in reference to comedy, "He wrote the book," he is referring to the most Perfect of Fools, Ed Wynn.

There was one he was enormously fond of. "Oh, I never told this on a stage," he vowed, giggling merrily. "You know, I've worked sixty years and never once did anything off-color, but this story . . . I absolutely adore. Oh, God, how I wish I'd dared do it," he'd sigh.

It seems there was a parade on in Manhattan, and it was a very warm afternoon. Crowds lined the sidewalks, watching the parade. Down the street came a very tired old prostitute. "See why I couldn't tell this?" asked Ed, with a certain amount of glee. "*Anyway* . . . she's very, very tired, and her feet hurt, and she's hot, and it's been a long, hard day—you see, the fleet's in. She tries to get a look at the parade, but she can't get near enough to see it through the crowd, and besides her feet hurt her so damn much from walking . . . Now, over *there* she spots a fire hydrant, and she walks over to it . . . Oh, anything to sit down on! So she sits down on top of the hydrant . . ." sighed Ed, "and slowly sinks to the ground."

One can only wish there were a videotape machine invented earlier, so that Ed could have been recorded telling that one.

Or for that matter, Ed telling anything.

Comedy is the unexpected replacing the expected. The cigar box that is opened—and a snake pops out. If you'd like a formula, try one + one = three. You were expecting two. Three surprised you. Translated into a joke, it would probably run like so: "Of course she's not a beautiful girl, but when it comes to cooking— she stinks."

By the way, although jokes are usually based on a rhythmic tier of three . . . ba-doom, ba-doom, ba-*dang* . . . three in itself isn't a very funny number. Oh yes, certain numbers in jokes are funny. Nine is funny. Eight isn't. Twenty-four is a dull number; twenty-nine isn't. Odd numbers get laughs; even numbers don't. Don't ask why.

The most marvelous practitioner of that art of the unexpected has to have been the old stone-face, Buster Keaton. Wynn respected Buster's ability to such a degree that he insisted Keaton join him as often as possible on those early television shows circa 1950. Ed knew Buster needed the work—that was part of it—but he also knew that Buster was a genius, whose comedy would make Wynn look even better. (That's the Jack Benny rule for longevity. Let everyone else on the stage get laughs—it only serves to make you look better.)

Wynn and Keaton doing pantomimes were a treat, and to sit in with Buster as he explained a gag he'd thought of the night before, while acting it out for you, was the kind of basic training the Yale Drama School could never provide.

Buster had evolved a sort of parody on *The Count of Monte Cristo,* and in his rasping voice he talked and acted it all out, down to the last slow take and pratfall. The scene called for him to be a prisoner in one cell, Ed in the next one, both of them grizzled old men. Between them was a thick wall. All in pantomime, Buster rapped on the wall. Ed rapped back. Soon they communicated. Then they discovered that the blocks that made up the cell wall between them could be moved. Ed moved one out. Buster moved one out on his side. Ed took another, Buster took another, and the pace quickened, until there was a space wide enough in that wall for the two of them to see each other. Pandemonium: Buster came through the opening, fell on Ed, embraced him! Neither of them had seen another human being in twenty years—*quelle* scene!

"Then," rasped Buster, acting it out, "down the hall there's the sound of a guard coming. We panic. I rush back into my cell and I start putting back the blocks. Ed does the same from his side. We hurry to replace that wall just the way it was. We finish it. The wall is perfect—not a trace of a change. We're safe! And then Ed looks down on the cell floor, and we pan down, and then up to his face as he does a take. *There's still one block left!* Where the hell did *it* come from?"

The two went out and played that sketch for nine or ten joyful minutes, live, in front of the cameras . . . and they got the laugh Buster promised us, but for Ed it wasn't big enough. He fretted over the row of TV cameras that stood between him and his audience, blocking the view. "Damn it," he'd sigh, "You just can't get laughs out of cameramen's asses!"

IF YOU'VE never seen Mr. Keaton in *The Cameraman*, then you can't know where Red Skelton got all his routines twenty years later in *Watch the Birdie*. SPENCER BERGER COLLECTION

There is preserved on a precious scratchy 1950s kinescope a sequence in which Keaton, most effortlessly, managed an impossible feat. Playing an errand boy in Wynn's grocery store, he inadvertently dumps a bucket of molasses on Ed's floor. Then his feet are caught in it, and in desperation he manages to get one foot up on the counter. He stands there, stork-fashion, because the second one is still stuck to the floor. Painfully, Buster manages to get his other foot up onto the counter, and for one miraculous moment he's suspended in mid-air, sans any visible means of support . . . before he inevitably lands on his prat in the molasses. Perhaps Nijinsky might have managed it . . . but he wouldn't have got the laugh Buster did . . .

For that early era of television comedy was still largely visual. Not yet had the medium been taken over by a corps of brash young stand-up comedians in dark blue suits who stood out there holding the hand mike and spraying a stream of one-liners about their home life, their nagging wives, their vacations in Florida and Vegas, and their nagging children and their nagging bosses. A good many of the old stalwart comics were still available for guest shots. Bert Lahr to play sketches, Willie Howard and Eugene to revive "Pay the Two Dollars," Señor Wences with those fabulous ventriloquist routines ("Easy for you—difficult for me") . . . and Professor Lamberti, he of the wild wig and the xylophone solos.

To watch Lamberti's act, even somewhat cleaned up for the TV audience, was another sort of education. Keep it simple, make yourself an amiable fool . . . and you can get away with any sort of gentle smut.

The Professor would announce that he would now play us a lovely ballad, "Wishing Will Make It So," for the music lovers everywhere. As he played on his xylophone, behind him, unseen by him, a lovely girl would appear and begin to do a demure striptease. After the first chorus, she'd go off, to great applause. Lamberti would happily play an encore. Again she appeared, behind him, to remove more clothing. End of chorus. Loud cheers from the audience, at which Lamberti would delightedly bow. "I never realized you people were such music

The great Professor Lamberti plays background music for Rita Hayworth, who never, alas, removed more than the one glove. SPENCER BERGER COLLECTION

lovers!" he'd muse. "You know, I once played seventeen choruses of this song at an American Legion convention?" After the fifth or sixth chorus cum strip, amid the cheers, Lamberti would lean across his xylophone, his hands waving the mallets upright. "You know something?" he'd confide. "I'm the only man I know who can play with six knockers at once."

Take that line out of context, and it's merely a schoolboy's locker-room smirker. But embed it in nine minutes' worth of a jovial clown's act, and even your aunt from Duluth would collapse with laughter.

Comedy is also anarchy. Nothing works better than controlled destruction. For years, Willie, West, and McGinty portrayed three fumbling workmen on a construction site, systematically bringing it all down about them, in a superbly timed series of mayhem jokes. The great Durante built his comedy personality about his persecution complex. In his chaotic world, everybody was against Jimmy. If he attempted a song, the musicians who accompanied him despised him for his talent. "I'm surrounded by assassins!" he'd cry, when the band hit a clinker. Demoniacally, Jimmy would systematically demolish a grand piano and hurl pieces of said Steinway about the stage, and end up by flinging the bench into the orchestra pit. Between our laughing at Jimmy and his tantrums, and howling at his antics as he inveighed against the world, there was a lesson to be learned about the comedic value of rage. As well as the title for a novel I was to write, purloined from the great Durante's act, *Don't Raise the Bridge, Lower the River*. When I handed Jimmy a copy, with his words emblazoned on the cover, he was delighted. "Son of a gun, you made me hysteric!" he chortled.

You yourself don't necessarily have to be funny so long as you have enough insane gags, visual and physical, to keep the audience happy. No two men ever proved that better than Ole Olsen and Chic Johnson, who made a fortune on Broadway with a collection of raffish madhouse material they called *Hellzapoppin*. On your way into their theatre, the gags began—a man wandering up and down the aisle, carrying a palm in a pot,

FRIEND TO UMBRIAGO, destroyer of pianos, idol of music lovers, the great Schnozzola. The eminent Mr. James Durante, from whose pungent philosophy the author gratefully helped himself—"Don't Raise the Bridge, Lower the River!"

calling for his wife. He would reappear all through the evening, and the palm grew and grew, until the final curtain, when you came out, and there would be a full-sized palm tree in the lobby, with that same poor soul up on a branch, still calling for his wife . . .

Ole was the tall one and Chic was the short one, and when they came to television, they brought along scenes which were straight out of the wheeziest days of vaudeville. Hotel rooms where doors opened and girls ran screaming out of closets, followed by apes, followed by zoo keepers. Courtroom scenes in which Ole as a judge pelted the assemblage with pig bladders; cars which exploded and collapsed; props which fell down on people, splashing them with water; props and props and more props, and always, in case the scene didn't finish with a big enough prop laugh, there were those midgets which Olsen and Johnson considered indispensable. The midgets kept dashing here and there, frantically inundating the actors, creating pandemonium. If you couldn't find a tag for an Olsen and Johnson sketch, you simply wrote, "Midgets here." "But we never call them midgets," cautioned Ole, sternly. "They are little people— remember that." So we'd rewrite, "Little people here," and it would get a laugh.

No one needed to worry about jokes around those two. Over the years, they'd amassed an encyclopedia of jokes, hundreds of replacements, all written down, indexed, bound in leather volumes, and stacked in a library that traveled with them. You needed a foot joke, you pulled out "F" and dug . . .

But somehow or other, all those O & J noisy madnesses, the prop trains that fell apart, the dead ducks which dropped out of the flies when Chic Johnson shot at a fleeing policeman with his shotgun . . . the juggling acts which ended up in a sea of broken crockery . . . none of it translated well onto the small television screen. Remember, those were the days of the nine- and the twelve-inch screen—and their physical comedy didn't survive miniaturization. Perhaps all those swarms of yelling midgets— excuse it, little people—dashing madly in and out of slamming doors, broke up live theatre audiences. On the home screen, they resembled a horde of angry ants. And nobody ever got much of a

Two DEANS of the school of cornball comedy, pratfalls, explosions, midgets, and collapsible cars that is (alas?) no longer with us: Olsen and Johnson. LEONARD MALTIN COLLECTION

laugh out of ants . . . unless they were inside the comedian's baggy pants.

So another lesson. Television comedy had to be smaller, and more sharply focused. Study the elegant double ballets of Laurel and Hardy, slower paced and quiet, which build inevitably up to the comedic explosions. The focus is microscopic. The laughs are huge . . . and those two-reelers have been running steadily for two decades, until the sprocket holes on the film must have worn out, long since . . . and who remembers Olsen and Johnson?

Television was to be more fertile for quiet comedians like Victor Borge, with his understated comedy at the piano . . . or for Peter Lind Hayes and Mary Healy, who could intersperse pleasant cross-talk, casual asides, with comedic song and dance . . . Or Dave Garroway, who provided a clever and inventive half hour. Anarchy didn't return until the great Ernie Kovacs moved in, and began to bend the medium to his own devices.

Comedy writing was a treadmill, and only the young and healthy had blood pressure that could survive those weekly schedules. There was one intensive period back in those days of live television when George Axelrod and I were engaged in writing scripts, separately and in tandem, for the dour Dane, Mr. Borge, for Peter and Mary, as well as the five kernels of rube-type corn per week that Axelrod was devising for a radio show called "Grand Old Opry," down in Nashville. (Where they greatly enjoyed such gems as "Say, why did the cow jump over the moon? . . . Because the farmer had such cold hands.") It made for an intense work schedule, especially since every so often we were also called in to create an original dramatic half hour for Mr. Boris Karloff, who was at the time essaying an original mystery drama each week.

We managed to keep up this backbreaking schedule. We didn't know enough to realize it was impossible. Besides, we had to; comedy didn't pay as much in those primitive days as it would when the Hollywood studios were to move in. So we covered for each other at rehearsals, and we were able to function, running back and forth across town with rewrites. Luckily, on the Borge show there were two collaborators, Bob Quigley and Eddie

Now you see, Stanley, if I merely pull this ring . . .

Lawrence (The Old Philosopher), who could cover for me when I had to rush over to a script crisis *chez* Peter and Mary, or uptown to a rewrite for the amiable Mr. Karloff.

Mr. Borge, who has probably never fancied himself a schoolmaster, did teach us a basic lesson. Not about comedy, but about comedians. Most of them have no sense of humor. And it never pays to be too funny, especially at the expense of melancholy Danes. The pianist-comedian made his TV debut in a half hour on which we worked very hard to create comedy that was pleasant, witty, and—to use a dreaded word around the networks—smart. We surrounded him with a cast of great bit players that included Art Carney, Charlotte Rae, and our own Eddie. We devised a piece of musical material that parodied the current "Hit Parade," which Victor insisted to the audience had its antecedents years ago in old Vienna, back in 1870, and we had singers in costume doing all the current hits, such as the rhythmic "Orange Colored Sky"—in German. The effect was great. It still works. Try it.

Then we gave him a pantomime routine in which he attempted to play Chopin's "Minute Waltz," and couldn't, while a procession of people, the window-washer, the delivery boy, the maid, a school kid, all came into Victor's living room, sat at his piano, ripped off the Chopin with ease, and left him to struggle with it . . . It was a deft show, which ended with the announcement on the screen, "For those of you who have just tuned in, you have just missed the 'Victor Borge Show.'"

The show was a hit, and the network and the sponsor were well pleased. Even Borge managed to force a smile. But by the end of the second week, Quigley had departed. Somehow he wasn't being reverent enough. By the end of the third week, I was pink-slipped, as well. Why? Later, I found out. Borge had inadvertently discovered that I was simultaneously the author of an hour TV script which was in rehearsal at the "Philco Playhouse." "Dot's a dramatic show," he muttered. "Nobody who writes drama could write for *me* . . ."

What he meant was—he didn't need help.

So we all of us went on to other writing and producing jobs, and Borge lasted another few weeks, and departed the TV half-hour field to return to concerts. But he didn't leave empty-handed. He has done that sketch about the "Minute Waltz" many times in the years since . . . usually sans credit. And/or payment. Why should he pay? He's made us immortal. Anonymous, but immortal.

There's a certain stock kind of comedy that involves the naughty-boy syndrome. Go back to the very first days of Martin and Lewis, to the period when their act scored instantaneous success. The chemistry they projected was traditional; plenty of comedy teams before them had employed the same basic formula, comic and straight man, rowdy kid and teacher . . . but for them the formula struck gold. There stood amiable, handsome Deano at the mike, trying to sing a ballad, and Jerry constantly interrupting with one-livers, with funny faces, and bursts of irreverent guffaws. Jerry was so identifiable—someone everyone empathized with—that brash kid who entertains at parties, the goof who keeps the high-school cafeteria in stitches, the happy dunce, the show-off, the lovable nut. Incorrigible boy, he should be spanked, stood in the corner, sent to his room . . . but beneath our disapproval we're vicariously enjoying the kid's complete disrespect . . .

Later, he went out on his own and extended the character—now he was Jerry, the goof, against the world. Mr. Ordinary, in trouble with the authorities, knocking his head against the machinery, falling into the pitfalls . . . but always coming up covered with roses.

Leave it to the *Cahiers du cinema* boys to discover all those hidden nuances and overtones in M. Jerry . . . as if an entire generation of silent film comedians before Jerry hadn't worked exactly the same side of the comedy street. Charlie Chase, Harry Langdon, Ben Turpin . . . Snub Pollard . . . Fatty Arbuckle . . . Oliver Hardy . . . all of them had portrayed the various facets of simple schnookdom. If you're looking for a guaranteed laugh, work out a way to let society kick you in the pants. But always make sure you get the girl in the eighth reel.

Jerry was funny for a long time in films; almost two decades in which (as he would be the first to remind you) not one of his films, either with or without Deano, ever failed to turn a large profit. There was a period when Jerry was making yearly two or three black-ink numbers at Paramount and that faltering studio had practically no other successful pictures to sell. Small wonder that Jerry's ego expanded to the point where he was writing his own scripts, directing them, telling the cameraman where to point the lens, conducting the musical score, producing, and completely dispensing with anyone else's critical judgment. Especially that which might occasionally caution him that the last scene had run on a bit too long, or that perhaps he needed a rewrite, or a retake . . . or editing . . .

Besides, the French considered him a genius. What else does a comedian need? Jerry agreed with them . . . completely.

I'd never had the rare privilege of working with and for a genius, until a few years ago, when Mr. Lewis agreed to play the lead in a film I'd written, one which was based on that same Durante-titled novel, *Don't Raise the Bridge.*

The script for said project had been written and rewritten and rewritten again by me at the behest of a London-based film producer, Walter Shenson. Walter is a meticulous man, and after two years' worth of conferences, we'd dotted every comedic "i" and crossed every comedic "t," to our mutual satisfaction. Every scene, every character, every speech and sequence in that screenplay had been assembled like the circuits of an IBM electronic brain. It had to be so, because the plot was intricate and convoluted, and every second of it had to work . . . or the whole thing would collapse like some sick soufflé.

Then we acquired Jerry Lewis as our leading man . . . but not as our director. This time, it was agreed that he would function solely in front of the cameras, an arrangement that all hands considered favorable for success.

Our star arrived in London and installed himself in the vast penthouse suite of the Hilton, surrounded by his staff, his press agent, and banks of portable tape recorders, cameras, and every piece of sophisticated electronic equipment ever devised by the Germans and the Japanese. The tape recorders weren't for pleasure, they were for posterity. Jerry tape-records himself from dawn to dusk, in meetings, conferences, interviews, and even in

According to *Les Cahiers du cinema*, M. Jerry Lewis *est un génie veritable*, and M. Lewis is the first to agree.

the most casual conversations. He is a traveling archive of self . . .

Walter and I and Jerry Paris, the director, a first-rate comedy man, arrived for our first pre-production conference. Jerry greeted us cordially, congratulated us on the high quality of the script, and proceeded on to other, more pressing matters . . . the new Nagra tape recorder he'd purchased that morning. He clowned for us (and it), he sang, he told jokes, he stood out on the terrace of the penthouse and blew blasts across Hyde Park on the antique British bugle he'd picked up that morning on Portobello Road, and then he clapped us all on our collective back and vowed, "Fellas, this is going to be one hell of a good comedy!"

After fifteen years of working for comics, and making changes, I spoke by reflex. "Do you feel completely comfortable with the character of George as he's written—?"

Shenson kicked my ankle. I got the message and shut up.

Later, in the car, going home, I swore I couldn't believe it. The star wanted no changes? Impossible . . .

Shenson, equally bewildered, allowed as how I might be right, but thought that we should leave sleeping stars lie.

Imbued with a false sense of security, we proceeded to Shepperton Studios, and on the first day of shooting, Jerry appeared, right on time to the minute, ready for his first scene. The script girl held open the book, Paris outlined Jerry's movements, and we started to do a walk-through. "Ah, I come in the door here," said Jerry, "and I say something, and then I go over to this beautiful doll here who's my wife, and I kiss her and I say something else very nice, and then she says her line, and then I answer with something very funny, and then I go out the door, okay?"

"Excuse me," said the script girl, "but these are the lines you say, exactly, Mr. Lewis." She read out his speeches. Dialogue which contained necessary exposition for the plot, and a certain amount of characterization, words which had been meticulously polished for two years now. "Honey, that's very nice stuff," said Jerry, "and I love the way you read it, I really do, you maybe ought to be at the Old Vic, but I don't want to memorize any of those lines, because if I do, I'll lose all my spontaneity, see? So I'll just make up what I say and it'll come out very, very funny, you'll see. Okay, everybody, shall we get started?"

We had a seven-week shooting schedule ahead of us, and one hundred and forty-odd pages of screen play to shoot, a story in which the leading character was the storm center of a series of complicated machinations . . . and said star refused to learn his lines. He proposed to improvise for the next thirty-five days. It was the ultimate in ego trips. In the manner of a nightmarish "Twilight Zone" story, that naughty-little-boy character Jerry had been playing for all those years had finally taken over his master's personality . . . Surrounded by a topflight cast of British character comedians, all of them prepared down to the last intake of breath, he persisted in improvising. "Learn your lines!" demanded Paris. "I'll be *stale!*" Jerry insisted. On went the battle, every morning. Finally, somebody asked him the obvious question. Why had he agreed to do the picture if he hadn't thought the dialogue was good? "Oh, it's not that the script isn't good," Jerry conceded. "You think I'd've agreed to do a piece of junk? It's just that I know I can come out and make it better. You want me stale?"

To that question, there was only one reply. Not that we could supply it to Jerry. Only the audience can do that.

Even the most precocious naughty little boy has to grow up . . . even in France.

Sometimes the trick in being a successful comedian is to be gifted with an extra helping of memory. Milton Berle is quite frank about his. "They always say I steal from everybody," he once told me. "For years Berle has been known as The Thief of Bad Gags. But believe me, that's not the case. I just happen to remember better . . ."

Working with Berle is something akin to having an IBM memory retrieval system as your star. The man's mind is a storehouse of one-liners, comedy *schtick*, bits and pieces, song parodies, and verbatim transcripts of every act, large or small, he's ever seen or played with in his sixty-odd years of performing. Yes, it's that long. As a child, Milton was toted by his mother over to Fort Lee, New Jersey, where he performed as an actor in early Chaplin two-reelers, and with that as your day-nursery training who needs kindergarten?

The King of Comedy and I once spent two pleasant weeks in Paris on a most improbable assignment, while he served as host of a TV special starring a troupe of ice skaters. For years, I'd heard horror stories which emanated from people who'd worked for Berle when he'd been the first TV comedy star, for Texaco, but in Paris, on a pleasant assignment which involved a jovial series of introductions and a minimum amount of work, Uncle Miltie was a pleasure.

He did give the producer an early ulcer when he sat in on the first production conference. "There is one rule on this show," he announced. "Berle does not skate—nor does he intend to learn how. Berle could hurt himself out on that ice."

That proviso involved a special set of trick shots, in which expert skaters doubled for Milton's shots on ice. But outside of that one ukase, he made no other problems. All he wanted was that everything be done capably, efficiently, and with dispatch. "Berle cannot stand inefficiency," he warned.

Making a show in the vast and drafty Palais des Sports, with a cockney British camera crew, a French television director, skaters who were German, Austrian, and Italian, a musical conductor who was Polish, and with the cameras being directed from a mobile booth parked yards away, outside the arena, there were many moments when the entire enterprise lapsed into an insane ice-bound Tower of Babel. Milton would sit quietly by, wrapped in an overcoat, in an arena seat, a large box of Montecristo No. 1's tucked under his arm, puffing happily away ("I really only did this show so I could get to Paris and buy some Havanas," he confided), and watch the various minor foul-ups down below without ever once losing his temper. "No use getting sore," he said. "Suppose Berle yelled? Who'd understand me?"

As we whiled away the time waiting for his sequences to be taped, he entertained me and everyone else in the arena with a constant series of one-liners. The French stagehands smiled politely as he translated his jokes into double-talk gibberish. News people came for interviews. Milton had just finished making a film in Hollywood, one in which he had portrayed a straight part. It was *The Oscar*, and Berle had surprised everyone with his ability to act. "Why am I a surprise?" he complained.

"Being a comic is acting all the time." When somebody remarked that he'd received great notices for his work in that
less-than-wonderful epic, Milton nodded sagely. "It won't mean
a thing, pal," he said. "Remember what I tell you—better to be
a shit in a hit than to be a hit in shit . . ."

To keep us all amused, he did card tricks. His manipulative
skill was superb. Professional card dealers pride themselves in
being able to deal seconds, i.e., the second card beneath the top
card, without being detected. "That's for amateurs," said Milton.
"Watch me—Berle can deal *fourths* . . ." And he did, amid
clouds of fragrant cigar smoke. "Only trouble is, after I do this,
nobody will play gin with me," he moaned.

Then erupted a crisis of massive proportions, with skaters
milling about helplessly all over the rink, musicians missing cues,
and the director screaming French invective over a faulty p.a.
system to anyone in earshot. It was finally all too much for Berle
to stomach. He stood up in his seat, his eyes narrowed, and all
the joviality went out of his manner. In the old days of the Texaco
show, Uncle Miltie had carried a whistle around his neck which
he blew to achieve order. This day he didn't need the whistle.
The cold steel in his voice communicated, even through that
babble of polyglot tongues around us in the arena. "All *right!*"
he yelled. "Cool it—this is Berle talking to you!" He grabbed
a nearby mike. "Now, we're going to get this goddamned show
on the tracks, right?" Every one stopped and stared at the cigar-
smoking star who had finally asserted himself. "Now," he said,
"from this point on, we're going to have a little organization
here—or the King of Comedy walks—*comprenez?*"

Whatever it was he induced, be it fear, tension, or what, his
leadership asserted itself. From then on, we managed to keep the
project functioning smoothly until the closing shots, which consisted of Berle making a farewell speech to the camera, and giving
the closing credits, while in the background a highly proficient
group of skaters did fantastic arabesques on the ice.

"Put my closing speech on cue cards," instructed Berle.
There was no one available to do so. He pointed a cigar at me.
"You're the writer—*write.*" I went out with a French assistant
and found a heavy-nibbed pen and procured some large cards.

The speech was printed on cards; it ran to two full cards. Then arose a major problem in logistics; everyone else was busy. Who could hold the two cue cards for the King of Comedy to read? "They're your words—*you* hold them," instructed the star.

Well, in show business there are times when you have to do everything . . .

I stood behind the camera, cue cards at the ready. Out on the ice, with the fact that he wasn't on skates carefully masked from the cameras, Berle prepared to do the scene.

It was my big moment. After all those years locked away in offices writing, backstage in dressing rooms revising, or up in control booths watching monitors as a somewhat frustrated non-participant, I was finally out there, working—an integral part of the show. You never know when you'll get your big chance.

Nervously, I held up the cards. The director gave the cue, the music blared out, all over the Palais des Sports the bright lights went on, and out on the ice all those skaters began whirling through their routine.

"And so, folks, it's goodbye from us here at the Palais des Sports, in gay Paree," read the King of Comedy, and he continued to follow his words that I'd written out on the idiot cards, right on down to the bottom. With a flicker of his eye, he gave me the cue to drop the first card. ". . . and it's a fond farewell from—" I dropped the card.

Berle stopped. He sighed.

"*Schmuck,*" he said, with infinite scorn. "It's *upside down.*"

Ninety-odd whirling skaters slowly came to a halt and stared at the two of us.

"You know something?" remarked Berle. "I must be getting old. In the old days, I'd've fired you right here on the spot. But on this budget, we can't replace you, can we?"

On the second take, we got it right.

"It's a good thing for you that you're very literate," Berle said, as he walked carefully off the ice.

I believe it was meant as a compliment.

Some years back, I worked on a unique television show that was CBS's first color venture. "The New Revue" emanated from a small studio up on the twenty-second floor at 485 Madison Avenue, and it was a variety show designed to demonstrate to Mr. Paley and his brass section the possibilities of the network's new color system. (Which was fated to be discarded in favor of NBC's, alas.)

Once a week, we performed a miracle of miniaturization in a vest-pocket studio where there was hardly room to turn the cameras. Singers, dancers, jazz performers, comedians, all cheerfully took their turn before our avant-garde color cameras, while we tried out the possibilities of Dr. Goldmark's excellent system.

One afternoon, an agent sent over a young fellow from the Midwest for an audition. The kid, he promised us, could do brilliant mimicry and had developed, at parties, a remarkable set of impromptu original routines. All he needed now was his first break. It was a show day, and upstairs the technical crew was getting ready to put the show on the air, but we agreed to take out a few minutes and give him some time during the afternoon break.

He arrived at our fourteenth-floor office, and there, in the tiny room, he went through his stuff. In a matter of seconds, he had us reeling with laughter. For once, the agent hadn't oversold his client; if anything, the kid was better than he'd promised. He not only had an uncanny knack for mimicking old ladies, hillbilly types, pompous businessmen, and assorted oddballs, but he could also reproduce the sounds of engines, machine guns, airplanes, power mowers . . . anything we asked for he could do. Brilliantly.

His audition was interrupted by an urgent phone call from upstairs. One of the performers scheduled for this afternoon's show had missed connections from the Coast and couldn't make it on time, and we were suddenly confronted with a gaping three-minute hole in our rundown . . .

"We can definitely use you," the young comic was told.

"Oh, gee, great," he said, cheerfully. "Do you have any idea when? I mean, I don't want to be pushy, or anything, but—"

We had a very good idea when. Upstairs, in half an hour or so.

While he stood there gaping at us, the producer called his

agent and hurriedly arranged a deal for a one-time guest shot. Then we sat down and began to block out what he should do in front of the cameras.

"Hey, is this some kind of a gag?" he demanded.

"No, just be funny," I told him. We hastily blocked out a three-minute spot from the stuff he'd done for us—a mini-scene in which he satirized a World War II movie (five Marines in an attack boat, about to make a landing on a Japanese island) . . . the hillbilly, the tough sergeant, the kid from Brooklyn, the coward . . . all complete with sound effects. "Okay, let's go upstairs," I told him.

Still bewildered, he rode upstairs in the elevator with me, as we discussed his cues, and how to improve one or two of his lines. A waiting make-up man went to work on him, the wardrobe lady supplied him with the proper color shirt and tie, and within twenty-odd minutes he was thrust in front of the bright lights for an impromptu camera blocking.

He'd arrived at CBS to audition at four-thirty, and by five-thirty he was standing in front of the cameras, doing his imitations and his characters on a network show, which has to set some sort of record for being discovered, even in the frenetic, ulcer-inducing world of television.

"I *still* don't believe it," he said, when he'd finished.

"Oh, don't fret," I told him. "This sort of thing happens every day around here."

The audience of a dozen or so stagehands and cameramen had laughed heartily. When the show ended, the control-booth phone rang, and one of the executives who'd been watching the show wanted to know where we'd found that kid with the crazy imitations—he looked very promising. He had an idea he might be useful around other current CBS shows . . . and what was the name again? "Winters," we told him. "Jonathan Winters."

"Where'd you find him?" asked the program executive.

"He found *us*," said the producer. "And just in time, too."

Out of the CBS elevator and into a long and successful career went Jonathan.

He's one of the very few comics I've ever worked with who

MAJOR Hugo Von Und Zu Schteffer, née Maude Frickert, and also the world's most successful salesman of garbage bags, Mr. Jonathan Winters.

is an original. His is a unique talent. An incredibly accurate ability to mimic, to create characters, blended with a huge helping of surrealist humor, and a genuine sense of the ridiculous. And that's about as far as you can go when you try to analyze Winters. Any man who can paint a charming landscape and then title it *Two Birds Watching Doris Day's Cat and Dog Drown* absolutely defies logic. One doesn't write comedy for the man—one simply tries to tune in on his wavelength, to stimulate his mind, to touch the keys on his console, set off charges which stimulate him to take off and go into monologues, or pantomimes, or to create characters . . . and when he's finished, it all comes out much funnier than you ever hoped it might be.

As the old show business truism puts it, "Either you have it, or you don't," and that about wraps it up for now about comedy, folks. Even those who have it can't tell you where it comes from . . . nor should they waste time trying.

But we're not going to go out without a laugh for closing, are we?

Jonathan came to visit a while ago, and we all went out for dinner to our local, a small, excellent Chinese restaurant in the heart of the low-rent district, in nearby beautiful downtown Norwalk. As we made our way to a small booth in the Good Earth, one of the customers, a local lady, stared at him as if she was certain she knew him. She plucked timidly at my arm. "Please excuse me," she said, "but that man with you looks a lot like the television star . . . Jonathan Winters. Is that possible?"

"Don't be ridiculous," I told her. "What would *he* be doing in a place like this?"

It got a laugh from our table. Jonathan smiled politely.

The Chinese waiter brought the tea and the crispy noodles. Then he stared at Jonathan. *"You!"* he said. "You a funny man!" He grinned.

"You bet!" agreed Jonathan, his appetite restored.

And are there any more questions about comedians?

CHAPTER TWELVE

•••••••••••••••••••••••••

Leland

I HAVE COME to the Lincoln Center Performing Arts Library to do research on a new book, one that deals with a half century of American popular music, based on interviews that are being taped with the composers and lyricists who wrote the songs.

As we make our way through the stacks—cavernous, quiet rooms full of filing cabinets and piles of cardboard cartons stuffed with scripts, old photos, scrapbooks, clippings, and theatre programs, all manner of precious, as yet uncatalogued memorabilia deposited in the Library by generous donors—the man who is taking me through, Paul Myers, the librarian, pauses at a particular collection of cartons.

These, he tells me, do not contain anything directly concerned with composers or lyricists, but there is quite a cache of material here that I should find interesting. It has been donated by Leland Hayward's widow; these cartons are the entire contents of his office files, most of his library, and many copies of the plays he produced. "I believe you knew Mr. Hayward quite well, didn't you?" he asks, politely.

It is a startling question. Of course Myers does not know what he's asking. Know Leland?

This book I'm here to do research on had its origin in Leland's office, with him as midwife . . .

It's impossible to associate all this dusty material here with a living Leland. I cannot consider him as a pile of cartons on a library floor, nor was his life something that should be stuffed into neat filing cabinets. What's here are merely the artifacts of his career. Letters, contracts, memos—old playbills and copies of opening-night wires, canceled checks. Perhaps, ten years from now, some Ph.D. candidate will use them to footnote his doctorate on Hayward, L., Broadway producer, circa 1945–71.

Pity the good scholar; he will never have known the man who left behind all this paper. His doctorate will be factual and pedantic. Not at all like the one I might write about my friend Leland . . .

One which I had perhaps better begin now . . . before *I* become a pile of cartons, stacked on some other library floor . . .

At one time, he was a Hollywood legend—and he fitted that easy cliché description far better than most of his own famous clients. Name any major star of the '30s and '40s—Fonda, Jimmy Stewart, Hepburn, Garbo, Astaire, Ingrid Bergman, Bill Powell; list a few of his high-priced author clients—Dashiell Hammett, Ben Hecht and Charles MacArthur, Gene Fowler, Donald Ogden Stewart, Edna Ferber, Lindsay and Crouse . . . but why is there any need to take inventory? Isn't it sufficient to remember that when he quit the agency business and sold his client list to Jules Stein, of the infant Music Corporation of America, so blue-white and perfect was the calibre of his assembled talents that by buying their contracts MCA was immediately launched into the top echelon of agencies?

One afternoon, years later, he looked up wearily from his desk, where he'd been engaged in a furious telephonic battle for the services of an MCA client he needed for one of his own projects. "Just think of it," he said, with a grimace. "They're trying to beat the hell out of *me*. Without me, they'd still be booking dance orchestras. Sonofabitch, I created my own monster!"

When he left Los Angeles to move his activities east, it was specifically to try his hand at producing on his own. "I saw all those conceited bastards who called themselves producers making so damned many mistakes," he said. "I figured I couldn't possibly do any worse than *they* were doing." His first shot at the brass ring, a new play based on John Hersey's *A Bell for Adano*, with Fredric March in the lead, was a smash, and for the next three decades his list of Broadway successes was—and still is—also blue-white and perfect. He was to beam fondly at SRO signs under the marquees of his shows; from *South Pacific* and *Mr. Roberts*, to *State of the Union*, *Call Me Madam*, *Wish You Were Here*, *Gypsy*, and *The Sound of Music*, he specialized in hits—with class.

Anent that last monster success, *The Sound of Music*, he had his own favorite ironic footnote. "You know something about this show?" he asked one afternoon as he sat at his desk, counter-signing profit checks that totaled well over a million dollars—the latest dividend for his backers. "Damn show never really got a good review from anybody. Movie's grossed over a hundred million so far. Now I ask you—what the hell do critics know?"

He had other successful careers. Very early on, he'd learned to fly, in those primitive, open-cockpit days of single-engine biplanes. His good friends then were leather-helmeted types, the fabled Jack Frye, who was to found TWA, and Elwood "Pete" Quesada, who became an Air Force general. During World War II, he and a group of his Hollywood pals established a flying school near Phoenix, to accelerate the teaching of young airmen for our Allies. Thunderbird Field played a major part in increasing the badly needed supply of trained airmen for the British, the Chinese, and for our own forces. "Christ, at one time we had thousands of acres of desert under option down there, for expansion," he would recall. "John Connolly, our business manager, kept coming around and nagging us to take up those options on the land. Not us. We were too busy flying and teaching all those kids to pay him any attention. Fifteen dollars an acre—miles and miles of open land. If we'd bought it—why, we'd own half of downtown Phoenix today!"

Then he'd grin. "But the truth is I didn't want the damn land. I really hated Arizona . . . and I still do."

It was the same John Connolly with whom he went into business soon afterwards, to establish their own airline. Southwest Airways eventually became one of the principal feeder carriers, up and down the Pacific Coast and points south. "It's marvelous owning your own airline," he once confided. "See, whenever you get on someone else's plane, like one of old Howard

Hughes's, you get to go right up front and sit with the pilots . . . which really is the only damn place to be."

Up front . . . that was where he always wanted to sit.

He was a voracious reader, a passionate listener, a brain-picker with an insatiable curiosity. That was his one obsession—to be ahead of the pack. Money was something one could always make—early on, he'd acquired the knack. But to be in at the very beginning—to have the news ahead of everyone else—that was his genius and his particular joy. Whether it was the set of galleys of the latest potential best-seller, or the playscript that had just come out of the author's typewriter—the young actor who would be the next star—the latest invention of science, or the move that would take place on the political scene tomorrow . . . all of it was Leland's meat and drink. He thrived on getting there fustest—and then selling off at a fat profit to others not so alert.

I'd heard about Leland Hayward for years. Usually around my father's office, and then his name was prefaced with a muttered derogatory prefix. The two men frequently went to the mat over the services of one of Hayward's clients, or the rights to a property he was auctioning off to the highest bidder. "Toughest trader I ever met, your old man," Leland once said, years later, thinking back to some of the deals, such as the monster sale of *Life with Father* to the Warners. "Jake fought me tooth and nail—for everything. But he was honest. Once he said we had a deal, that was it. Not many of those guys around, believe me . . ."

"He told me the same thing about you," I murmured.

"He did, eh?" Hayward grinned . . .

So he was something of a myth until 1958, when we had our first face-to-face encounter. Which was less of a meeting than it was a runaway marriage. In the morning, we were strangers. I'd left my Connecticut home at eight-thirty, headed for New York and a spell of meetings. When I'd left the house, life was placid and relatively routine. By noon of that day, I was affianced to Hayward, and things would never be completely routine again. Not for the next decade or so.

In those days, Leland was up to his Savile Row–tailored hips in television. He had a contract with the CBS network, which was paying him a hefty yearly retainer to come up with exciting new concepts for their prime-time schedule. Whatever sum the company was paying him, Hayward was worth it. He hadn't done much television, but the shows he had done were legendary. Back in 1953, he'd come up with the first mammoth TV special, the "Ford 50th Anniversary Show," which enraptured a national audience for ninety minutes, culminating in a wow finale as Mary Martin and Ethel Merman, seated on two simple stools, belted out a joyous medley of American song hits.

"That wasn't easy," he related. "Remember, they were both top stars, and not given to working with anybody else, least of all a female. I had to play a little game to get them. Neither of them was set for closing of the show. But I went first to Merm and I told her *Mary* was set to close the show, but that she didn't feel it was right unless she had Merm to do it with her . . . and the next day, I told Mary the same thing—that Merm was set to close it, but that *she* wouldn't do it without *Mary* . . . and within an hour the two of them were on the phone, making mad love to each other, like the Bobbsey Twins!"

After that triumph, Leland had created for NBC the original concept of a broad series of bold "spectaculars," shows which were to have as much impact on early television programming as had any of his old friend Pat Weaver's long-running "Today"/ "Tonight" institutions . . .

That first morning, I went into town on the train beside a lady named Elizabeth Bullock, a CBS story editor whom I'd known well from the days when she bought free-lance half-hour material for "The Web" and "Danger." Neither of us planned it, but Liz was to be my sponsor *chez* Hayward, our inadvertent marriage broker. I read the paper while, beside me, Liz plowed through stacks of magazines, foreign newspapers, and erudite quarterlies that dealt with science, psychology, overpopulation . . . What was all that for? Certainly, it was light-years away from the usual stack of mayhem/blood & gore mystery material that Liz usually lugged in and out of the city.

It was for a television concept Leland Hayward was developing. CBS had put her to work with him, combing through anything, animal, vegetable, and mineral—absolutely *everything* that

LELAND HAYWARD relaxing on the set of the "Ford 50th Anniversary Show" with his two favorite leading ladies, Ethel Merman and Mary Martin.

pertained to the events of this year, 1958. Hayward's concept was vast—but a bit undefined for Liz's precise mind. He simultaneously stimulated her and sent her frequently climbing the wall. "He's got me digesting *all* this material," she sighed. "You know, he's the most interesting man I've ever worked for, but right now I'm lost. I don't know where we're going. I think we need some specific ideas—or a point of view—a road map . . . *something* . . ."

I nodded sympathetically and went back to my crossword.

As our train nudged its way into Grand Central, and we prepared to joust with the day's small crises, Liz suddenly grabbed my arm. "I just had a thought," she said. "How would you like to come up to Leland's office with me—and perhaps you could toss around some ideas together? We need a new, fresh mind—it could be you . . . Or are you too busy?"

Anyone who's ever labored in the frenetic creative bullpens of television programming knows that shows aren't written, they're argued, torn apart, shouted over, cursed into existence. In my time, I'd been in enough of those pressure sessions, from which I'd emerged with little except frustration and a sick headache. With Leland Hayward . . . it might be the same old thing, true, but wouldn't it at least be interesting to have touched bases with him . . . once? Afterwards, I could always return to conferences with producers who spent their days repackaging cops-and-robbers, and situation comedies about young married couples and the hysteria attendant on Dad bringing the boss home to dinner without prior warning . . .

I rode uptown with Liz Bullock to 655 Madison Avenue, and we took the elevator up to the twenty-fourth floor. There, Hayward occupied a lone penthouse suite, one that commanded a fine 180-degree view of the midtown area. The waiting room was hung with a series of posters that recalled his past successes— *South Pacific, Mr. Roberts, Anne of a Thousand Days, A Bell for Adano, Call Me Madam, State of the Union* . . . the display was impressive. At a glass-enclosed booth was a switchboard, and inside it sat a grey-haired lady who seemed to be involved in an endless series of intricate long-distance phone calls to Florida, California, Paris, Berlin . . . an atlas of exotic destinations. Soon

I would learn that the telephone was Hayward's most basic tool. He could never travel anywhere, be it by car, or boat, whatever, without keeping several umbilical telephone cords open to the outside world. From dawn until midnight, he kept in constant touch with friends, enemies, with business acquaintances, with complete strangers whom he'd decided he must speak to at that particular moment. Old Alexander Graham Bell would have been gratified to see and hear the optimum use Hayward made of his invention.

The story goes that as far back as 1932, when Hayward moved his business to new offices, he spoke to his secretary, Miss Malley, about getting a distinctive telephone number. "Who do we know in the telephone company?" he inquired. "Heavens, Mr. Hayward," replied that lady. "We know *everybody* in the telephone company."

That same Miss Malley was still guarding the outer door to Hayward's office, as she would until the last day of his tenancy. She was short and a bit stout. Her responses were brief, but always to the point. No job, however exotic, seemed to dismay her. She was the repository of vast stores of useful information; without ever losing her cool, she directed office traffic, handled correspondence, arranged theatre tickets, booked transportation on a moment's notice, and kept Hayward's fast-moving affairs always on some sort of track. Over the years, I learned that her name had originally been Kathleen Malley, that she had, in her years as his factotum, also married and become Mrs. Kavanaugh and raised her own family. But for as long as there would be Hayward, buzzing her on the intercom and calling "Get me Ingrid Bergman—she's somewhere in Europe, and I have to speak to her right away," there would be a Malley to find that lady and to make the proper connection for him forthwith . . .

Hayward was seated behind his desk, talking one one of his phones. A lean-faced man, his hair close-cropped, he was crooning softly to somebody on the other end—somebody who was obviously anxious for news of this current project. "Don't you worry, Beauty," he was saying. "It's going to be the goddamndest most marvelous thing we ever tackled. I'll be back to you with some details tomorrow—and meanwhile, don't stop thinking up great numbers for us to do, right?"

He hung up. "Jerry Robbins," he said. "And we have to get together some concrete ideas for him right away. You can't leave a genius hanging there, can you? Liz, who's this?"

Liz explained who I was, introduced me, and suggested that I was a bright, capable fellow who might be of some assistance to Hayward in putting together a working concept for this . . . project.

Leland nodded cordially. A phone on his desk buzzed, and he grabbed it, and we listened for another four or five minutes, while he spoke to someone in Boston who seemed to be having trouble with a new show, and who needed his advice on re-casting.

While he suggested a list of names, I examined the Hayward nerve center. A large desk piled high with playscripts, books, papers, more phones, and a magnificent, attenuated, scrawny cat, in bronze . . . done by Giacometti. Around the room were endless shelves also overflowing with books and more books, a table piled with current magazines, a small baby grand on which were enlarged color photos of people and flowers—his work; he was a dedicated camera nut—and on the walls a framed Klee and a Picasso harlequin, both of museum quality.

Leland hung up and promptly inquired what thoughts I'd had on the project. "Give me your ideas—shorthand them," he instructed.

I had no ideas, unfortunately, until he explained what *he* had in mind. Could he fill me in a bit more . . . precisely?

"No," said Leland, happily, "but I'll give you a little blueprint of what we want to do . . ."

He began to talk. Enthusiastically, vividly, in broad strokes, he started to outline a plan for a giant television show that would encompass everything that had happened in our world in the year 1958.

In years to come, I was to have firsthand evidence that Hayward was one of the greatest salesmen that ever made a pitch. Whoever coined the old phrase "He could sell smoke" must have had Leland in mind. Others can bear witness to Leland's ability to charm cynical actors into contracts, or to woo unwilling

leading ladies, to sell truculent studio heads expensive packages.
I was to see him hold hypnotized a conference room full of
hard-nosed oil-company executives with an improvised spiel
which he casually reeled off from four or five sketchy notes on
file cards in his hand . . . and when we drove away from that
session, he turned to me with a conspiratorial grin. "Boy, I love
spitballing," he admitted. "And we didn't have anything at all
to sell them," I said, somewhat redundantly. "That's what made
it even more fun," he said, chuckling.

This particular morning, he sold me smoke as enthusiastically as if I were Henry Ford II, or some Nobel Prize winner
whose services he needed. To a complete stranger, on a one-to-
one basis, he pitched . . . and the fantasy show which took shape
as he described it became as vivid and exciting as if the damn
thing was coming at me from a seventeen-inch screen . . .

It sounded great. Much more stimulating than any of the
nightly mediocrities which came out of that idiot box in the
living room . . . but the precise architecture was a bit vague.
Details? They seemed to involve scenes from hit Broadway
plays, exciting ballet by Jerry Robbins, film clips, interviews
with great scientists and football players, live news pickups from
all over the world, chats with Charles deGaulle, Carl Sandburg,
Bertrand Russell, Haile Selassie . . . Leonard Bernstein leading
the Philharmonic in some sort of original music by old Igor
Stravinsky . . . Eisenhower exchanging ideas with a panel of
4-H Club kids . . . Walter Lippmann being interviewed by
Spencer Tracy—the whole structure soared upwards and hung
there in front of us—a behemoth, a mind-boggler, a Macy's
Thanksgiving Day parade—a feast—a hugely fascinating first-class
bill of gorgeous goods.

That, of course, was another one of Leland's talents—the
ability to build towering dream ediflces to order. He opened up
wide vistas into infinity and tempted his potential buyer like a
cultural Mephistopheles massaging Dr. Faustus' ego. The under-
lying sales message was fiendishly subtle—and effective. *These
are the greatest and most important talents in the whole damn
world*, went his subtext. *Forget the second-rate . . . You deserve
the best.*

That morning, his pitch was startlingly effective. All that seductive blue sky he'd mapped out started my own creative juices drooling. As he talked, so vivid were his descriptions that they engendered responses I didn't even know I could come up with—never mind that there was no structure, that he'd piled film stars upon heads of state, that a piece of documentary news banged up against Hank Fonda doing a reading from Maxwell Anderson's *Valley Forge* without much rhyme or reason . . . that the "rumble" ballet from *West Side Story* seemed somehow to be making a comment about juvenile delinquency rather than serving as entertainment . . . that the whole thing was a traffic jam of disparate ideas. So what? It didn't matter at all. It sounded marvelous.

"Okay," he said. "*Now* have you got any ideas?"

Yes, I did. Where were they coming from? I didn't know, or care. His electricity had turned me on—but good. Half an hour ago my world had been tightly bound up in stifling situation comedies, as rigidly formatted as Molière. Now, as if set free, I was on my feet, pacing his carpet, and throwing ideas at him, embellishing on his random vistas, stretching my own horizon to spread it across the panorama he wanted. That morning, I took a short course in creativity. Never again would I question what happens at a Billy Graham revival meeting.

Remarkably, it was after twelve. Leland was nodding at Liz Bullock. "You're right," he said. "We need this guy." Then he smiled at me. "How soon can you start?" he asked.

The question startled me; ideas were still churning through my mind. "Haven't I already started?" I asked.

"Yeah, you bet your ass you have," agreed Leland, and took another long-distance call.

Shortly after that first meeting at the summit, a financial understanding was concluded between our respective business people, and my telephone in Connecticut became another way station in Hayward's intricate network of communications. My job was to bring a semblance of order to his concept, to try and reduce it to coherent prose, and while I sat at a typewriter at home, hammering out pages that would serve as part of a CBS sales brochure, I was interrupted regularly by his calls. "Good morning, Mr. Wilk," I might hear, at 8:36 A.M. "This is Miss Malley, Mr. Hayward wants to speak to you." Was he already in the office? Certainly not . . . he was being put through the office switchboard from his Long Island home, or perhaps from the back seat of his car as it sped into town, and the burden of his call was that he'd just read a review of a remarkable new book, something on genetics, or on the latest exploration of outer space, and an advance copy was on its way to me to be read, digested, and added to our prospectus. All through the day, a fusillade of sporadic calls came at me. We needed something by Dr. Pitirim Sorokin, of Harvard, on the decline of civilization. Could we include a whole section on female beauty? That afternoon, he'd arranged for it with a museum director. An English poet had been in, who had some absolutely marvelous ideas on children's fantasy games—I must talk with him. I must not forget the original music we were hoping to include by Aaron Copland . . .

Would I make notes on the show for Charles Eames, the designer, who was a firm friend of Hayward's and who would be doing all the graphic material we needed? The calls continued until late at night, when finally he read himself to sleep . . .

Several days a week, Hayward insisted that I spend time with him sorting out ideas over lunch. Such meetings always took place at his private table in the bar at the now departed Colony. There we'd repair, a yellow pad and pencil between us; he would order a double Wild Turkey for himself, a double Bloody Mary for me, and we would confer. Around us, Gene Cavallero's regulars—all the beautiful people—gossiped and picked at their gourmet lunches while we concentrated on our CBS business for a stated period. "What the hell," he'd say. "They're paying for the lunch—so let's give them something for Mr. Paley's money." And after we'd built a couple of notions into some segment that might work for the show, we'd eat an expensive lunch and talk . . . usually about show business. Over that Colony table-cloth, a good deal of Hollywood and Broadway history came to life for me . . .

Some of it is already well documented elsewhere . . . How he'd been born the son of Colonel William Hayward, a prominent

New York lawyer, who had gone overseas in World War I as the commanding officer of the 369th Infantry—the first all-black fighting unit in the Army . . . "Lord, I can even remember when they came marching home after the war," he mused fondly. "You know, they had a military band which was led by a wonderful musician named Lieutenant Jim Europe, a guy who wrote jazz. When that band struck up its syncopated beat, and my father's unit came marching up Fifth Avenue, strutting and stepping to Europe's music, well, it was the goddamndest thing you ever heard. People all over the city were really jumping . . ."

Young Leland was sent off to Princeton, but the academic life was not for him. He left school, by request, and his early years were spent, in the '20s, working at a brief stint on a newspaper, but more often in speakeasies, with cronies. Eventually he fell into a job with United Artists as a press agent, which employment took him traveling across country. In Hollywood, he hung around with the right crowd—even though at the time nobody really knew that he and David and Myron Selznick and Lewis Milestone were ever to achieve any status at all. "We all starved together," he said. "None of us had a buck . . ."

What was his first deal as an agent?

"Oh, hell, I can't even remember, it was so long ago," he complained. "But I think it was probably when I sold a story by Ben Hecht. Ben was a pal of mine and he'd given me something to read back in New York. I heard all around me how the studios were looking for material—talkies had just come in, and all the producers were scratching around, looking for stuff with words . . . I remembered I still had Ben's thing in my bags somewhere, so I dug it out and sold it to Metro for $1,500. Called Ben long distance and told him afterwards. He thought it was great. Why not—he was busted, too. Then I came back to New York and went into business with John Rumsey at the American Play Company," he said. "But I made a deal with Myron Selznick out on the coast, to be our California man—and *then* we started swinging." Leland paused to think. "I ever tell you about the great Paramount talent raid? I guess it was back in 1931 . . . That should show you how stupid the studio guys were . . . so *smug* . . .

"See, there was Paramount, with Adolph Zukor running the show, with Lasky, and with old B. P. Shulberg handling production. The most powerful outfit in the whole business—making fifty, sixty pictures a year . . . and Zukor was out to take over everybody. He hated the Warners—they had Vitaphone and they were making money fast—but as far as Zukor was concerned, the Warner boys were strictly Johnny-come-latelies . . ."

One Friday afternoon, after the close of business, one of Myron Selznick's subordinates came into his boss's office to report on a minor oversight that concerned the contracts of three of the Selznick-Hayward clients. Kay Francis, Ruth Chatterton, and William Powell, all enfiefed to Paramount, and all huge box-office draws, elite stars at the top of Zukor's long list. It seemed that some underling in the Paramount business offices had forgotten, in the press of the day's affairs, to go through the routine formality of notifying Selznick's office that Paramount was taking up the options on the three stars; the option dates for the trio happened by chance to come up on the same day, that memorable Friday. "Just a mistake, I guess," said Selznick's aide. "I'll call them up at Paramount on Monday and remind them, right?"

Hayward's eyes twinkled. "You've got to remember that Myron was a helluva businessman, and he had a personal vendetta against everybody in the studios, especially Zukor— who had given Myron's old man, Lewis J. Selznick, a really rough time years back. Myron was always out to revenge himself against anybody who'd been such a bastard to his father, and he saw this as a chance. He told the guy in his office to keep his mouth shut. Then he got hold of me, and told me what had happened. 'You know something?' he said. 'Legally, those three people are free agents, right?' 'Right,' I agreed. 'So what?' I asked. We sat there looking at each other, and after a minute or two, Myron said, 'I'll bet Jack and Harry Warner would really *love* to get three classy stars for Warner Brothers, don't you think?' That's all we needed to say to each other. We got Jack Warner on the phone that night, and we went over to his house next day for breakfast and offered him Kay Francis, Ruth Chatterton, and Bill Powell—at a terrific price, of course—up to close to a

million before it was done. Jack practically fell off his chair—
he was drooling at the idea. But he couldn't make the final commitment until he called his brother Harry in New York, to get
the okay on the money side. My God, what a spot for them—
they'd been scratching around the business for years, with Rin
Tin Tin and Monte Blue . . . now they had their Vitaphone and
they had money . . . but here we were offering them a package
of class—their first taste of it . . . and the chance to stick it to
Zukor, as well. Well, old Harry Warner yelled and screamed at
our price, but he couldn't resist the temptation to steal three of
Zukor's hottest stars right out from under Zukor's nose, could he?
. . . So by Sunday night we'd drawn up the papers and the deal
was made, dated as of Monday morning. We'd put Warner
Brothers into the class business . . ."

And what transpired at Paramount thereafter?

Leland shook his head. "Man," he sighed. "That was when
it really hit the fan. Monday morning, the *Hollywood Reporter*
came out with a big headline, announcing the deal at Warners
for our three clients, and that was the first news Zukor or anybody else at Paramount had ever gotten an inkling of it. Man—
you should have heard Zukor screaming on the phone at us. He
accused us of every kind of treachery—he told us he'd sue—he
barred us from the Paramount lot—but it was no use. That
poor little bastard in the contract department who'd missed up
on a technicality on Friday had really blown it . . . and made *us*
rich."

How long did the Zukor ukase against Selznick and Hayward continue? "Oh, until he needed somebody else we represented, natch," said Hayward, matter-of-factly. "But the hell
with all that ancient history," he'd add, reaching for the check.
"Let's get back to *this* goddamned show we're stuck with."

Conferences, meetings, conference calls, reading and study
and the digesting of more and more material, all continued with
rising intensity. The mail deliveries began to resemble the pre-
Christmas rush at 655 Madison. Down at CBS, Liz Bullock and
assistants went through more stacks of magazines, books and
newspapers. Messengers from their office would regularly come

trotting up to Hayward's penthouse to dump the latest digests onto his desk. Leland himself was the eye of this paper hurricane, happily dredging up more and more, having material airmailed in from Europe, calling authors and critics and scientists all over the world, voraciously devouring whatever addenda they would pass on to him . . .

Eventually, we had our preliminary sales piece, seven or eight pages of prose that we hoped would generate some of the excitement that we needed in order to induce some sponsor to open up a corporate checkbook and pass over some of the thousands of dollars that developing such a behemoth would have to cost.

Leland scanned it. "I think we'd better put in some sort of a very *rough* budget," he mused. "Something very vague, that doesn't commit us, but gives the guy at least an inkling of what we're going to need . . ." He sent for Herman Bernstein, his business manager, who presided over Hayward's theatrical affairs from a smaller office in the penthouse.

Herman Bernstein had long since acquired the Broadway reputation of the sharpest and most reliable manager in town. A quiet gentleman with a soft southern accent, his financial acumen was the mainstay of various top-level Broadway showmen as well as Hayward—Herman Shumlin, Guthrie McClintic, Howard Lindsay and Russel Crouse, all leaned heavily on Herman, and Herman never once collapsed beneath their collective creative weight.

The Bernstein mind operated with the sort of precision that would have caused envy at IBM. Should Leland toss him a new playscript at 5:30 P.M. and request an instant analysis, the following morning Herman would appear, report on the quality of the script, suggest proper casting for the various parts, supply a detailed breakdown of production costs, be able to name the precisely correct theatre for the show—as well as to suggest, down to the last few hundreds of dollars, what said play's eventual weekly gross might be. And all of this would come forth from Herman's brain, sans a single note on paper.

Herman came in, picked up the sales presentation for the

proposed Leland Hayward TV production to be called "Year End Review," and agreed to give us his estimate of its probable sales cost the following morning.

What he studied went:

Leland Hayward presents: YEAR END REVIEW

The night? Within a week or so of December 31, 1958.
Where? On a full station lineup of the CBS Television Network.
The cast? Well . . .
Brigitte Bardot, Admiral Rickover, Mary Martin, General de Gaulle, Roy Campanella, Sherman Adams, William Holden, a satellite named Jupiter, Tim Tam, seventy-six trombones, a dozen Venezuelan southpaws, Ernie Kovacs, Art Buchwald, Tito, Bing Crosby, Queen Elizabeth, the Man from Schweppe's, Nikita Khrushchev, the Moiseyev dancers, Nehru, Frank Sinatra, the New York Stock Exchange, Yves St. Laurent's latest silhouette, Van Cliburn, the Witch Doctor, Rafael Trujillo, and whoever wrote the year's best-selling novel . . .

It went on like that for six or seven pages, suggesting Spencer Tracy as a host, with graphics, film, live spots, the "rumble" ballet from *West Side Story* interviews with world-famous personalities, comedy scenes, Carl Sandburg reciting his own poetry . . . The whole thing designed to leave our prospective sponsor gasping with greed and ready to envelop the show, to drape it with his sales message . . . and to pick up the check.

Herman Bernstein was back the following morning, and he carefully replaced the outline on Leland's desk. Then he stood in front of Leland, staring for a long moment at what he'd read.

"Well, Herman?" asked Leland, tilting back his chair, his stockinged feet reposing on some of the stacks of scripts on his desk. "What do you think the goddamned thing might cost?"

"I'll tell you," said Herman, thoughtfully. "I really wouldn't want to commit myself to any specific figure, not at this time. But anybody buys this show for television, they better have an awful lot of money to spend . . ."

"Oh, I assumed *that*," said Hayward, happily.

"So maybe you just better not put a definite price on it," said Herman. "Do it on a cost-plus basis."

"That's a great idea!" said Leland. "An open-end commitment—but we put a floor beneath it. Say we'll start at half a million, and tell the guy we'll need escalation clauses, just in case. Does that sound right to you, Herman?"

"Half a million," mused Herman. He shrugged. "Well, better to aim high than be caught short . . ."

"After we hook him for the first half million," said Hayward, "he'll *never* haggle over a couple hundred thousand more or less . . ."

"No," mused Herman. "I guess he won't . . ." And he went back to his office, and reality.

When the CBS program department received Hayward's proposal, it induced a series of shock waves. But since Leland's contract had been arranged with Mr. Paley himself, there was no recourse for the CBS executives but to accept this bold concept as viable TV entertainment, and to proceed to try and sell it to some bold sponsor . . . or, at least, to go through the motions of doing that. The outline was set in type by the excellent CBS graphics people, a handsome brochure was printed, and "Year End Review" was passed out to the sales department.

Silence descended.

What was happening?

"They're scared of it," Leland remarked. "It's too big—and they won't have any controls. That always gets them worried. What they'll try to do is to beat the thing to death with a sofa cushion . . . But the hell with that. When the right sponsors show up, they'll adore it!"

While we waited for Mr. Corporate Right, Hayward was busy with other projects. With Richard Rodgers and Oscar Hammerstein and Richard Halliday, he was engaged in preparing a musical vehicle for Mary Martin, based on the story of the singing Trapp Family; with his good friend Jerome Robbins, he was involved, with Arthur Laurents, Jule Styne, and Stephen Sondheim, in another musical project for his other favorite

musical leading lady, Ethel Merman. Simultaneously, he and I
went on building new dream projects.

One of the television ventures he proposed was to be a
ninety-minute special to salute the emergence of the newest
state, Alaska. "The 49th Star," it was called, and after much
discussion, we both knew it would never be anything but
routine. Having an actor read "The Shooting of Dan McGrew,"
was about the limit of our creative thrust. "You know what we
need?" he asked, over his customary Wild Turkey. "Some kind
of wild dramatic stuff, the kind of thing old Ben Hecht was
good at. Too bad we haven't got him around to give us a few
ideas . . . Christ, what an imagination Ben had . . . He could
sit at a table with you all night, spinning yarns, and you lost all
track of time, he was so full of material. All that newspaper stuff
he'd picked up in Chicago . . . Did I ever tell you about the deal
I made for Ben on *Scarface?*"

"Howard Hughes was just a kid then, a very rich one, trying
to bust into the picture business, and he had this notion about a
gangster and he wanted Ben to write the script. Ben had done
a picture called *Underworld,* and it was one of the first gangster
pictures . . . Well, I called Ben up and offered him the job, and
he said he'd never heard of this guy Hughes and how did we
know he was good for the dough? I tried to explain that Howard
had a fortune, but Ben wouldn't budge. He finally agreed to
write the script for Hughes at a specific figure—$1,000 a day,
paid in *cash.* Every day at 5 P.M. Hughes said fine, so Ben sat
down at the typewriter up in the house he was living in, in
Hollywood, and at the end of each day, I'd go up there and pick
up the pages he'd written, take them down to Howard's office—
he had this ramshackle little suite in the back of one of the
rental studios. Howard would come out and hand me ten hun-
dred-dollar bills. Then I'd go back up to Ben's house, drop nine of
those hundreds on Ben's desk, and keep the tenth for my com-
mission . . . and you know, at the end of nine days, Ben had
worked so fast that he had the whole damn thing finished? I
kept asking him to slow down—hell, I *needed* those hundred-
dollar-a-day commissions—but not old Ben—he wanted to be
done with the damned thing and that was it, the script was

finished. And believe it or not, that's the script they shot, with Muni . . . Nine thousand bucks, for writing a great picture— one that made Howard millions! . . . Old Ben really outsmarted himself on that one . . ."

One hundred dollars a day. Quite a difference from the size of the fees that Hayward was taking ten per cent from, in years to come, for Hecht and MacArthur, and for other clients whom he'd pushed into the upper-income tax brackets. "Yeah . . . I remember the deal I made for Edna Ferber, on *Saratoga Trunk,*" he said. "I told Edna that we were going to make a real break with tradition—we weren't going to sell her damn book—we were going to *lease* it to the studio that wanted it. The hell with them owning it and remaking it forever—they could use it for seven years, after which it would revert to her. Well, Edna thought that was a dandy idea—she liked money a whole lot— but she wasn't sure any studio would go for the deal. So I told her, 'Listen, what the hell have we got to lose by asking?' and she agreed to go along with me. I sent every studio a telegram offering the book for $175,000, seven-year lease, no trading. Wow!—you should have heard the outraged screaming. Your old man called me up and *he* yelled, too. I said, 'Listen, Jake, if you don't want it, all you have to say is that Warners passes, right?' But he went on, he told me this was highway robbery, and piracy, that I was ruining the business, the studios couldn't afford to make such a deal, if one of them did it, then it would set a terrible precedent. I said I knew all that and it had been nice talking to him, but I had to take another call—it was a producer at Metro . . ." Leland leered like a happy small boy. Was there such a call? "What difference?" asked Leland. "Your old man said, 'Before you take that call, I just want you to know we've accepted your terms, and we consider that *Saratoga Trunk* belongs to Warners.' 'For only seven years,' I insisted. '*All right— seven years!*' he yelled, and hung up." Hayward chuckled. "I could guess what he was saying after he hung up . . ."

By the end of our first year, Hayward's files were over-flowing with stacked outlines for new television projects, all neatly in order. There were such presentations as our "Male and Female," which called for the services of such talented, albeit

disparate, ladies, as Arlene Francis, Lauren Bacall, Marya Mannes, Brigitte Bardot, and Marianne Moore, a female tug-of-war
team captained by Dr. Margaret Mead—arguing out male/female
problems with a masculine contingent whose roster included such
Hayward cronies as Yul Brynner, Hank Fonda, John Steinbeck,
Truman Capote, and whatever other male Leland might have
encountered at a dinner party the previous evening. There was
a project to be called "U.S.A. Today," in which every available
scrap of the week's media—the press, magazines, books, TV—the
works—was to be scanned and digested and tasted, reviewed,
and discussed. "We'll do the whole thing with only one great
host!" Leland said enthusiastically as he strode up and down his
office, throwing out ideas like an inexhaustible Roman candle.
"Yeah, one host," said Herman Bernstein, as he tiptoed out
of the office, "and about one hundred and ninety-six people on
the staff, feeding him . . ."

Gypsy, the musical saga of Rose, Gypsy Rose Lee's mother,
finally went into production. Leland had called up his roster of
backers, and most of the financing was in the bank. It sounded
as if it would be a big hit—were there any "pieces" left open?
Leland shook his head. "Save your money," he warned. "It's not
much of a gamble, sure, but the payoff is going to be lousy. You
know what a unit of this show is costing? Seven thousand dollars.
Christ—this thing is going to end up running four hundred
grand before we open!" He shook his head angrily. (Although,
fifteen years later, Broadway costs have more than doubled.)
"Listen," he lectured, "when my wife Maggie Sullavan decided
she wanted to come back to Broadway and we found that play
by John Van Druten, *The Voice of the Turtle*, I took a look at
it and it was three characters, one set, and I figured, hell, this
is no big deal, let's take a good shot at it, out of our own pockets.
The show was to come in for twenty-five thousand—no more.
So Sullavan and I got hold of Alfred de Liagre, the producer,
and we bought pieces for each of the three kids—a couple of
thousand for the three. That was 1943. You have any idea how
much we've gotten in return, out of profits?" He scribbled some
figures on his desk pad, and then looked up, shaking his head

in amazement. "About seventy-five times for each dollar we put in! . . . Now, even if *Gypsy* is a smash and we make back all our investment, I figure you probably won't end up getting back more than two dollars for each dollar you invest. That stinks. And how much longer do you think we can go on producing shows with that kind of costs to buck?"

It was a good question in 1959, and it's even more pertinent fifteen inflated years later.

As is usually the case with the early phases of a Broadway birthing, Leland's days and nights were now taken up with a constant series of wrangles and arguments. Who were the contestants? Author wrestling with composer, lyricist battling with performer, director, costumer, performers and agents and lawyers, all going to the mat over endless problems, artistic, emotional, and, more often than not, financial.

The Hayward office anteroom was crowded with all manner of insistent visitors. The office phone never stopped ringing; as she had been for more than four decades now, Miss Malley was in charge of arranging audiences for the various pleaders at court. Everyone connected with the show seemed to have some axe to grind, and Leland's cluttered office desk was the arena where all the razor-sharp edges ended up in clangorous combat. Throughout this guerrilla warfare of egos, Leland maintained an amiable calm. David Merrick, his co-producer, was off somewhere else, busy with another show he said he much preferred to *Gypsy*—a musical version of *Destry Rides Again*. Leland mediated, soothed, calmed down tempers. But so acrimonious were all the pre-rehearsal arguments that one evening a full-dress council of arbitration took place up in the office, at which he presided, and at which everyone concerned, plus agents and lawyers, could be heard. He spent long hours that night trying to keep his fledgling craft from being scuttled before it had ever been launched . . .

I arrived the next morning early, and there he sat, red-eyed, weary, but alert, and ready for this day's new harassments. I'd already heard about the previous night's session. He described the wranglings that had taken place at some length, and with pain. "Grown people," he said. "How can they all behave this way?"

Anyone else, any rational businessman, I suggested, would have tossed in the towel long ago, and given up the whole thing as a bad deal . . .

"Yeah, I guess that's absolutely right," agreed Leland, yawning.

Then why not let everyone stew in his own juice?

He pondered that course of action, and then he shook his head. "Oh, I couldn't do that," he said.

"Even at the risk of your own sanity? Why not?" I persisted.

"Because," he said, softly, "it's going to be such a hell of a good show."

That was the salesman's credo . . . But what about the merchandise?

Gypsy gave its first performance at a run-through, one warm Saturday afternoon, on the vast bare stage of the Winter Garden, for a large invited crowd of working actors and actresses. Jerome Robbins came out before the assembled jury of his peers, let us know the general layout of the nonexistent scenery, positioned the action of his show in time and in place, thanked us for coming, and stood back, to let the show take over.

The music began to tinkle from the piano in the pit. There on the stage came the kids, auditioning for the amateur show in Seattle, in the '20s. As the two little sisters began to pipe out the words of "Let Me Entertain You," from the back of the Winter Garden echoed a familiar, stentorian voice, commanding, "*Sing out, Louise!*" Down the aisle, a small dog in her arms, came Ethel Merman, up went a delighted, spontaneous roar of affection, adoration, and welcome from the audience. So noisy was it that even the redoubtable Merm needed a couple of seconds to recover from the impact. She'd been off the stage for a few years, but now she was back, and they wanted her to know they loved her. In a matter of minutes, *Gypsy* had been well and truly launched, with the muzzle velocity of a howitzer blast.

Rarely has a musical ever seemed as exciting as the barestage Sunday matinee of *Gypsy*—sans costumes, with no orchestra . . . with the only visible stage lighting emanating from the talent on show. Merman, Jack Klugman, all of the elements,

the Laurents libretto and the Styne and Sondheim score, Robbins'
staging, even in this rough state, "worked" so well that when the
final scene ended, with Merman singing her now famous "Rose's
Turn," there was another Niagara of applause and cheers.

This isn't nostalgia talking. Ask anyone else who was rocked
there that afternoon.

Next morning, Leland peered at me across the desk through
eyes tinged with even more fatigue. He didn't waste time asking
whether my wife and I had enjoyed the show; he was already
grappling with the next phase of his problems. "The thing that
worries me is, if the show's so good without costumes and
scenery, can that stuff make it any better? Or will they weigh
it down?"

His fear was justified. *Gypsy* became an opulent, well-
dressed production, but it somehow never again re-achieved the
excitement, the raw energy of that Sunday afternoon performance. Steve Sondheim had the same feeling; a decade later, he
looked back on his show and said, "We were a hit, sure, and we
ran two years, but that was all."

All, that is, until the summer of 1973, when a revival of
Gypsy opened in London, with Angela Lansbury in the lead.
When she came out at the end of the second act to do "Rose's
Turn," suddenly, miraculously, the old electrical charges were
flickering. When she finished, the normally staid British audience
stood up and cheered. It was run-through time again.

The business affairs department at CBS had been instructed
to arrive at a weekly fee to cover my services as writer/consultant/
sounding board/telephone pal/luncheon companion, and that
largess enabled me to write my first novel. But somebody at CBS
decided that there had better be established a set of fees to cover
my services in the remote event that any of the Hayward projects
might be sold to a sponsor who had sufficient nerve and money to
put it on the tube.

My agent and I sat across the desk from a relatively sane
and sober CBS lawyer named Tom Ryan. We agreed on a price
for my services on a half-hour weekly show. How about for an

hour? We struck a bargain. "Ninety minutes?" asked Ryan. The price went up substantially, to five figures. What did it matter? This was all hypothetical . . . none of this would ever come to pass. Ryan puffed on his pipe, made notes, and then looked up and asked, "Suppose the show runs *two* hours?"

What an impossible dream! We snickered. He persisted. He wanted CBS protected in the event of such a contingency. But such a probability was fantastic. Who would have the capital, much less the energy, to mount a hundred-and-twenty-minute TV special?

Finally, we arrived at a fantasy figure, to cover my fantasy services, in the event of such a fantastic happening . . .

Two or three months passed. I journeyed back and forth from an office at 485 Madison, up to Hayward's, waiting for some tangible reaction to one—or any—of the television projects we'd prepared.

Across the hall, a group of comedy writers met each day with Nat Hiken and Billy Friedberg; their job was to furnish scripts for Phil Silvers, who was playing the hugely successful character of Sergeant Bilko. One of the Hiken-Friedberg crew, a quiet young man, discovered that I was privy to Hayward's uptown inner sanctum. Apologetically, he requested a boon. He'd written a stage comedy. Two other producers had optioned it, but with no success. Now his agent had submitted it to Hayward; weeks had passed, with no response. Could I possibly check and see what had happened?

Leland rarely read playscripts. As a successful producer, he was inundated with new ones; he had readers on whom he relied. Sometimes he might scan one himself, but unless you backed him into a chair, thrust the play in his hand, and stood over him while he read it, the chances of his opening up a manuscript and concentrating on it were dim.

The next time I was in Hayward's office, I leafed through the piles of scripts on his desk. Far down below, I found *One Shoe Off*, by my friend. I slid it out, and placed it on top of the pile. Perhaps there, with it staring him in the face, he might pick it up.

I went back downtown and assured the novice playwright that Hayward would do so.

But when I checked the pile, a few days later, his script had been smothered by a fresh batch of submissions. Grimly, I slid it out and replaced it on top.

No use. Within days, it had been shoved to one side and buried again. We played this game several more times, without success. "It's not easy," I told the writer.

"How come it's easier to write a comedy than it is to sell it?" he sighed, and went back to constructing adventures for Bilko.

I made one last try on his behalf. I put his script into Hayward's briefcase, in hopes that when he went home for the weekend, he'd have to read the damn play.

It came back the following week, amid a sheaf of magazines and airline timetables.

Sadly, I had to report failure. But my friend wasn't dismayed—in fact, he had great news! Two producers, Mike Ellis and Bill Hammerstein, had read his play and offered him a summer tryout at Bucks County Playhouse. Next time I was uptown, would I pick up his script from Hayward's desk and bring it back to him—he needed all his copies now. "I wish *he'd* read it," he said, wistfully.

"Let him come and see it, instead," I said, and went back uptown, found the script, and returned it to my friend. When it opened at Bucks County that summer, it was retitled *Come Blow Your Horn,* and it was successful enough there to be brought to Broadway. From that point on, my friend Neil Simon was to write no more adventures for Sergeant Bilko . . .

Without warning, one of our paper tigers emerged from hibernation, rejuvenated, now even more awesome. "The hell with doing a show about one single year!" Hayward called, on the phone from somewhere. "We've got some guys at one of the agencies interested in doing the thing as a review of the whole damned decade—"

Which decade?

"*This* one!" Leland said. "The '50s. Get down here and let's start revising the outline—we're going to make a pitch next week!"

The scene in the conference room at Young & Rubicam might have been titled "Daniel in the Lion's Den (Revisited)."

On one side of the long table sat several sober agency executives, flanking half a dozen or so sober gents in dark blue suits—potential sponsors, the General Electric Company, Major Appliance Division. Across from this phalanx, thoroughly outnumbered, flying solo, was Leland, with two men for his ground crew. Myself, and a program executive from CBS, Dick Lewine.

In front of Leland were a few file cards, on which I had typed brief notes to remind him of the substance of this proposed TV special. All of the elements—ballets, guest stars, musical numbers, scenes from great plays—would be presented with the careful proviso "we would *like* to have . . ." That was to keep us legally off the hook, lest any of these normally sane businessmen might lose his cool and buy this behemoth.

Hayward stod up and cleared his throat. "I'm glad you guys came here today," he said, "because it finally gives me the chance to tell somebody about the goddamndest television show anyone ever had the nerve to suggest. It's probably impossible to do, but if we ever did do it, I have the feeling it'll probably be maybe the best damn show ever produced . . ."

He had them all hooked with that opening paragraph.

It was a lovely mixture of the best of his pal Jimmy Stewart's shit-kicking awkwardness, combined with the affable enthusiasm of a Spencer Tracy, all intermingled with the down-home gosh-we're-all-folks-here manner of his other good friend, Hank Fonda. And you can be certain that their names were to be casually dropped in the ensuing forty minutes or so, while Leland ran down the description of the bill of goods we'd prepared . . . a super-salesman, maître d' of entertainment, cheerfully describing his ninety-minute super-feast.

When he'd finished, he glanced at his watch and casually murmured something about having to get uptown for a meeting with Mary Martin, Dick Rodgers, and Oscar Hammerstein . . . Then he shook hands all around, and walked out of the room, leaving behind a stunned group to caucus.

"You think they bought it?" he asked, as we walked towards the elevators.

"They *liked* it," I said. "But buying?" Buying meant conferences. He'd offered them a production that would involve well past half a million dollars. No corporation hands that sort of money out from the treasury without a certain amount of deliberation . . .

One of the agency men came running out to the lobby, waving his hand frantically, to stop our progress. He wanted Dick Lewine to step back inside. For clarification? "No!" he panted. "They want to *buy* the show—they want a definite price, and somebody's got to give them one!"

Leland patted Lewine on the shoulder. "Well, Dick," he said softly, a broad grin on his lean face, "I guess we're stuck with doing the goddamned thing, eh?"

We got into the elevator, leaving Lewine to wrestle with the cost problem.

"I don't believe they're really going to buy it," I said, stunned.

"Oh, I do," said Leland, carelessly. "They adored it."

The production of "The Fabulous Fifties"—which is what our great white whale was to become—involved a solid year's work. The show concerned itself with history, with politics, with life and birth and death and accomplishment—all our yesterdays of the past ten years. The brilliant renaissance-man designer, Charles Eames, came in from California to cope with visual design and graphic sequences. Jay Blackton, the conductor, spent hours in a sound cutting room, putting together a musical montage of the song hits of the past decade, while Marshall Jamison, who'd been appointed to be the producer, struggled with me daily to bring some semblance of order out of the drama, comedy, and prose sequences we'd derived from the monster pile of source material. All of it had to be digested, dramatized, compressed . . . and there was always more coming at us.

"More entertainment hunks!" commanded Leland, and proceeded to engage such hitherto TV-holdouts as Rex Harrison and

Julie Andrews, in a recital of songs from *My Fair Lady*. They went cheek by jowl with a condensed version of Anne Morrow Lindbergh's book *Gift from the Sea*, snatches of brilliant comedy by Mike Nichols and Elaine May, interwoven with Bob Smith's *Where Did You Go? Out. What Did You Do? Nothing.* If Jackie Gleason agreed to re-create a number from his current hit show *Take Me Along*, it would have to follow a moment of reality, perhaps film of the ascent of Mount Everest by Sir Edmund Hillary, and if young Dick Van Dyke was to do a brilliantly choreographed number about man's growing inability to cope with a computerized society, then we had to find another way to dramatize a batch of statistics by having them commented upon by Betty Comden and Adolph Green . . .

"How the hell do we *find* Sir Edmund Hillary?" Leland barked at Malley one morning. Half an hour later, she returned and announced that the gentleman was at that moment in New Zealand. How she had managed to come up with that information with such dispatch will always be her own secret, but when Hayward demanded to know his telephone number down there, she had to shrug and admit defeat. "Who the hell do we know who's around New Zealand?" Hayward mused, as if that far-off land were no less accessible than Asbury Park.

A lucky flash of memory provided me with a possible solution. One of our mutual friends, the theatrical director John Fearnley, had embarked on a cruise of the South Seas a few weeks before. "Find out what ship he's on and send him a cable," Hayward instructed. "He can do a recording of Hillary right there and mail it to us!"

Malley shortly returned with the name of Fearnley's ship, a list of its ports of call, plus times of arrival and departure. The cable went off forthwith.

"I can remember it to this day," says Fearnley. "I was out on deck, enjoying a cruise, thousands of miles away from New York, and the steward handed me a cable. In it, Leland asked for a favor, told me Sir Edmund Hillary's home address, and requested that I go see him when we docked and make a tape recording, and then it gave the text of what he wanted him to say . . . and he'd pay all the expenses. It was signed, 'Love,

Leland.' He didn't bother to put on his last name. He just assumed I wouldn't know anyone else named Leland . . ."

Several weeks later, the tape arrived, from thousands of miles away, expertly recorded in a New Zealand radio studio, under Fearnley's direction.

"He did it!" we chortled, all of us impressed by the logistics that were involved in this feat.

"Of *course* he did," said Hayward, carelessly, as if he dealt regularly with crises in New Zealand. "What ever made you think he couldn't?"

So much writing was involved that eventually A. J. Russell joined the crew, to share some of the burden in concocting comedy sequences and narrative. Scenes kept being added, talk for Eric Sevareid and Henry Fonda, all sorts of segments that Hayward would think of overnight and bring into the office for exploration the next day. So cluttered were the desks with source material that it was difficult to find a place for our typewriters. The decade of the 1950s was turning out to be a Pandora's box of probables. No matter how we pruned and cut and sharpened, we were always timing out a show that could run for an entire evening on CBS.

Late one afternoon, Leland called us in. "I've been worried about the time thing," he said, cheerfully, as if no one else had considered the problem. "I've got it licked. GE has just agreed to buy another half hour of network time—so now we're doing a two-hour show, okay?"

An extra thirty minutes. Now we could use some of the film on jet travel, now we might be able to schedule that review of ten years' worth of TV, with film clips of "Kukla, Fran, and Ollie," and the immortal Fred Allen, and Jack Benny, and "Arthur Murray's Dance Party," and . . .

I spoke to my agent a day or so later, and casually mentioned that our show would now run for two hours. He snickered. What was so amusing? "I'm just thinking of the look on Tom Ryan's face when *he* gets the news," he remarked. "Thanks to him, you get a lot more money. Remember?"

I'd been too busy, after six months of slogging through Hayward's mammoth project, to remember anything as mundane as a contract. A year ago, the whole thing had seemed utterly improbable. A two-hour television show?

But now, nothing seemed out of reach.

Most of the program was taped and completed by December. We had an air date for the end of the month. Musical numbers, comedy scenes, news film, dramatic vignettes—Eames' superb visual tapestries; his documentary which we nicknamed "The Deads," in which a seemingly endless procession of the photos of the great people we'd lost in the previous decade all paraded quietly before us; the musical medleys; our film editor Beatrice Cunningham's cunning montages of news and entertainment clips . . . most of it was done, tape-edited and ready for viewing. That monster banquet which Hayward had so casually proposed to a roomful of GE executives all those months ago . . . somehow it was completed, save for a few live introductions, which we planned to do in the studio, on the actual night the show would be televised.

We came into the CBS studio on West Fifty-third Street, and began to run the whole thing down at our first dress rehearsal. On the monitors around the studio, the product of our year's work unreeled, interspersed with the live segments that involved Fonda and Sevareid.

Late that afternoon, I stood beside one of the TV cameras as we focused on the closing segment, in which various members of the cast discussed the future and prognasticated on what we could expect for the 1960s . . .

The cameraman turned to me. All afternoon, he'd been watching "The Fabulous Fifties," both live and taped. "Tell me," he asked, casually, "How does it feel to have written an Emmy-award show?"

I blinked at the question. What show was he referring to?

"*This* one," he said. "Don't you *know* how great it is?"

"No," I said, truthfully. "I guess I've been working so hard on the damn thing I've lost contact with it . . ."

It was the absolute truth; there was no humility involved. For a year or so, life had been a lunatic roller-coaster ride—meetings, interviews, consultations with Shelley Berman and Nichols and May, days spent deep in CBS cutting rooms with technicians and with Bea Cunningham, hours reviewing news film . . . conferences with Marshall Jamison, timing and re-timing of dialogue and scenes . . . Who could tell if the sum total would be any good at this point?

The CBS cameraman could.

And he was absolutely right. "The Fabulous Fifties" got a huge viewing audience, and it held that audience for the entire two hours. The reviews were full of high praise, and eventually the show was to run off with all the awards ever given for TV that year. It's even been shown at the Museum of Modern Art, as an example of the best of television of that era.

But television, even the best of it, has no permanence. A book sits on the shelf. A film is re-run, a play is revived. Even a newspaper can be stored away. Outside of "I Love Lucy" re-runs (which go on forever), television has all the permanence of cigar smoke . . .

I spoke to my agent late that spring. It had been a long, jobless period since "The Fabulous Fifties." Hayward was off and running on other projects, films, plays that took him out to California, or across to Europe. He'd done his blockbuster—now he needed even wider horizons and larger targets. And I was eminently employable. My phone had stopped ringing. No more calls from Templeton 8-5100, Hayward's office; no calls from other potential employers.

"I don't really know what it is," confessed my agent. "There's that old saying—you win an Academy Award and it's a sure passport to unemployment. Maybe you'll just have to wait until 1970 . . . when somebody does the *next* two-hour special about a decade."

It was to be nearly four years before I heard from Leland again.

The telephone rang in our rented London flat. New York calling; Miss Malley on the line. "Mr. Hayward wants to talk to you," she announced.

How had she found my number, from three thousand

miles away—when we weren't even properly listed in the London telephone directory.

She brushed aside that question. "You ought to know better," she said. "When he needs to get hold of you, I find you . . ."

"Hello, Beauty!" he sang out—as if we'd parted four or five hours previously on Madison Avenue, rather than years before. He was coming to England for a tryout of a new play, *The Film of Memory,* a book he'd long wished to do; it would star Vivien Leigh. But he had a project he wished to discuss with me—would I be able to give him some time in the next week? It was something absolutely marvelous, exactly the sort of thing I was perfect for, he'd fill me in when he saw me. And with that for a teaser, he hung up.

Several days later, another call. This time, he sounded less ebullient. "Down here in Newcastle-on-Tyne," he announced. "Godawful place. Lots of problems with the play. See you in London next week, right?"

Sunday morning, the phone rang again, and the energy level of his voice was low and fatigued. "Bombed out," he said. "Couldn't lick the damn thing. Well, you take your loss and get the hell out . . ."

Did he want me to come down and take a look at the play?

"Nothing to look at," he said. "Closed it last night. Call me the minute you get back to New York."

He was gone again.

A year later, I arrived back in New York and rang his office. "Where the hell have you been?" he demanded. "I've been waiting for you!"

About that project he wished to discuss last year—

"No, no," said Leland. "I don't even remember what the hell it was. But I've got something else damned exciting going on—how soon can you get up here?"

The next day, we were off and very much running again, on some new television project that involved his old favorite topic, the war between men and women. Now it would be Gloria Steinem and perhaps Jackie Gleason—the cast was updated, but the subject was still valid . . .

Leland seemed a little older now, a bit greyer, somewhat

stooped, less forthright, but with undiminished curiosity and energy. He'd moved to a new home in Yorktown Heights, where flowers bloomed, and where he could prowl his garden on weekends with a Hasselblad, snapping color pictures of the most interesting blooms. Those he fancied he had framed giant-sized, and they hung on his office walls, amid signed photos of old friends. Irving Berlin, next to begonias. Above a spray of vivid roses, Howard Lindsay and Russel Crouse. Mary Martin, next to a flowering cactus; Dick Rodgers and Oscar Hammerstein surrounded by lilacs.

Luncheons were longer, and were at a different place, across the street at the Carlton, where he had a regular table. No more Wild Turkey—he'd had serious intestinal problems, and he was allowed to sip nothing more stimulating than some Coca-Cola, or a bottle of Poland water, "Yeah," he sighed, one noon, "it's a long way from the days when I used to go out on the town with my buddies . . . Gene Fowler and Ben and Charlie . . . Did I ever tell you how old Gene got himself to New York? He worked in Denver, on a newspaper, but he didn't have the price of a railroad ticket. One day, an undertaker asked him if he'd be willing to accompany a coffin to New York. Some poor guy, probably a TB case, who'd died in Denver . . . Fowler figured that was a fine idea. Picked up the ticket, rode east for five days with the coffin, delivered it, and here he was, ready to get a job in the big city. My God, we had good times in those days . . . perpetually in speakeasies . . . But don't knock it, that's how I got my first client—by hanging around night clubs . . ."

Which first client? There had been so many names on the Hayward roster.

"Why, old Fred Astaire, of course," Leland said. "I went into a place called the Trocadero, and the owner came over and started crying on my shoulder about how lousy business was. Some new joint had opened down the street and was taking all the play away from him. What the hell, they were all cutthroats and thieves then—most of them were gangsters. Anyway, this mug said to me he needed an attraction, to get the crowd back in. 'What kind of an attraction?' I asked. 'Well, somebody like those Astaires,' he said. Fred and Adele, his sister, were big stars already, dancing in *Lady Be Good*. I didn't know them—they'd never heard of me—but I was young and I had the guts of a burglar, so I asked this guy how much he'd pay for them, and he told me a figure, and I said I'd get them for him. Went around to the theatre, got backstage, got in to see Fred, and made them an offer. I think it was about four thousand a week. They didn't know who I was, but they sure knew what four thousand a week was—and they took it. That's how I got Fred as a client . . ."

Had he stayed on as an agent thereafter?

"Hell, no," admitted Leland. "I had this crazy notion, even then, that I ought to be a producer—not the theatre, but movies. They looked like a great soft touch, so I went around and got my job with United Artists, and eventually I became pals with a very bright guy, Sidney Kent—helluva nice guy; he ended up running Fox, but at the time he was at First National. He was making some pictures here in New York—he put me in charge of one of them. You know who was the director? Frank Capra . . . *Capra*, for God's sake. Here I was, not even out of my twenties yet, and Kent went back to Hollywood and left me to get this thing made. I don't think Capra knew much more than I did at the time . . ." Leland snorted with laughter. "End of the first week's shooting, I paid everyone their salaries. We kept on going; second week I paid everybody off, and then I was out of money. I called Kent out on the Coast and asked for next week's dough. He said he'd get it to me in a while—they were having some financial trouble at the studio. I kept calling—I said, 'How the hell do you expect me to keep them working without any money?' You know what his answer was? 'That's why I left you in charge,' he said. 'You're a bright guy—you'll think of something!'"

"Oh Lord," Leland sighed. "When I think of the lying I did, the stories I had to make up, and the finagling I had to do to keep all those people working for the next three weeks. I'd get maybe half what I needed from the Coast, and I had to spread it around so everybody would be at least eating and sleeping . . . Because I damn well couldn't afford to have anybody quit on me—hell, I had no money to hire a replacement!"

He nibbled at his scrambled eggs, then shook his head.

"All that conniving . . . for what? The picture had to be one of the worst dogs ever made—*For the Love of Mike*. A disaster. Which is why I went back to being an agent. I let the other guys make the production mistakes. I sat back and sold them the best talent around—at the highest price I could gouge out of them. Hell, during the war I found Gregory Peck in a Broadway play—he was young and good-looking and he could act. I got on the phone and started calling producers on the Coast. They needed leading men so badly, by the time I finished I had Greg booked for half a dozen pictures—and he'd never even been in front of a camera! I had them all fighting over him as if he was gold . . . which he turned out to be, thank God . . ."

Many times, I brought up the prospect of Leland setting down his memoirs. That rough-and-tumble era of Hollywood's early days; his would be a definitive chronicle.

"Nah," he said. "Too many of those people are still alive . . . and if I told the truth, a lot of feelings would be hurt . . ."

Perhaps those Hollywood rough-and-tumble specialists with whom Leland had carried on a love/hate affair over the years, Sam and J. L. and L. B. et al., were still around, but too many of his own old reliables were going.

Herman Bernstein had died . . . For a man as meticulous with other men's money as Herman had always been, his death was to reveal him as a Broadway Dr. Hyde with his own dollars. Vast amounts of his accumulated earnings were nowhere to be found, not in banks, nor in safe-deposit boxes . . . Over the years, Herman had quietly loaned his cash to less fortunate friends, out-of-work actors, producers going through dry-hole seasons. But he'd never kept records, not even the customary terse "marker" that would prove the obligation to his executors. So much of Herman's assets had been passed out to anonymous debtors that, at his funeral, Howard Lindsay prefaced his eulogy with the remarkable request . . . would all those who owed money to our late friend Herman please to take it as an obligation to his family that they come forward and identify themselves?

It was a Broadway fable for a Damon Runyon.

Gone was Harry Kurnitz, one of Leland's most witty pals,

who had done the successful adaptation of the French comedy
that was called *A Shot in the Dark.* "You know, when Harry was
a kid, he was awfully poor," mused Hayward. "Lived down on the
Bowery, and, my God, how he struggled. He told me the most
he could ever afford for a real binge was to go buy a ten-cent pack
of cigarettes, and for a few cents at the corner druggist you could
get tincture of cannabis—that's marijuana. Harry would pour the
stuff on the cigarettes, let them dry, and sit at home and smoke
and get mildly high . . . So maybe that explains why he liked to
spend money—after he got it . . ."

Hemingway . . . Gene Fowler, Charlie MacArthur, Ben
Hecht . . . vanished—so many of the circle of client-cronies.
"Look at that goddamn *Front Page*," he remarked, after the
Hecht-MacArthur comedy had been successfully revived. "See
how well they put it together—it's like a Swiss watch. Everything
works. You come out of that show, and you wonder how anybody
can sit through this aimless drivel that passes for playwriting
today . . ."

It was not only contemporary writing—or the lack of it—that
bothered Leland. Avante-garde "plays" such as *The Beard*, with
its vacuous, ugly duologue between a "Jean Harlow" and a "Billy
the Kid," offended his sense of good taste, certainly. But what
disturbed him much more deeply were the rising tremors of
anarchy that were coming from the SDS generation. That nightmare scene of the late 1960s—the one which caused so many of
us to toss fitfully in our sleep after the 11 P.M. news—filled him
with as much dread. Perhaps more. "After all, I remember the
goddamn Depression, when they marched on Washington—and
those guys were desperate, believe me . . ." All the old structures,
the truths and rules by which we lived—the whole system (good,
not-so-good, awful, but at least it was a *system*) was threatened
by an oncoming generation of unwashed, uncombed, unshaven,
but well-fed revolutionaries. "Sure, things are lousy," Hayward
would complain, ticking off forbidding statistics that ranged from
the incidence of venereal disease among the under twenties, the
breakdown of marriage, the diminishing buying power of the
dollar, and whatever else he'd gleaned lately, "but I sure don't
see what the hell is so great about bombs. Maybe I am a re-

actionary," he would concede, "but these half-assed kids are just running around like actors without any script. Look, if you run into a problem with a show, you work your ass off to fix it, or rewrite, or go find somebody else who can give you fresh ideas. But I'll be goddamned if I ever agree that you improve a sick show by setting fire to your theatre."

Later on, when his own son became involved in the production of *Easy Rider*, Leland's reaction to his first viewing of the film was ambivalent. Parental pride in Bill's considerable contribution, along with that of Peter Fonda and Dennis Hopper, was mingled with Leland's own distaste for the sense of values mirrored on the screen. "Isn't it crazy?" he asked. "Can you imagine a movie in which you bleed when the two guys get blasted at the end—and they've been out seeing America with money that they made by pushing dope?"

But his business acumen, his ingrained sense of what would sell, also helped him recognize *Easy Rider* as an incipient box-office success. "Picture's going to make a helluva lot of money," he mused. "Of course, everybody over forty is going to loathe it, but it's not made for old farts like us. It's the kids—and they're the audience now. I saw the picture with a bunch of old-timers, and to a man they hated the thing. So does Columbia—and *they're* going to *release* it! They don't really know why it's good, you know," he confided. "Those guys wouldn't know a good picture if it leaped up and bit them in the nose. I was out in Palm Springs one night last month, and after dinner Leo Jaffe"—he was then the head of Columbia—"came over and said, 'You know, we're a little peeved at Dick Brooks over *The Professionals*.' I asked him what he was sore about—how could you get mad with a guy who's given your company such a big box-office winner? 'Well,' Jaffe complained, 'Dick never told us it was going to be so good . . .'" Leland snorted with disdain. "I'll tell you one thing about old Harry Cohn. He may have been a bastard and a bully, and a tough man to deal with, but nobody ever had to tell Harry when one of his pictures was going to be good. He *knew* . . . before anybody else—and he went out and fought for better terms for it, up front!"

When the box-office returns of *Easy Rider* began to mount steadily into seven-figure piles of profit—depleted in purchasing-power dollars, but nonetheless negotiable—the success was an ironic footnote to Hayward *père's* last two film projects. Years back, he'd made *Mr. Roberts* for Warners, and it had been a hit, true, but when he subsequently originated two of his own, the results were unpleasant. The movie of his old friend Ernest Hemingway's *The Old Man and the Sea* had floundered and sunk, and his film biography of another of his early idols, Charles Lindbergh, *The Spirit of St. Louis*, which starred another firm friend, Jimmy Stewart, had crashed after takeoff, not in the Atlantic, but in a sea of red ink.

Lately, there seemingly weren't any new scripts around that sparked his creative interest. Fewer and fewer projects came into 655 Madison that would send him to the telephone, to start wooing directors to come back to the theatre, to track down nomadic stars for a marquee. As for television, it had become a much less challenging medium. What sort of excitement could be derived in adapting old stage successes into ninety-minute shows—or in concocting variations on the law-and-order theme? And as for a repeat of his review of the '50s . . . well, that wouldn't happen for another two or three years . . .

Suddenly, however, an idea soared into view. The firehouse bell began to ring, and the Pavlovian excitement it induced in Leland was a replay of the earlier, swashbuckling times. What mammoth vision had floated seductively into the penthouse, to start his creative juices flowing? It would have to be more impressive in size and scope than anything even he had ever tackled, or proposed—and it certainly was that. It was nothing less than the oncoming celebration due in 1976—the two hundredth anniversary of the founding of the Republic.

The scheme of such a project—one that encompassed the entire history of the United States—satisfied Leland's desire for the ultimate, filled him with anticipatory glee. Over the Carlton luncheon table, throwing out notions, he might have been Michelangelo, licking his lips at the sight of the bare ceiling of

HAYWARD with his long-time chum, General James Stewart, on the set of the film version of the late Charles A. Lindbergh's life, *The Spirit of St. Louis.*

the Sistine Chapel. Daily, his vast edifice expanded, without the
slightest regard as to cost or logistics. If the show was to be done
at all, it certainly could not be simply one two-hour presentation.
"Hell, you couldn't possibly do it justice that way," he burbled,
happily. "What we've got to do is to build a *series* of annual
yearly celebrations—once a year for every year, until 1976—and
then, for a climax, we wrap the whole thing up into one big
blockbuster! Nine years of American history . . . with a terrific
finish!"

Such a series would have to be the biggest and the most free-
ranging television entertainment ever contemplated. Actors, performers, any and all creative talents, politicians, statesmen—none
would dare say nay to participation. "None of the networks would
have enough guts to try it," he predicted, correctly.

But one sponsor was sufficiently interested to invest a sizable
sum in preliminary research—Hayward's earliest TV client, the
Ford Motor Company, for whom he had created the historic
"Ford 50th Anniversary Show" long years ago. Hayward was
commissioned to develop a detailed prospectus for Henry Ford's
personal judgment.

And he was off and running again, surrounded by a few
old hands. Marshall Jamison was soon back at his old desk,
struggling with the piles of research material, the stacks of books
and plays that crowded the office suite. Nearby, Malley spent
hours establishing preliminary contact with potential partici-
pants . . . Frank Sinatra. "Let's see, he could do a batch of early
American folk songs right down to today, maybe, with Joan
Baez, or Bob Dylan . . . with Lennie Bernstein doing the musical
accompaniment . . ." Katharine Hepburn and Jimmy Stewart.
"A couple of scenes from great American plays, O'Neill, and, of
course, Maxwell Anderson's *Valley Forge*." Charles Eames, out
in California. "He has to handle all the visual stuff—absolutely
nobody can do graphics better than Charles." Jerry Robbins.
"He'll choreograph us an original series of ballets that will do
the history of show business the way nobody's ever done it
before."

Each morning, he would arrive at his office with some new

thought, an idea, or a fact that he'd encountered the night before. "Did you know that Audubon was the first guy who ever banded birds for scientific research, in 1803? Now what the hell do you think we should make out of that?" Perhaps he'd heard something on the news that had started his conscience ticking over. "What are we going to do about the Indians? We can't just show some old battle out of a Western—that doesn't do it. What will make an impact—that nobody's done before?"

Like Egyptians piling endless stacks, we gradually assembled a mammoth prose pyramid—a huge structure that we offered as the living record of two centuries of American accomplishment. It would be orchestrated by great American composers, footnoted by our best writers, commented upon by the humor of Will Rogers, and Thurber, Benchley, and E. B. White, illustrated by Wyeth and Hopper and Frederic Remington, Jackson Pollock, and Maxfield Parrish. It would touch on war and explorers, railroads and airplanes and Dr. Jonas Salk, Mississippi River boatmen and Babe Ruth, John D. Rockefeller and Edna St. Vincent Millay, Al Jolson and Arthur Miller and . . .

When it was all down, at last, on paper, forty-odd pages of it, neatly typed, a prospectus so far-ranging that it boggled the mind of the beholder, Leland was satisfied. But it was not feasible to hand it over to a potential reader; that wouldn't do it justice. The whole thing was taken into a studio, where professional actors read it aloud, music was added . . . and the monster began to twitch, and show signs of life.

Three representatives of the advertising agency came up to the office one fine afternoon, and sat down and listened, while one of Leland's tape recorders recited the hour-long proposal.

When the final climactic peak had been attained, Leland glanced at his listeners. "Well?" he inquired, cheerfully. "How'd you like our little show?"

"There's a lot there," sighed one of the men, choosing his words with great care.

"Yeah, I know," said Leland. "But it's a big subject. We're going to need every bit of those nine years' worth of time."

"That's for sure," said the second executive, fervently.

"It's a sonofabitch, though, isn't it?" asked Leland, with a measure of pride.

The three men nodded.

"What we'd better do is to arrange a conference out in Dearborn," said the ranking member of the delegation. "It's going to be up to them to decide." If you've been around adevrtising agency men long enough, you learn how to read between their equivocations, and to plumb their definite maybes.

They departed.

"Do you think they bought it?" someone asked.

Leland knew. "They're scared stiff of it," he said, a bit ruefully.

His analysis of his client was intuitive . . . and correct. For whatever reasons that would be forthcoming—and no longer would the corporate decision be taken by one impulsive executive, not when such huge sums were involved—the Dearborn brass regretfully passed. They were impressed—but not nine years' worth.

Perhaps Leland was relieved. He was far from a well man now. What could he have done if his old friend Henry Ford had said yes? . . . Neither he nor the Ford Motor Company was in any position to make such a long-term commitment.

No, his last hurrah would not be so elephantine in scope. But when it came to pass, his finale would have, in an ironic way, more impact.

I was in California in the late spring of 1970, working on a television show, when a friend called to inquire if I'd enjoy escorting her to the theatre, to see the opening of a new play called *The Trial of the Catonsville Nine*. What was the play about? She was somewhat vague; all she knew was that it dealt with recent American history . . . something about a protest against the war in Vietnam.

We went downtown to the Mark Taper Forum, parked, and

went upstairs to the theatre. There, standing in front of the box office, was Leland.

A bit greyer, but erect, surveying the arrivals with the roving eye of the watchful showman. Three thousand miles away from his comfortable country home, as I was from mine. What was he doing *here?*

"Come to see the play," he said. "What else?"

"Why this one?" I asked, still perplexed.

"Because I *own* it," he said, somewhat testily. "If you'd come around to the office a little more lately, you'd've known that."

We filed into the new theatre and sat down together. The first performance of this new work began, prefaced by a tape-recorded speech by Father Daniel Berrigan, his disembodied voice welcoming the audience in the soft darkness, and explaining that he was not present because he was a fugitive from justice. "For you, our friends and hearers and audience and jury," he said, "we pray a light boon and favor from *The Trial of the Catonsville Nine*—the purging from your hearts also of the inhabiting demons of pity and fear . . ."

If I had been expecting the usual glittering Leland Hayward entertainment, something, say, of the nature of a deft Norman Krasna comedy, *Kind Sir*, or a *Who Was That Lady?* . . . had I assumed this would be another lighthearted Lindsay and Crouse political satire, *The State of the Union* . . . the recorded voice of Father Berrigan brushed away that promise. What followed on the Mark Taper arena stage was stark, vital . . . immediate. A trial of nine individual consciences, with the audience as witness, as jury to their testimony . . . eventually, a tortured self-examination for all of us.

During the intermission, nobody said much. Gordon Davidson, the director, broke some of the tension by jocularly pointing out two FBI men who had been assigned to cover this opening night, in anticipation of Berrigan's possible appearance. "Look," he said, grinning as he pointed out two men hanging on the edge of the lobby crowd. "They've adopted a certain amount of what

they think is a good disguise for this audience—they're wearing
turtleneck sweaters!"

The second act was lengthy and diffuse, and yet the power
of the work was all too obvious. When the trial had ended, and
a newsreel clip flashed on the screen which showed the actual
Catonsville Nine—not the actors—in the specific act of burning
draft-board files as a protest against injustice, we stood up and
filed out, in thoughtful silence.

All evening, the paradox of Leland's association with such a
production had perplexed me. *The Trial of the Catonsville Nine*
was light-years away from the sort of entertainment he'd spent
his life sponsoring. How did one equate his espousal of the passionate, dedicated cause of the Berrigans, et al., against the op-
pressive authority and injustice of an implacable government of
man, not God, with his earlier audience-pleasers—Mary Martin
and Ezio Pinza crooning "Some Enchanted Evening," or his old
friend Hank Fonda limning Mr. Roberts, and that jolly naval
crew? Political—certainly he'd handled the current scene before—
but only to the shallow depths of the TV version of "That Was
the Week That Was," for NBC. This staged trial of Berrigan's
friends was a serious, gut-wrenching evening of encounter. Was
Leland seriously contemplating bringing it east? It was heavy
stuff for the fantasy world of Broadway. If, in the past, he had
always been a pragmatist showman, aligning himself with attractions that could be counted on to sell the maximum number of
ten-dollar tickets, he certainly didn't have one in *The Catonsville
Nine*. And as for the substance of the play, plenty of Americans
in 1970—and he himself, not so long ago—would be quick to
react angrily to those draft-file burners . . . *subversive law-breakers
—let 'em go to jail where they belong!*

The following day, he would be on his way back to New
York, but he insisted that I call him, for one of our usual brain-
picking sessions. He wanted a firsthand reaction.

"Well," I said, still bemused. "It certainly isn't *The Sound
of Music*, is it?"

He laughed at my sardonic comment, but he was impatient

for an answer. What about New York—would the show go there?

It was too long, too wordy, but the acting was fine, the direction equally good, and the subject material strong as a rock. Yes, I wanted it to have a chance . . . but perhaps not in the fiercely competitive canyons of Forty-fifth Street. Why not off-Broadway?

"Yeah, yeah. Well, I'll talk to you when you get back," he said, and went off the line to take another call . . . leaving me in California with a question of my own, still unanswered— Why do *you* want to produce it?

His strength wasn't what it needed to be. His speech was slower and more thoughtful. Walking down the crowded Madison Avenue sidewalk, one was conscious that he was only a quiet shadow of the old jaunty, bareheaded Leland. But remarkably determined. He'd decided to get Father Berrigan's play on this season of 1970–71, and he wasn't about to give up on that promise. Throughout the summer and fall, after Berrigan had been arrested by the FBI and sentenced to a term at Danbury Federal Penitentiary, Leland would go to visit his author as often as the authorities permitted. "It's the first time I've ever discussed rewrites and changes in a prison waiting room," he said, with a grin. "But the guy is marvelous. I really like spending time with him . . ."

No matter how taken Leland was with Berrigan, and with the justice of the man's cause, he was a realist about the production. Raising money for it in this lean season would prove to be a frustrating crusade. Not only were his heretofore eager backers shying away from this altruistic venture, but the process of finding others, of beating the woods for replacements, was obviously for a younger, more energetic manager.

No one needed to remind Leland of the old rule—100 percent of nothing is never as valuable as 50 percent of something. Somehow, this damned play had to be produced. Why? Finally he told me. "Because this guy is saying something people have to listen to. This goddamned war in Vietnam is wrong, and the only way we can call it off is to get people upset about it . . .

What the hell good is the theatre if we can't use it to make them *know?*"

But wasn't it his own good friend, Sam Goldwyn, who had once said, "I don't do stuff with messages. If I want to send a message, I call Western Union"?

"Never mind what Sam said," Leland snapped. "That's ancient history. I want to get this play on. This is *our* history."

Finally, he found his modus operandi, one which definitely guaranteed the production. T. Edward Hambleton, the modest, self-effacing gentleman behind the Phoenix Repertory Theatre company, had also seen Berrigan's play, and was equally impressed with its statement. With Flora Roberts, Berrigan's literary agent, as broker, Hayward and Hambleton made a marriage of much convenience. Under their joint auspices, *The Trial of the Catonsville Nine* opened that winter, not at a forbidding Broadway theatre on the cold sidewalks of midtown, but up in the most remarkable surroundings of the Good Shepherd–Faith Church, on West Sixty-sixth Street.

Actually, though—what could have been a more appropriate setting?

The critics were impressed, the notices were good. Leland relaxed behind his desk at 655 Madison, and permitted himself the luxury of one small quip. "I send the notices up to Danbury to Father Berrigan, and he's very pleased," se said. "Of course, if he didn't like the way we did his show, he's not going to be able to get down here and call for rewrites, not for a while . . . is he?"

For nearly thirty years, he'd been producing. And if his last was not his most financially successful venture, it didn't seem to matter a damn. The show was running. Nothing else mattered.

One afternoon in January, I dropped by Leland's office for a brief chat. The desk was piled high with scripts and the usual books and magazines, but Leland was not behind it. He was lounging on the office sofa, his feet, as always, unshod, shoes kicked off. What was new?

I mentioned that the latest Broadway news had to do with the revival of *No, No, Nanette*, which had just opened up in Boston. Nothing much had been expected of it, but within moments of the opening number, a brand-new hit had been launched. "Sure, sure, I heard," he said, impatiently. "Going to be a smash. What else?"

We gossiped on, discussing various aspects of this remarkable thirty-year-old musical's rebirth, and then I mentioned something about the creative crew which had originally written it. Had anybody paid attention to the fact that Irving Caesar, the lyricist, with Otto Harbach, of all those wonderful Youmans songs, "Tea for Two," "I Want to Be Happy," et cetera, was still over in his Brill Building office, very much alive and kicking— and the voluble repository of reams of vivid recollections of the show's original production, back in 1923?

"What the hell would you want to do about him?" Leland asked.

"Just what I'm always nagging at *you* to do," I told him. "I'd sit with Caesar and ask him to talk into a tape recorder, so we'd have the history down, somewhere . . ."

"I'll bet that would make a helluva magazine article," Hayward mused. "Maybe you could sell it to somebody like Clay Felker, down at *New York* magazine."

"I don't know the guy," I told him.

"I do," he said. "Malley?" he called.

She emerged from her office and stood waiting. "Get me Clay Felker," said Leland. "Tell him it's goddamn important."

A few moments later, the desk phone buzzed; Clay Felker was on the line. Leland chatted with him for a few moments, and then explained an idea for a possible article on Caesar. Felker commissioned me to write it forthwith. His only proviso was that it be in hand before the show opened in New York.

I hung up, and turned to find Leland beaming, a crew-cut Cheshire cat. "Now you'd better get the hell out of here and go see Irving and get him talking," he said.

I shook my head in admiration. "That," I said, "was the fastest deal I ever saw anybody make. I only wish I'd been born twenty years earlier, so I could have had you for an agent . . ."

Leland grinned up at Miss Malley, who stood by, patiently awaiting his next instructions. "I guess I *was* a pretty good agent in my time, wasn't I, Malley?" he said, softly.

Miss Malley allowed herself a brief smile. "Yes, Mr. Hayward, you were," and she went back to her post outside.

"You were the best, Leland," I said, "and you damn well know it."

"Right," said Leland. "Get the hell out of here and go write that article."

In time, the piece on Irving Caesar was on its way down to Clay Felker. When it finally appeared, in late February, it was titled "The Caesarian Birth of Nanette." I forwarded the first copy to Leland.

Leland may have read it, but one cannot be certain. The advance copy sat on the bedside table of his hospital room. Shortly afterwards, he died.

Some new tenant sits in that penthouse now, performing some routine 9:30–5 mercantile job. All of Hayward's personal possessions are long gone; his phones, finally mute, are back with Ma Bell. Dispersed are the tape recorders on which he might have set down more of the history he'd made for all the years he functioned.

What remains is that pile of cartons and files, in the library, waiting for the librarians and Ph.D. candidates to collate and index the man into his proper historical perspective.

Leland would probably be bored stiff by his new academic status. Once he had made today's history, it was instantly stale. Old news.

He adored tomorrow . . .

And these pages? Perhaps they also belong in those cartons, for the edification of that future Ph.D. candidate.

Sorry, friend. They're only an outline of the book that Leland might have talked.

But then, the two of us seemed to specialize in outlines . . .

Index

Abbott, George, 86
Abdul, 42, 44
Adoree, Renee, 9
Air Force, 112
Allen, Fred, 30, 265
Allen, Gracie, 30
All in Fun, 162–63
Anderson, Alan, 105, 114
Anderson, Maxwell, 86
Andrews, Julie, 264
Anhalt, Edward, 138, 146, 148
Anne of a Thousand Days, 242
Arbuckle, Fatty, 224
Arlen, Harold, 26
Arnold, H. H., 99, 137, 138, 148, 149, 150
Astaire, Adele, 269–70
Astaire, Fred, 237, 269–70
Atkinson, Brooks, 98
Axelrod, George, 163–75 *passim*, 190, 221

Bacall, Lauren, 185, 189, 190, 192, 256
Baker, Phil, 162, 163
Baker, "Snowy," 38
Banjo Eyes, 95
Bankhead, Tallulah, 175–81 *passim*, 183
Bardot, Brigitte, 256
Barry, Philip, 142
Baxter, Warner, 60
Beard, The, 272
Behrman, S. N., 85
Bell for Adano, A, 237, 242
Bennett, Richard, 86, 162
Benny, Jack, 30, 213, 265
Berg, Gertrude, 175
Bergman, Ingrid, 130, 237, 243
Berkeley, Busby, 60, 61, 128
Berle, Milton, 228–31
Berlin, Irving, 88, 94–95, 96, 104, 116, 130–31, 133, 160, 269
Berman, Shelley, 266
Bernie, Dick, 126, 128
Bernstein, Herman, 251–52, 253, 256, 271
Berrigan, Daniel, 279, 280, 281, 282
Big Sleep, The, 74
Binyon, Claude, 116
Black Mask, 63, 66–76 *passim*
Blackstone, Harry, 53, 90
Blackton, Jay, 263
Bloch, Ray, 178
Blue, Monte, 40, 41, 250
Bogart, Humphrey, 130, 149, 184–85, 188–89, 190, 192
Borge, Victor, 221, 222–24
Boys from Syracuse, The, 88
Brady, William A., 11
Breck, Walter, 52–53

Brice, Fanny, 24
Broderick, Helen, 27
Bromfield, Louis, 184–85
Brooks, Dick, 273
Brooks, Mel, 172
Brown, Lew, 27
Brown, Michael, 172
Brustein, Robert, 77
Brynner, Yul, 256
Buchanan, Jack, 84
Buchman, Harold, 22–23, 27
Bullock, Elizabeth, 240, 242, 244, 246, 250
Burns, George, 30
Burrows, Abe, 160
Butterflies Are Free, 48
Butterworth, Charlie, 116

Caesar, Irving, 283, 284
Call Me Madam, 238, 242
Cambanellis, Iakovos, 197
Campbell, Mrs. Patrick, 183
Cantor, Eddie, 30
Capote, Truman, 256
Capra, Frank, 270
Captain Blood, 112
Carillo, Leo, 60
Carney, Art, 222
Carson, Robert, 148
Casablanca, 112
Case, Nelson, 178, 180
Cavallero, Gene, 247
Champion, Gower, 93
Chandler, Raymond, 74
Chaplin, Charles, 207
Chartock, Capt., 104, 105, 114
Chase, Charlie, 34, 138, 224
Chasen, Dave, 16, 18
Chatterton, Ruth, 249
Chodorov, Jerome, 138, 149
Churchill, Winston, 178
Clark, Bobby, 19, 20, 30
Clash by Night, 175
Coca, Imogene, 162, 163
Cohn, Harry, 57, 273
Cohn, Jack, 57
Columbia Pictures, 57, 273
Comden, Betty, 264
Come Blow Your Horn, 261
Compton, Betty, 27
Conn, Billy, 118
Connolly, John, 238
Constantine, King, 193–94, 197, 198, 202, 204
Cook, Joe, 16–18, 30–31
Cooper, Gary, 130
Copland, Aaron, 247

Cornell, Katharine, 84, 209
Cortez, Ricardo, 69
Coxe, George Harmon, 71
Cross, "Stump," 98
Crouse, Russel, 237, 251, 269, 279
Crump, Owen, 149
Cunningham, Beatrice, 266, 267
Curtain Going Up, 163–73 *passim*
Curtiz, Mike, 112, 114, 115, 121, 122, 123, 124, 126–28, 130–31

Damaged Goods, 10
Daniels, Bebe, 60, 69
Daniels, Marc, 104–5, 106, 134
Dannay, Frederic, 75–76
Dassin, Jules, 192, 193, 195, 198, 199, 200, 201, 205
Davidson, Gordon, 279
Davis, Bette, 60, 130, 149
de Liagre, Alfred, 256
DeMilhau, Louis, 133
Destination Tokyo, 130
DeSylva, Buddy, 27, 88
Dolan, Robert Emmett, 161, 162
Don't Raise the Bridge, Lower the River, 217, 225, 227–28
Dowling, Eddie, 89–90
DuBarry Was a Lady, 88
Dubin, Al, 59
Durante, Jimmy, 30, 88, 217

Eames, Charles, 263, 266, 276
Easy Rider, 273, 274
Einfeld, Charlie, 60
Eldredge, David, 82–93 *passim*
Ellis, Mike, 261
Europe, Jim, 248
Evans, Maurice, 84, 88
Ewell, Tom, 93, 163

Fearnley, John, 264–65
Felker, Clay, 283, 284
Feller, Pete, 106
Ferber, Edna, 12, 237, 255
Fidler, Jimmy, 130
Fields, Dorothy, 87
Fields, Herbert, 28, 87
Fields, W. C., 20
Fifty Million Frenchmen, 27–29, 87
Film of Memory, The, 268
Fine and Dandy, 15–16, 31
Fitzmaurice, George, 40
Flaming Forest, The, 9
Fletcher, Lucille, 177
Flight of the Phoenix, The, 138
Flynn, Errol, 130
Fonda, Henry, 237, 256, 262, 265, 266
Fonda, Peter, 273
Fontanne, Lynn, 86
Forbstein, Leo F., 59
Ford, Henry, 276, 278
Ford, John, 140
For the Love of Mike, 271
Forty-second Street, 59, 60
Fowler, Gene, 237, 269, 272
Foy, Brynie, 69
Francis, Arlene, 256
Francis, Kay, 249
Freud, Sigmund, 208
Friedberg, Billy, 260
Frisco, Joe, 131
Front Page, The, 272
Frye, Jack, 238

Garbo, Greta, 237
Gardner, Erle Stanley, 71–72, 74
Garfield, John, 130
Garroway, Dave, 221

Gaxton, William, 27, 28–29, 87, 88, 161–62
Geddes, Norman Bel, 28
Gendel, Max, 123–24, 128–29
George, Grace, 11
Gernsback, Hugo, 65
Gershwin, George, 27
Giant, 12
Gift from the Sea, 264
Gilbert, Edwin, 149
Ginsberg, Henry, 12
Gleason, Jackie, 264, 268
Goldwyn, Sam, 282
Gomberg, Sy, 140
Gorney (songwriter), 29
Gottlieb, Morton, 80
Grable, Betty, 154
Graham, Irvin, 172
Graham, Sheilah, 130
Grant, Cary, 130
Green, Adolph, 264
Green Ice, 71
Guthrie, Bill, 149
Guys and Dolls, 47–48
Gypsy, 238, 253–54, 256, 257, 258–59

Haas, Mr. 55–56
Hadjidakis, 194
Hale, Alan, 116
Halliday, Richard, 253
Hambleton, T. Edward, 282
Hammerstein, Bill, 261
Hammerstein, Oscar, 253, 262, 269
Hammett, Dashiell, 68–69, 71, 237
Harbach, Otto, 283
Harburg, E. Y., 26, 29
Hardwicke, Sir Cedric, 175
Hardy, Oliver, 34, 138, 221, 224
Harrison, Rex, 263
Hart, Lorenz, 27, 85, 86, 88
Hayes, Helen, 88
Hayes, Peter Lind, 221, 222
Hayward, Bill, 273
Hayward, Leland, 236–40, 242–74, 276–84
Hayward, William, 247–48
Hayworth, Rita, 154
Healy, Mary, 221, 222
Healy, Ted, 30
Hecht, Ben, 135, 237, 248, 254–55, 269, 272
Heflin, Van, 138
Heindorf, Ray, 122
Helen of Troy, N.Y., 77
Hellinger, Mark, 189
Hellzapoppin, 217, 219
Hemingway, Ernest, 75, 272, 274
Henderson, Ray, 27
Henry, Hank, 99–100, 104, 111, 115, 122, 123, 134
Hepburn, Katharine, 237
Her Cardboard Lover, 162
Hersey, John, 237
Hiken, Nat, 260
Hillary, Sir Edmund, 264, 265
Hitchhiker, The, 177
Holden, William, 138
Holm, Eleanor, 60
Holtz, Lou, 24
Hooray for What?, 26–27
Hoover, Herbert, 49, 50, 52, 56
Hopkins, Harry, 102
Hopper, Dennis, 273
Hopper, Hedda, 111, 130
Horwath, Sam, 84, 85, 86, 92
Howard, Eugene, 24, 215
Howard, Sidney, 86
Howard, Willie, 24, 215
Hughes, Howard, 238–39, 254, 255
Huston, John, 69

Ives, Burl, 98
I Wanted Wings, 148

Jacobs, Seaman, 210
Jaffe, Leo, 273
Jamison, Marshall, 263, 267, 276
Jazz Singer, The, 27, 37, 49
Jessel, George, 19
Johnson, Chic, 217, 219, 221
Jolson, Al, 10, 11, 13, 30, 37, 49
Jones, Henry, 98

Kalmer, Bert, 27
Kanter, Hal, 206, 210
Karloff, Boris, 221, 222
Keaton, Buster, 212–13, 215
Keeler, Ruby, 49, 60
Keighley, William, 138
Kennedy, Arthur, 138, 142, 144, 145–46
Kent, Sidney, 270
Kerr, Walter, 18
Kind Sir, 279
Klugman, Jack, 258
Kogan, Ed, 120
Kovacs, Ernie, 221
Krasna, Norman, 138, 149, 279
Kurnitz, Harry, 271–72

Ladd, Alan, 138
Lady Be Good, 270
Laemmle, Carl, 57
Lahr, Bert, 25, 88, 215
Lake, Veronica, 154
Lamberti, Professor, 215, 217
Lamparski, Richard, 207
Langdon, Harry, 224
Lansbury, Angela, 259
Lasky, Jesse, 249
Laurel, Stan, 34, 138, 221
Laurents, Arthur, 253, 259
Lawrence, Eddie, 221–22
Lawrence, Gertrude, 13
Lawrence, Joe, 103
Leave It to Me!, 87
Lederer, Charlie, 151–52
Lee, Gypsy Rose, 256
Lee, Manfred, 75–76
Leigh, Vivien, 268
Leslie, Joan, 116
Lessy, Ben, 162
Lester, Jerry, 162
Lewine, Dick, 262, 263
Lewis, Jerry, 224, 225, 227–28
Life with Father, 239
Lindbergh, Anne Morrow, 264
Lindbergh, Charles, 274
Lindsay, Howard, 237, 251, 269, 271, 279
Lloyd, Harold, 36
Locke, Sam, 140–44 *passim*, 148
Loesser, Frank, 47–48
Loew's, Inc., 57
Louis, Joe, 116, 118
Louisiana Purchase, 88
Low, Warren, 150
Lugosi, Bela, 33
Lunt, Alfred, 86
Lyons, Leonard, 178

MacArthur, Charles, 237, 255, 269, 272
McClintic, Guthrie, 251
McCullough, Paul, 19–20, 30
Maddow, Ben, 138
Makarios, Archbishop, 194, 197, 198, 202, 204
Malley, Kathleen, 243, 247, 257, 264, 267–68, 276, 283, 284
Maltese Falcon, The, 68–69
Maney, Dick, 181
Mannes, Marya, 256
Mantz, Paul, 138
March, Fredric, 237
Marshall, George C., 99, 100, 107, 108
Martin, Charles, 176, 177, 178, 179, 181
Martin, Dean, 224

Martin, Mary, 87, 240, 253, 262, 269, 280
Marx, Groucho, 77
May, Elaine, 264, 266–67
Mayer, L. B., 57, 111
Mead, Margaret, 256
Medford, Harold, 138, 142, 149
Memphis Belle, 138
Mencken, H. L., 75
Mercouri, Melina, 192–201, 202–5
Merman, Ethel, 88, 240, 253–54, 258, 259
Merrick, David, 257
Merrill, Gary, 98
MGM, 57
Milestone, Lewis, 248
Mr. Roberts, 238, 242, 274, 280
Montgomery, George, 138, 150
Moore, Marianne, 256
Moore, Victor, 24–25, 87, 88
Moran and Mack, 13
Morris, Jack, 82, 86
Muni, Paul, 149, 255
Murphy, George, 116
Music Corporation of America, 237
Myers, Paul, 236
My Fair Lady, 78, 264

Nathan, George Jean, 75
Nebel, Frederick, 71
Nelson, Barry, 138, 144, 150
Nelson, Gene, 98
Never on Sunday, 195, 199
New Faces of 1952, 172
Nichols, Mike, 264, 266–67
Nixon, Richard M., 135
No, No, Nanette, 283, 284

O'Brien, Edmond, 138, 142, 144, 150
Odets, Clifford, 175
O'Hanlon, George, 158
Old Man and the Sea, The, 274
Olsen, Ole, 217, 219, 221
Onassis, Aristotle, 194, 201, 202
On Borrowed Time, 86, 162
O'Neill, Eugene, 20
Only Angels Have Wings, 138
Oppenheimer, George, 151
Oscar, The, 230, 231
Oshins, Julie, 98, 102, 104, 114, 116, 133
Our Gang, 34, 138

Paley, William S., 232, 247, 253
Paramount, 57, 225, 248–50
Paris, Jerry, 227, 228
Parsons, Louella, 111, 130
Peck, Gregory, 271
Perrigo, Lucia, 184, 187–88
Philadelphia Story, The, 142
Pinza, Ezio, 280
Pollard, Snub, 224
Porter, Cole, 27, 28, 29, 87
Powell, Dick, 59
Powell, William, 237, 249
Prinz, LeRoy, 121–22
Professionals, The, 273

Queen, Ellery, 75–76
Quesada, Elwood ("Pete"), 238
Quigley, Bob, 221, 222

Rae, Charlotte, 222
Rain or Shine, 16
Ramblers, The, 19
Rathbone, Basil, 149
Reagan, Ronald, 116, 138, 149–50
Resisting Enemy Interrogation, 142
Richard II, 84
Rin Tin Tin, 37, 41, 250
RKO-Radio, 57
Roach, Hal, 34, 36, 38–39, 137–38
Robbins, Jerome, 243–44, 245, 253, 258, 259, 276

Roberts, Flora, 282
Robinson, Bill, 162, 163
Robinson, Edward G., 149
Rodgers, Richard, 27, 85, 86, 88, 253, 262, 269
Rogers, Will, 46
Room Service, 171
Roosevelt, Eleanor, 101, 102, 103
Roosevelt, Franklin D., 59, 60, 100, 101, 102
Rose, Billy, 175, 176
Rosenstock, Milton, 96
Ross, Anthony, 98
Rothschild, Jerry, 136
Rox, John, 163
Rubin, Stanley, 152
Ruby, Harry, 27, 77
Rumsey, John, 248
Russell, A. J., 265
Ryan, Tom, 259–60, 265

Saratoga Trunk, 130, 255
Saroyan, William, 88–89
Sarthou, Joseph, 58–59
Sarthou, Mme., 58
Scarface, 254–55
Schwartz, Arthur, 94
Seferis, George, 194, 197, 202, 204
Selznick, David, 248
Selznick, Lewis J., 249
Selznick, Myron, 248, 249, 250
Sevareid, Eric, 265, 266
Sherwood, Robert E., 102
Shaw, Joseph T. ("Cap"), 66, 67, 68, 69, 71, 74, 75
Shenson, Walter, 225, 227
Shevelove, Burt, 93, 163
Shot in the Dark, A, 272
Shubert, Lee, 80–81, 82, 85, 86
Shulberg, B. P., 249
Shumlin, Herman, 251
Sidney, Bob, 95, 115, 116, 121, 122
Sillman, Leonard, 172
Silvers, Phil, 260
Simon, Neil, 260, 261
Sinatra, Frank, 276
Sinclair, Robert B., 138, 141, 142, 143, 144
Skouras, Spyros, 39
Sleuth, 80
Small Wonder, 92–93, 163
Smith, Al, 49
Smith, Bob, 264
Smith, Kate, 116
Smith, Kent, 138, 145, 150
Smith and Dale, 20
Sobol, Louis, 178
Solomon, Leo, 210
Soma, Larry, 56
Sondheim, Stephen, 253, 259
Sound of Music, The, 238, 253
South Pacific, 238, 242, 280
Spirit of St. Louis, The, 274
Star Is Born, A, 148
Stars in Your Eyes, 88
State of the Union, 238, 242, 279
Stein, Jules, 237
Steinbeck, John, 256
Steinem, Gloria, 268
Stevens, George, 12
Stewart, Donald Ogden, 15–16, 31, 57, 237
Stewart, James, 237, 262, 274
Stone, Ezra, 98, 99
Streetcar Named Desire, A, 78
Strike Up the Band, 30
Styne, Jule, 192, 253, 259
Sullavan, Margaret, 256
Swift, Kay, 15, 16, 31

Take Me Along, 264
Talbot, Lyle, 60
Target Tokyo, 151

Teasdale, Veree, 60
Theodorakis, Mikis, 194, 204
This Is the Army, 95–96, 98–116 *passim*, 119–23, 124, 127–31, 133–34
Three Stooges, 30
Tibbets, Paul W., Jr., 152
Tiger Rose, 40–41
Time of Your Life, The, 88–90
Tobias, George, 116
Tobin, Genevieve, 28, 29
Toots Shor, 180
Tracy, Spencer, 262
Trahan, Al, 25
Trial of the Catonsville Nine, The, 278–82 *passim*
Trosper, Guy, 138
Tucker, Sophie, 87
Turpin, Ben, 224
Twelfth Night, 88

Underworld, 254
United Artists, 270
Universal Studio, 57
Ustinov, Peter, 13

Van Druten, John, 256
Van Dyke, Dick, 264
Velez, Lupe, 40, 41
Voice of the Turtle, The, 256
Vorhaus, Bernard, 138

Walker, James J., 27
Wallace, Irving, 149
Wallis, Hal, 121–22, 124, 130
Warner, Abe, 58
Warner, H. B., 40
Warner, Harry M., 37, 58, 130, 249, 250
Warner, Jack L., 42, 58, 111, 122, 124, 130, 148–49, 190, 249, 250
Warner, Sam, 37
Warner Brothers, 27, 28, 36–37, 39–42, 55, 57, 58, 59, 60, 69, 249–50
Warren, Harry, 59
Washer, Ben, 100
Weaver, Pat, 240
Weber and Fields, 142
Weeks, Larry, 100, 122–23
Weinberg, Sydney, 52
Welles, Orson, 177–78
Wences, Señor, 215
When Willie Comes Marching Home, 140
Where Did You Go? Out. What Did You Do? Nothing, 264
Whitfield, Raoul, 71
Who Was That Lady?, 279
Wilk, Jake, 11–13, 22, 29, 36, 39–44 *passim*, 55, 57, 58, 60, 68–69, 72, 74, 80–89 *passim*, 239, 255
William, Warren, 72
Williams, Bert, 11
Williams, Herb, 24, 25
Willie, West, and McGinty, 217
Winchell, Walter, 123, 124, 128, 129, 178
Winter, Ella, 15
Winters, Jonathan, 232–33, 235
Wish You Were Here, 238
Withers, Grant, 40
Wyler, William, 138
Wynn, Ed, 25–27, 30, 209, 210–13, 215

Yankee Doodle Dandy, 112
Yip, Yip, Yaphank!, 96
Youmans, Vincent, 283
Young, Nedrick, 138, 149

Zanuck, Darryl, 60
Ziegfeld, Florenz, 29
Zukor, Adolph, 249, 250